MW01013392

HARWELL HAMILTON HARRIS

Harwell Hamilton Harris

By LISA GERMANY
Foreword by KENNETH FRAMPTON
Introduction by BRUNO ZEVI

Published in Association with the
University of Texas Center
for the Study of American Architecture

UNIVERSITY OF TEXAS PRESS

AUSTIN

First Edition, 1991

Requests for permission to reproduce material from this work
should be sent to Permissions, University of Texas Press,
Box 7819, Austin, Texas 78713-7819.

♾ The paper used in this publication meets the minimum
requirements of American National Standard for Information
Sciences—Permanence of Paper for Printed Library Materials,
ANSI Z39.48–1984.

Publication of this work was made possible, in part, by a grant from
the Amon G. Carter Foundation, Fort Worth.

Library of Congress Cataloging-in-Publication Data

Germany, Lisa.
   Harwell Hamilton Harris / by Lisa Germany ; foreword by Kenneth
Frampton ; introduction by Bruno Zevi. — 1st ed.
      p.   cm.
   "Published in association with the University of Texas Center for the
Study of American Architecture."
   Includes bibliographical references and index.
   ISBN 0–292–73043–8 (cloth : alk. paper)
   1. Harris, Harwell Hamilton, 1903–   —Criticism and interpreta-
tion.   2. Regionalism in architecture—United States.
I. Title.
NA737.H295G4   1991
720′.92—dc20   90–44616
                                                         CIP

Frontispiece: Harwell Hamilton
Harris on the grounds of the
State Fair of Texas at the
construction site of his *House
Beautiful* Pace Setter House,
Dallas, 1954–55.
Photograph by Squire Haskins

*Unless denoted otherwise, all
photographs and drawings are from the
Architectural Drawings Collection,
Architectural and Planning Library,
General Libraries, University of Texas at
Austin.*

Contents

For Kate and Cap,
—Allan and T. D., too

Acknowledgments

 I N 1984, I FLEW TO RALEIGH, North Carolina, to spend a week interviewing Harwell Hamilton Harris. The Center for the Study of American Architecture at the University of Texas School of Architecture in Austin had asked me to be the curator of an exhibition of his drawings that were soon to be acquired by the university library, and it was my job to go over the drawings with Mr. Harris and to gather enough information and insight to write a small catalogue to accompany the show. Mr. Harris has since told me that he and his wife, Jean, had almost despaired of finding me on the arriving flight from Texas, when finally I emerged from the gate, the last passenger to disembark. He has recalled that I spotted them across the room and smiled, and that he then knew that we would get on, that it was the beginning of our special relationship.

I very much like the picture that his memory creates, and I wish that I could believe in that smile which dissolved their apprehensions and inspired their confidence. But I remember a different scene, one in which a young reporter, specializing in architecture, finds herself faced, not merely with the subject of a profile or an examination of styles and ideas, but with an extraordinary life, a career that encompassed the whole of the Modern Movement and had more than a few moments of glory and pathos. I remember a young writer who had realized moments before her flight landed that she was woefully unprepared for the job before her, and I remember the reason for her tardy exit from the aircraft—it was to take a last, long, hard look at a picture of Harris's 1937 Granstedt house in Hollywood, hoping against hope that she, with something like Superman's X-ray vision, might see through the photograph and behind it to the truth about Harris's architecture. It was a pause that amounted to a kind of prayer for the days ahead.

But if my smile was nervous, so too were those of the Harrises. Jean had come to the airport even though she was in considerable pain with her heart ailment because my arrival was an event in their lives, one, she told me privately later, for which they had waited twenty years. Mr. Harris had his drawings out ready to show me, and we started work immediately. He had an agenda for our long hours together, and I frequently felt that the questions I asked were premature or ill-conceived—he often responded to them by simply looking at me and continuing with what he was saying. There was a quality of melancholy about him in those days, and I felt, of course, that I had neither the authority nor the stature to live up to the high hopes he had had before my arrival. He told me late one afternoon that, when Frank Lloyd Wright had wanted his story told, he simply sent Henry Russell

Hitchcock at the Museum of Modern Art a postcard inviting him to Taliesin. I knew that this was a remark made not merely in passing.

I think it was Jean, however, who broke the ice. It was she who introduced levity into our serious business. At elegant lunches and suppers that she insisted on preparing (at age 91), she described people and events in their lives with a wonderful, hilarious, I thought Dorothy Parker–like keenness. She was sometimes quarrelsome and I never wanted to argue with her for she intimidated me, but once during a disagreement we were having she said with a directness that was quite disarming, "Look, I trust you, and I know you are going to win some battles, but," with her eyes squinting for emphasis, "you won't win this one." I don't quite know what happened, but somehow toward the end of the week Mr. Harris also seemed to relax. There was no more talk about battles, only a common interest in producing an accurate, interesting exhibition and catalogue. To their everlasting credit, neither Harris ever sought to influence my ideas after they had taken the form of written words. Harris corrected factual errors—for instance, a board might be twelve inches rather than fourteen—but he was too honest, too respectful of my opinion to shape my analysis of his career.

I think that he would have preferred for the catalogue and the book to be more strictly architectural. He understood, however, that I wanted to know why he had become an architect and why his sensibility had taken the particular shape that it had. "How did you feel, personally?" I would ask, and so he answered my questions in lengthy conversations, and telephone calls, and long, beautifully expressed letters. Mr. Harris let me get to know him and he did it with grace and a commitment to goals that were not entirely his own. I think the book is far richer for these contributions, but I know without a doubt that I am. For this I am profoundly grateful.

The Amon Carter Foundation generously supported the book as they had previously supported the exhibition and catalogue. They were patient, helpful, and, above all, interested. Harwell Harris designed a house for Ruth Carter Stevenson in 1957, and her support of studies devoted to his career is a beautiful testimony to their remarkable client-architect friendship.

I am indebted also to John Kyle at the University of Texas Press. Jack formed a deep admiration for Mr. Harris's work when he was an editor at *Progressive Architecture* in the 1950s. He never forgot Harwell Harris, and when my catalogue came out he seized upon the idea of expanding it into the present book.

David Barrow, Mr. Harris's former student and the only architect he ever elevated to the status of associate, shared his own remarkable insights into Harris's work. It was he who purchased and donated the Harris drawings to the University of Texas, and it was he who allowed me to study and illustrate slides from his collection of Harris's architecture.

The Harrises' close friend Raleigh architect Frank Harmon became my friend when he invited me to accompany him and Mr. Harris on a pilgrimage to all of Harris's Texas buildings. Long road trips from Austin to Dallas, Fort Worth to Abilene, and Abilene to Big Spring gave us hours to talk about architecture and life, the subjects he so richly shared with Harris, and by so doing brought such pleasure to the elder architect's final years.

I'd like to thank T. C. Howard, whose office occupies the studio of Harris's studio-home in Raleigh, for befriending me during my week-long stay there and for adding yet another rich architectural dimension to Mr. Harris's life in Raleigh.

David Thurman, a graduate student in architecture while I was researching this book, added much to my knowledge of Harris's tenure at the University of Texas out of his own important study of Bernard Hoesli's career. Lila Stillson, the architectural drawings curator, made sure the collection was accessible to me and, with an architectural historian's diligence and imagination, prepared the book's useful index. Many former clients of Harris went out of their way to open their homes to me. Dr. and Mrs. Seymour Eisenberg in Dallas, Dr. and Mrs. J. M. Woodall in Big Spring, and (though I never made it to their home), Mr. and Mrs. Calvin Antrim of Fresno, California, are some who stand out for the tirelessness with which they praised Harris.

Finally, I'd like once again to express the enormous debt of gratitude I owe Austin architect Paul Lamb. He was the first to point out Harris's architecture to me, and continually afterwards he helped me to be sensitive to its subtleties. And, because I am not an architect, he cannot know how much I appreciate his letting me understand, through his own devoted study of Harris, something of what it must have been like *to be* Harris, creating and designing, thinking freshly about the sheltering forms that we call architecture. Perhaps in his calling to produce such forms Harris simply followed a universal and timeless impulse, but isn't it telling that two of our most eminent historians of the Modern Movement—Bruno Zevi and Kenneth Frampton—men of different generations and divergent philosophies, both find tremendous value in what he contributed to the field? Their essays do honor to this book.

Harwell Hamilton Harris died on November 18, 1990,
too late into the production phase of this book
for the text to be altered. It is with a sense of comfort and
humility that I remember his deep belief that architecture
is "not the art of books or of classrooms,
but the art that proceeds from the very fiber of things.
An art from within. Filling the imagination
with a swirling stream of living images."

Foreword

by
Kenneth Frampton

Harwell Hamilton Harris is virtually the last surviving member of the second generation of the southern Californian school—a generation that sought to render the American suburb as a place of culture. Heir to Frank Lloyd Wright in this regard, and to a line running back through Wright to Richardson and Olmsted, Harris belonged to those young pioneers who apprenticed themselves to Richard Neutra and Rudolph Schindler, in a Los Angeles that in the early twenties was still very much a frontier. There is no more touching testament to this moment of Harris's early maturity than the now familiar photograph of students visiting the Lovell Health House under construction, with Harris reticently situated to the right of the frame and Neutra, center stage, plans in hand, directing the works (see photo page 30).

Unlike his immediate contemporaries, Harris was prompt to renounce the post-Wrightian abstractions of Neutra and Schindler in favor of Wright himself. Harris chose to retrace his steps toward the Prairie origin, rather than to embrace the emerging, "international," machinist future. A certain stylistic shift, however, is detectable in Harris's late career, particularly after World War II, when he began to move away from Wright's textile block culture to come closer to the turn-of-the-century, neo-Japanese manner of Greene and Greene. Despite this vacillation, Harris would remain under the influence of Wright's canonical Hollyhock House of 1920 throughout his life. This work is evidently latent in Harris's larger domestic commissions, for example, his Harold English and Ruth Carter Stevenson houses of 1950 and 1957, respectively.

Harris was most fully himself when he came close to the immateriality of the Orient, as in the famed Lowe House of 1934 or the 1935 Fellowship Park House, Los Angeles. This Pacific Rim sensibility kept its hold on Harris right through to the Granstedt House of 1937 and the Weston Havens house of 1941. While Harris's later fascination with the orientalism of Greene and Greene overlaid this more transcendental sensibility, something of it still persists in his later North Carolina work, particularly the Sugioka and Bennett houses of 1967 and 1970, respectively.

Harris's conservative posture, the "cause conservative" in the Wrightian sense, took him away from the more radical, egalitarian line pursued by John Entenza, after World War II in the critical patronage that he extended through *Arts and Architecture.* In the activities of such figures as Charles Eames, Craig Ellwood, Rafael Soriano, J. R. Davidson, and Pierre Koenig this line led to the canonical Case Study Houses of the late forties and early fifties. In many ways this was the swan song of a much larger, neo-Wrightian movement to render the American suburb as a place of civility, a movement in which Harris played a somewhat isolated role.

Aside from Harris's singular personality as an architect, something must be said of his subsequent roles as educator and theoretician, above all perhaps because the so-called Texas Rangers, John Hejduk, Bernard Hoesli, Robert Slutsky, Werner Seligman, and Colin Rowe, owed the autonomy of their teaching as junior faculty to the patronage they enjoyed during Harris's tenure as dean of the University of Texas at Austin from 1951 to 1955. It says everything for Harris's pedagogical vision that these young turks would go on to revolutionize architectural education, not only in the United States but also to some extent in England and Switzerland.

Of the second attribute, namely Harris's stature as a theoretician, one work stands out above all the others, namely, the epoch-making address that he gave to the Northwest Regional Council of the AIA, at Eugene, Oregon, in 1954, under the title "Regionalism and Nationalism." In this remarkable text Harris distinguishes in a revelatory way between the twin faces of regionalism, that is to say between a chauvinistic retarditaire expression that is concerned more for the preservation of dialect than for the cultivation of ideas and an equally rooted but altogether more volatile dynamic that Harris would identify as a liberative impulse. Harris characterized this as the Regionalism of Liberation, as a manifestation that was particularly in touch with the emerging thought of the epoch. In this regard, he saw the region as the locus of a transforming modernity. As he put it: "We call such a manifestation 'regional' only because it has not emerged elsewhere. It is the genius of this region to be more than ordinarily aware and more than ordinarily free. Its virtue is that its manifestation has significance for the world outside itself."

Harris saw with prophetic clarity the exceptional fragility of contemporary regional culture. Moreover, he appreciated the extent to which it must be constantly cultivated if it is to survive, a condition that has been amply borne out by recent experience, for where can we look for true innovation today save to those places on the so-called periphery, where we may still encounter a combination of economic vitality, political independence, and cultural continuity. Thus we find that the spirit of southern California between the wars is as present today in Porto or Barcelona as it is in Los Angeles. That a faint echo of such impulses can still be found today in other provinces of the United States, in the work of such architects as O'Neil Ford, Fay Jones, Mack Scogin, Antoine Predock, and Morphosis is surely in some measure due to Harris's life-long example, to his fundamental faith in the inherent strength and fertility of a modern regional culture whenever it may be found, be it in the California of his youth or in the Texas of his maturity.

L'Chaim! A Toast to H. H. Harris

by Bruno Zevi

Harwell Hamilton Harris at the Byron Pumphrey House, Santa Monica, California, 1939.
Photograph by Kellett-Imandt

Wᴵᴛʜ ʜɪꜱ ɪʀᴏɴɪᴄ ꜱᴍɪʟᴇ the Master affirmed, "We are going to win!" Sitting in the San Pancrazio Restaurant up on the hill of Janiculum, one could sense the presence of the American Academy in Rome. He was also challenging this type of institution, which he detested for its contents and forms. His prophecy came true. In fact, we have won at last.

Frank Lloyd Wright died in 1959. Thirty years have gone by, mostly wasted on evasions, escapism, and Postmodern horrors. But now, just at the beginning of the last decade of this century, organic architecture has indeed prevailed. It is an epoch-making event that very few people, even among ourselves, who are its protagonists, have noted. We are not quite aware of it. We are astonished.

As is known, organic architects are almost maniacally individualistic. They refuse to be labeled. Each one of them is quite prepared to be termed *organic* but only on the condition that there are no other organic architects in the world, either now or in the future. The triumph of organic architecture is, therefore, celebrated by hundreds and hundreds of architects in Japan, India, Europe, and North and South America but with no congresses, ceremonies, symposia, round tables, lectures, or meetings. Everyone is somewhat isolated; for instance, the followers of Frank Lloyd Wright are far removed from the disciples of Bruce Goff and the Friends of Kebyar. If they all got together our victory would be explosive.

It may be useful to mention a few other examples of this phenomenon. After Antoni Gaudí, John Wellborn Root, and Greene and Greene came Alvar Aalto. He was an organic architect, but he never recognized this appellation. The same applies to R. M. Schindler, William Wilson Wurster, Ralph Erskine, Reima Pietilä, John Johansen, Jean Renaudie, Fehling & Gogel, Gunther Domenig. They are all organic without realizing it.

What about Expressionism on the one hand and Deconstructivism on the other? How do they relate to the organic? Hugo Häring is surely organic but, after the Einstein Tower period, did Erich Mendelsohn remain so? It has been rightly stated that every meaningful building is, in some way, Expressionist. Is this, however, sufficient to raise Eero Saarinen or Paul Rudolph, Norman Foster, Richard Rogers, or Helmut Jahn to the level of organic? And can the Deconstructivism of Frank O. Gehry be assimilated into the organic?

In fact, we ought to be enjoying an exciting and fascinating festival but, with all these interrogatives, this is not taking place.

Nevertheless, we won. How did it come about? Here are a few schematic hints:

—We were told that a mass society required a mass architecture based on standardization. We opposed this with the need for personification and for the democratic value of the diverse.

—We were told that architectural language was codified according to principles proportion, symmetry, assonance, rhythm, equilibrium, and so on. We laughed in a most dissonant way and respected not even one of these so-called principles

—We were taught that the cradle of our civilization lay in Classicism, in the Greek and Roman world. Instead, we looked to the Middle Ages, to the Baroque, to the Orient, or, knowing and loving the past, we decided to stop looking back.

—We were told that we should simplify, get down to the essence of things and use the minimum instruments of communication. We, however, believe in complexity, and complex phenomena cannot be represented in simple formulas.

The oft-repeated question, What is organic architecture? has been answered many times in the last ninety years. In this book, where the work of H. H. Harris is also a stimulus for an implicit theory of design, it is again answered with great sensitivity and intelligence. Therefore, I could refrain from giving yet another answer, but ten or fifteen times a day I explain what organic architecture (or organic building, philosophy, or existentialism) is and, believe it or not, a new idea comes up every time. Here are those of this morning:

Supremacy of space: The meaning of the cavities where we live and move. The envelope is not important, even less the box. What is in it, the inside, is relevant. Therefore, never start with the outside, as do 99 percent of architects, including those who say they don't. From the inside out, from the central nucleus toward all directions. Then, make the nucleus dynamic by destroying its centrality. Organic architecture comes of age.

Broken volumes: The inside is the value to be molded, compressed and expanded, and perhaps manipulated. The outside is like a stamp, a form around the void, a container. It is a mistake to start working on the shell, presuming that if the volume is cut, fragmented, deconstructed, its dynamism will reverberate on the space within. It must be added, however, that if you know how to break the volume (the Dutch *De Stijl* group knew it already in 1917), you will be able to articulate your spaces. Of course, such spaces will be mainly visual and ideological, while organic space is social, human, functional, enjoyable.

Emancipation from rules: There is only one rule in organic architecture: do not believe in any dogma, do not follow any rule. We are persecuted and suffocated by "principles," "methods," "universal truths," "orders," or "Orders." The young architect swallows all this because he or she is passive and accepts what his or her masters have prepared. The hardest thing in architectural education is knowing how to slough off the principles, methods, truths, orders, and Orders that academic teaching has imposed on one. The vast majority of architects are unable to free themselves from what they have learned at Harvard, Yale, Columbia, Princeton, Philadelphia, Los Angeles, and so on. They remain crippled.

A style for every project: The traditional dilemma presented to the young architect was either Greek or Gothic. Then came an alternative: Greek and/or Gothic. Eclecticism had arrived, a cocktail of styles that, for the most progressive, included the Modern. Organic architects could not bear this divertissement. For them there must be no Greek, no Gothic, no mixture of the two, no Eclecticism, no style.

Mutability and conflicts: Organic architecture is not idyllic, rural, naturalistic, or peacefully balanced. It embodies the conflicts both of existence and of living, and their continuous changes. Organic architecture is not an escape. It represents the drama, contrasts, tragedy, and happiness of human beings. Light is its main instrument, light that can make space vibrate.

Now, as a footnote, I would like to look back to two or three episodes of American culture spanning the last fifty years.

In 1940 Walter Gropius and Marcel Breuer designed a housing development with 250 residences at New Kensington near Pittsburgh, Pennsylvania. For the Harvard students who, a few months before, had published a very polemical pamphlet against their teaching (*An Opinion on Architecture*, Cambridge, Mass., 1940), this project came as a source of surprise and pleasure. Buildings stood free on a dramatic land, no one was parallel or perpendicular to another; there were no elementary geometries, no square angles, no Bauhaus clichés. A different, softer approach to architectural language, what we in the Graduate School of Design defined as "organic," could be noted. At that time, we preached a tendency unheard of within the walls of Robinson Hall. Almost a scandal. We had a God and a couple of prophets. The God, of course, was the real, true, living one, Frank Lloyd Wright. The prophets (we did not know much about Bruce Goff) were Harwell Hamilton Harris and William Wilson Wurster.

For various reasons W. W. W. became more famous than H. H. H. Being named dean of the prestigious School of Architecture at M. I. T. certainly was decisive in this regard, and Wurster also benefited from the very active role his wife, Catherine Bauer (author of the splendid book *Modern Housing*), played in the field they shared. But it was Lewis Mumford who assured Wurster's place in American architecture by using his Reynolds House in San Francisco as a prototype and symbol for what, in 1947, he began to extoll as the "Bay Region Style." W. W. W., however, did not develop the Bay Region themes. Back in California, he fell in love with patio houses, an introvert affair, a box with a hole, with no dialogue between building and context.

On the contrary, H. H. H. remained faithful to the original message. His Hillside House for Weston Havens in Berkeley, California, was completed in 1941. It is contemporary with Gropius's and Breuer's New Kensington housing and precedes by five years W. W. W.'s Reynold's House. Indeed, Hillside is a rare masterpiece. There is no static box but incredible horizontal, vertical, and diagonal dynamism; no elementary stereometry but space grasped, accelerated, or slowed down, the whole enhanced by an orchestration of light. Apart from the products of Wright's genius, is there anything in 1941 that can be compared to Hillside? Nothing by Richard Neutra. Charles Eames's delightful House/Atelier in Santa Monica, California, dated 1949, has a less powerful space conception. On the other hand, George Howe's Thomas House at Mount Desert Island, Maine, dated 1939, is more significant for the extraordinary landscape outside than for the cavities within. I may sound monotonous, but as a Harvard student I stated that Hillside was a unicum. I reiterated this opinion in 1950 in my *History of Modern Architecture* and again in 1973 in *Spaces of Modern Architecture*. On the eve of the nineties I still confirm this judgment. It is a unicum.

From 1940 to today there is a leap of half a century. Now we are discussing Deconstructivist architecture, a new fashion fostered by Philip Johnson and Mark Davley with an exhibition held at the Museum of Modern Art in New York City. Shall we verify H. H. Harris's validity within the parameters of this new tendency?

The Deconstructivist stand is provocative. It denounces architects who make a myth of pure forms—cubes, cylinders, spheres, and cones—and are afraid of anything that might alter the sacred values of stability, unity, homogeneity, and harmony. Diametrically opposed to academic taboos, it proclaims the Modern architect's right to complex forms, disharmony, fracturing, disunity, instability, and conflict.

For a man like Philip Johnson, who was once a Classicist in a Miesian key, then a Classicist in an Eclectic key, then a Classicist in an awful Postmodern key, Deconstructivism represents courageous self-criticism of all his previous work. In general, Deconstructivism should be applauded because it canceled out the Postmodern shame. However, it is essential to note that it is a step behind organic architecture, in which conflict is incarnated not through psychiatric *a posteriori* applications but because it is in the reality, in daily life, and in the law of change that guides human destiny.

Among Deconstructivist architects, Peter Eisenman is the intellectual who endeavors to translate ideas in terms of space, while Frank O. Gehry is the artist who believes in open, unfinished work, in "cheapscape," in a "poor" architecture. They are both reference points in the culture of the 1990s. But perhaps one day they will discover that fifty years ago (and more, in the case of Wright) organic architects achieved what they are still looking for. Perhaps they will perceive that H. H. Harris is more than Deconstructivist because he is able to express disharmony and conflict without exhibiting them.

There is more to say about organic poetry, but it is fully dealt with in this book.

HARWELL HAMILTON HARRIS

Craftsman connections and rhythms of wood in the hands of a Modern architect. Harris, staircase leading from the street level of the Weston Havens house down to the entrance bridge, Berkeley, 1940–41.

1.

Forsaking the Formula, 1903–1921

Harris responding to the spirit of the land, rather than the rules of convention in the creation of his "sky house" for Weston Havens, Berkeley, 1940–41. Here, the underside of the trough-shaped bridge that connects the house to the land while it also protects the privacy of the lower patio from the gazes of incoming visitors.

© 1985 Henry Bowles

For OVER HALF A CENTURY, Harwell Hamilton Harris (now eighty-seven) has designed buildings that testify to the existence of a wholly American strain of Modernism. Born in Redlands, California, on July 2, 1903, and trained by Richard Neutra in the Los Angeles of the 1920s, Harris was one of the few native Americans to play a prominent role in the early stirrings of the Modern Movement in this country. As such, he was able to temper his Modern rejection of the past with a deep, almost spiritual appreciation of his American architectural forebears. Accustomed to and unmoved by the machines that thrilled Neutra and many other Europeans, Harris found inspiration instead in the naturalism of Frank Lloyd Wright and Wright's teacher, the great Louis Sullivan. By exploring and interpreting their ideas, he created a Modern architecture particularly suited to American values.

Here is an architecture that would rather be at home in nature than intrude upon it, that enjoys the idiosyncrasies of wood more than the precision of steel, and that rejoices more in the democratic single-family house than the high-rise mass housing projects relished by the more socialistic European architects. Harris was not only able to see the Modern spirit at work in Sullivan's ornamentation and in Wright's sculptural forms, but he was even able to distill ideas out of Greene and Greene's cozy, hand-crafted mansions that were in keeping with his own very lean aesthetic. Like the Europeans, he delighted in the freedom from the past that the Modern attitude made possible, but it was never enough for his buildings to be simply new and efficient. Nor was it necessary for them to be heroic. They had to be as warm as they were lean. To this end, Harris softened the Modern vocabulary and made it more palatable to the American public.

Harris's Modernism, gentle and modest as it was, never lacked confidence. He never felt compelled to make a point of it in the famous "less is more" manner of Mies van der Rohe. Moreover, he seems never to have accepted the notion that Modern architecture had anything to do with the creation of an "International Style." Harris designed houses that looked like they fit, not only in America but in their particular regions. Like the Pasadena architects Greene and Greene, Harris tried to give Californians houses that responded to the temperate climate of the place, just as later, in Texas, his houses turned inward to avoid the intense heat.

In many respects Harris's work existed outside a codified style. It was an attitude toward design, rather than adherence to a creed, that made Harris a Modern and linked him to other architects of the time. In publications ranging from early issues of *California Arts & Architecture* in the 1930s to books like Esther McCoy's *The Second Generation* of 1984, Harris's houses are always visually unlike their neighboring subjects whether those subjects are from the offices of those he knew quite well—like Neutra and Gregory Ain—or those he knew hardly at all—like J. R. Davidson and Raphael Soriano.[1] That his work was understood and appreciated says something not only about the strength of his Modern attitude and his ability to communicate it but something too about the rich diversity and complexity of the movement as it took shape in this country.

Harris is at the center of that complexity, responding in his own quiet way to the continuous spaces he admired in Frank Lloyd Wright's organic architecture, but making them lighter with a delicacy of feeling strongly influenced by humble Japanese dwellings. His own architecture often seems capable of demarcating the boundaries between Neutra's mass production aesthetic and the artistic naturalism of that most compelling of émigrés, Rudolph Schindler. With Neutra he was to learn about the Europeans; with Schindler and in far more subtle ways he was to learn about Americans—Sullivan, Wright, Irving Gill. (For instance, it was Neutra who first mentioned Gill to Harris, but it was in Schindler's Kings Road house that Harris saw Gill's sensibility interpreted and saluted.)[2] Schindler may have even taught Harris a little about himself, for, having fallen in love with America, this robust spirit never tired of giving it expression in his architecture, buildings, like his own house on Kings Road, that were to haunt Harris throughout his long career.

It would be some years before the young Harris would learn what Schindler in the twenties and thirties already knew, that Modernism was not everywhere as free and exuberant as it was in Southern California. Not until World War II, when Harris in his forties left the West Coast for the first time and traveled to New York, did he learn that Modernism could be restrictive, its adherents combative and political. However much he may have liked some of the European Modernists or admired individual buildings, he would never again be able to ignore the fundamental differences between his vision of architecture and theirs. Indeed, the presence here of so many Europeans, their vaunted positions of power and influence, seems to have inspired Harris to articulate America's virtues, her democracy and her pluralism, virtues he must have felt earlier needed no stating or defending. Although he was never a polemicist, Harris did, after his return to California, demonstrate that Modern architecture as it had developed there had not entailed a violent break with the past. Indeed, he seemed to be saying, it had not needed to. By allowing the lessons he learned from Greene and Greene and Bernard Maybeck to play a larger role in the look of his buildings he not only celebrated what he called a "regionalism of liberation," he also suggested that Modernism was evolving naturally here long before the arrival of the Bauhaus architects. This was to be a point taken up vociferously in the writings of his good friend Wayne Andrews, in the books of Lewis Mumford, and, closer to home, in the opinions of his wife, historian Jean Murray Bangs. But in the 1940s and 1950s the role Americans played in the early Modern Movement was merely a leitmotiv, occurring and recurring with a certain academic insistence, yet finally swallowed up in the larger melodic strains of the European influence in this country.[3]

Now that the twentieth century is waning and that movement that was so ardently based on the new would seem to have grown old, there is adequate distance to assess what happened, yet also a closeness that keeps it from being too glibly categorized. Perhaps it is possible to say that the aspects of Modernism that made it a style are the same aspects that were destined to make it go out of style, to relegate it to history. To the extent, however, that Modernism was an attitude, a devotion to originality, to function, to the task of engaging and inspiring a client or enhancing a landscape, then the Modern Movement is still with us. Harris had such an attitude, still has one, and it allows him to be as open and inventive and unselfconscious now as when, in California, he first took up his pencil and the world outside was an endless succession of orange groves and bougainvillea-draped water towers.

In 1906, a violent earthquake shook San Francisco and the charming Victorian city of the forty-niners crumbled and burned until it looked, wrote Jack London, "like the crater of a volcano." The next year the members of a small family—a mother, a father, and a four-year-old child—made their way home from Puget Sound, where they had been vacationing, southward to Redlands, California. As they neared San Francisco, the father expressed his interest in seeing what destruction the earthquake had wrought. Maybe the little boy looked up to see the ruins, for he was a curious, precocious child, but if so they left no impression. His imagination was engaged elsewhere. Looking over the side of the steamer, down into the water, the child could see a crimson stain rising to the surface. As he stared deeply into it he surmised that a fish had been caught in the propellers of the boat. In years to come, mention of the famous San Francisco earthquake would remind him of this. That is, it would remind him not of the destruction he might have seen (and no doubt did see) of the fallen city but of the destruction beneath the waves which he could not see and about which he would never know the full truth.[4]

Harwell Hamilton Harris, age four or five.
Courtesy of Harwell Hamilton Harris

This story from the early life of Harwell Hamilton Harris fixes the future architect in the California of the dawning twentieth century, a time which, for all its promise, was largely a period of unhurried change. The Victorian era had survived the close of the nineteenth century, and the sentimental tastes and rules of decorum that had defined it continued to prevail for some time as, indeed, the rebuilding of San Francisco soon made abundantly clear. Harris, too, long after he grew into manhood and even in the face of his strongly held Modern attitudes, retained personal habits that betray his Victorian upbringing. It was not simply a matter of his being always impeccably and conservatively dressed or consistently poised and formal (though he was all these things), but rather a matter of personal propriety, of a kind of quiet reserve. And, in the Victorian way, this propriety, this implacable reserve, was belied by an imaginative life that seems to have been all the more rich and intense for having been sublimated. Like the little boy on the steamer, the adult Harris was always compelled more by the images beneath the surface than by those of a more general, accessible nature.

To the peculiar characteristics of the Victorian era that shaped Harwell Harris there must also be added that he was an only child. Being a child, with a child's interests and curiosity, in a world peopled by adults forced Harris to become something of a loner. In the picture that emerges from descriptions of his childhood there is not the slightest trace of neglect but rather, one feels, a little too much adult scrutiny. It is unclear what his parents' long-term career expectations of Harwell were, but their feelings regarding his conduct would set up a dynamic whereby they would always remain authority figures. One sees him acceding to their wishes, becoming ever more the well-behaved, polite gentleman and developing an attitude of deference (still with him) that would make him feel younger than everyone else.

May Julia Hamilton.
Courtesy of Harwell Hamilton Harris

And yet as his life unfolded he began to make running annotations in the margins of his young mind. In that private realm he kept his own counsel, questioned the status quo, and gave himself over to the emotional, artistic aspects of his nature. When, as an adult, he happened upon some new ideas this was the aspect of him that was quickened. Indeed, he was so deeply shaken that to say he became an architect afterward hardly describes what happened. It would be better to say that he was *called* to architecture. Only such an old-fashioned word suggests the powerful reversal that would allow the annotations (or subtext) of his life to supersede the official text and bring into the light of day his inchoate but restless longing for expression.

The Hamiltons and the Harrises were Californians of a particularly romantic sort, the Hamilton grandfather having come as an early homesteader and the Harris as a forty-niner in search of gold.[5] Both Joseph Hamilton and Benjamin Butler Harris were southerners, and in their families there was a distinct gentility, a soft-spoken refinement, to which the young Harwell fell heir. His grandfathers had each fought on the side of the Confederacy in the Civil War, and the child was taken with a sword and Confederate flag belonging to Hamilton, who had been a colonel in Gen. James Longstreet's division. The war took Benjamin Harris to Texas because he could speak Spanish. Afterwards, he made a treacherous return to California, making notes that would one day constitute the first description of the Yosemite Valley and form the basis of a book on the Gila Trail. Having found no gold in Mariposa during his first stay in California, he decided to settle in San Bernardino and begin the practice of law. The families were destined to be united when a young Frederick Thomas Harris passed the studio window of a commercial photographer in Los Angeles and saw the pretty face of May Julia Hamilton looking out at him from one of the framed portraits.[6]

Although the lives of Harwell's parents were without the broad sweep and color of his grandparents', it is they who, in shaping the outward Harris, gave oxygen to the artistic spark latent in his nature. They did not mean to, of this one feels certain. They were not artists but rather pragmatists.[7] To them had fallen the task of consolidating and stabilizing the California lives their parents had so boldly embarked upon. And yet, it is doubtless *because* of their conventionality that their young son became a dreamer, an idealist, and, in his secret soul, a rebel.

"Our circumstances were moderate, our church was Methodist, our moral consciousness was ever present," Harris has written.[8] But beyond this very tidy, prosaic picture of his early life-style, Harris is at a loss to describe his parents as people. Something very essential is missing in his portraits of them, and while that something was neither love nor respect, it may well have been passion. Harris seems not to have been inspired by his parents. On what his mother was like he

Frederick Thomas Harris.
Courtesy of Harwell Hamilton Harris

has said, "Well, she was the smallest in her family."[9] A schoolteacher by profession,
he has written that she would have been "mortified" if his grades in school had
been less than excellent.[10] On the subject of his father, Harris's usual skills at re-
porting fail him again. "Well, he was not either an introverted or an extraverted
person, I don't think. . . . He didn't travel to speak of. He enjoyed hunting." It is, in
fact, with some surprise that one learns that his father was an architect. "He was a
good architect," Harris has recalled, "but he wasn't an outstanding one in any way.
He never thought of it as being something that you could be outstanding in, probably. . . . I don't think that it [architecture] was a subject that he was . . . very strongly
interested in. I mean he enjoyed the practise of architecture, but I don't think that
he had any thought of making any great thing out of it. And that may have had
something to do with my not [having been] more excited about it."[11]

Although Harwell would attend two schools his father had designed (one in
Redlands and another in El Centro), neither they nor his Mission Revival houses
would ever be more than buildings to the son, good buildings, sometimes, but not
architecture. And yet, as buildings they must have exerted a stronger influence
than he realized. Fred Harris, like his son afterward, did not have a formal architectural education. It was construction that had drawn him to the profession and
construction that the young Harwell saw when he went by horse and buggy to his
father's job sites. His duty at those times—to hold the horse while his father exam-
ined the work—ended in 1911 when the family purchased a car.[12] Harris was only
eight, but even such a small exposure at such a young age must have served its

Fred Harris, the W. F. Holt house, 1903, Redlands.
Courtesy of the Archives of the A. K. Smiley Public Library, Redlands, California

purpose well. At the very least, it may have stripped away the mystery and intimidation children associate with endeavors outside their immediate experiences. At the most, it laid the groundwork for his sublimely simple later structures, where the desired effect depended on expertly designed and crafted details that articulated their constructions frankly. Harwell Harris's working drawings and finished buildings were to be always characterized by a complete understanding and appreciation of how things went together.

Fred Harris was an architect of some repute, and at least two of his larger commissions for Redlands, the McKinley Elementary School and the home for W. F. Holt, show him enamored by the eclecticism that had become fashionable around the turn of the century.[13] But Fred Harris's interest in architecture also converged with the fashion for exposed construction of the early twentieth-century Craftsman and Mission Revival movements, a fortunate accident of taste for the developing child. In time and in spite of their seeming antipathy with the Modern Age, Harris would feel a great affinity for many aspects of these movements. His detailing—when in the 1940s he freed himself to look closely at the Arts and Crafts homes he had grown up in and around—demonstrated not only how inventive his Modern sensibility was but how natural, how second-nature, construction techniques were to him. What became art for the son, however, remained construction for the father, who, while Harwell was still quite young, relegated it to second place among his interests, advancing ranching (or, rather, farming) to first place.

When Harwell was born on July 2, 1903, his parents were living in Redlands, California. Harris has said that Redlands then was like a small Pasadena, inhabited by prosperous midwesterners who had come to retire in Southern California.[14] Their shingle-style houses with big porches sat in and amongst the ubiquitous orange groves planted by the Mormons a generation earlier. Something of a building boom was in process when the Harrises moved there in 1900 and they enjoyed a modest success, but in 1913, when a freeze wiped out a season's worth of crops and no one could afford new building, Fred Harris decided to pack up his family and move to a ranch in the far south of California close to the Mexican border.[15] The ranch, in the Imperial Valley, was about a two-mile car trip from El Centro, where Fred Harris continued his architectural practice and for which, with commissions from developer W. F. Holt, he had already designed some buildings.[16]

The new enterprise was not without its hardships. Not only was it necessary for Fred Harris to continue the practice of architecture, commuting twice daily, but Harwell also made the drive into town to attend school. Afterward, he waited in the public library until his father got off work.[17] The ranch had to be worked in their spare time, but that did not mean that it was merely a hobby. On the contrary, Fred Harris's purchase of the ranch—160 acres, of which only 20 had been leveled—was a very serious venture. He had maintained ranches throughout Harwell's life and even before as a young, unmarried man, but in the Imperial Valley his commitment was on a whole different scale. He and, what is more important, the ten-year-old Harwell threw themselves into it.

For six months Harwell watched as a gang of teamsters leveled the remaining 140 acres. Large scrapers pulled by mules had runners and long handles with ropes trailing from them. Fascinated, he observed: "The teamster would grab the dangling rope when he got ready to scoop up more sand. And he would pull the handle back and down. He'd take hold of the handle and yell at the mules who would hump their backs and pull to fill the scraper, and then to drag it to the place they dumped it. It was a constant movement back and forth, picking up sand here and dumping it there."[18]

During these years Harwell read a book entitled *With Men Who Do Things* that described, among other things, how the tunnel was built under New York's East River.[19] The ranch experience was his own very personal encounter with men who do things, and he learned what might be called a methodological approach to problems that shaped his own attitude. It was marked by a respect for obstacles, for their complex and seeming capricious nature, and, on the other hand, a confidence that patient, intelligent reasoning could overcome them. The tone of his re-membrances of planting alfalfa and Indian corn in the sandy terrain of his father's ranch is exactly the tone he would use later to identify architectural concerns:

First of all, the problem was to hold the land. The winds, which were quite strong and constant, would move the sand around. Where there was no sand hill yesterday, there could be one today, pretty good sized one, simply because of the wind and because there happened to be something else that the sand would form around, form behind. So one had to order water, which was delivered by canals, at such times that, when a certain amount of grading had been finished, one could get water on it to hold it. Well, there was the problem of keeping the wind from blowing the sand away, and there was the other problem of keeping the birds from eating the seeds before it could get covered, watered and growing.[20]

The child who ran errands for his mother on a horse-drawn sled through the sand[21] became the architect who described a dramatic roof overhang (in this case, the Birtcher house of 1940) with these words: "This is a nine feet overhang here. It's on the south side. We're interested in cutting off the sun but we aren't interested in making this any darker than necessary, so the whole outer three feet of it is perforated. These are wells through it . . . about 30 inches deep. The sun would have to be awfully close to vertical to hit the glass [wall] back here."[22] And in the realm of furniture design the same methodical approach became the standard. His comments on a tall table to be used for a buffet: "With the center of gravity near the top, there is danger of overturning when pushed unless the feet are broad. But if they were any broader, there would be the risk of kicking them when standing close to it."[23]

Identifying the problem, calmly, resolutely solving it, Harris was learning the plain, home-grown truth about functionalism. Elevating that knowledge to the level of art would come later. Significantly, however, his functionalist attitude was not put in the service of goals that were less mundane than planting corn but rather more mundane. For a building to succeed it was necessary to solve the simplest, lowliest questions of use.

If Harwell was learning on the ranch that the functions of machines and the outcomes of man's projects depended on working with nature, then he was also learning a respect for nature. As it happened, the landscape he was to know and love was on the brink of change, a change so drastic that in a very brief time it would become an alien, unrecognizable place. He would say later that his California was "a place and a time"[24] in order to separate himself from the California of the popular imagination, of the so-called golden dream, where, as Joan Didion would write in the 1960s, "it is easy to Dial-A-Devotion, but hard to buy a book . . . where the hot wind blows and the old ways do not seem relevant, where the divorce rate is double the national average and where one person in every thirty-eight lives in a trailer."[25] It is as if the giddiness and despair of the people who came to Harris's homeland were not only destined to alter the look of the land but even what he perceived as its benign mood. Didion's San Bernardino Valley "is a harsher California, haunted by the Mojave just beyond the mountains, devastated by the hot dry Santa Ana wind that comes down through the passes at 100 miles an hour and whines through the eucalyptus windbreaks and works on the nerves."[26]

For Harris the land really was a golden land, suitable for golden dreaming. Before the Dust Bowl, before the World Wars, before the divorces and capri pants, it was a place characterized by the gentleness of nature, a setting so lovely as to seem like Paradise. If the frontier aspects of the Imperial Valley experience animated the young Harwell, then the abundance and variety of the San Bernardino landscape were destined to make their own very deep impressions. He knew it first as a child in Redlands, a town protected from the Santa Ana by a stony ridge named Smiley Heights (for the famous brothers who settled the region), and then again after age fourteen at the outbreak of World War I, when the family moved to San Bernardino. He remembers the valley carpeted in wildflowers and bougainvillea and how hillsides looked like they were blanketed with a chenille bedspread, so even and endless were the orange groves covering them.[27]

In time and perhaps because this dream faded away and was lost even as he looked on, Harris's memories of Southern California grew to take in all the state. In California, he would say, "one finds the highest peak in the United States, Mount Whitney, and the lowest valley in the United States, Death Valley. The longest coast line probably in any state and the biggest ocean just outside it. Marvelous deserts, the Mojave in particular, and the spectacular valley, too, like Yosemite. Giant trees, the sequoia. Beautiful lakes, Lake Tahoe. The tall palms—and I can remember those particularly—usually in rows or in pairs, with their round tops elevated on long sticks above the round tops of the orange trees below . . . The tall, plume-like eucalyptus, the citriadora. The bougainvillea, which was like a giant red scarf over the water tower . . ."[28]

What Harris describes so wistfully is not a sentimental attachment to home and youth but the very foundation on which he built his attitude toward architecture. Southern California as it was in the first quarter of the century was the essential force in his development. And because his vision of it was a powerful one, it continues to be an ongoing force:

The variety in nature is something that is very much a part of me and something I like to take into account as far as possible in any building that I do . . . because we thought of nature as there first, and, although there was great development, the development for the most part hadn't been at the expense of the environment. We were building and doing purely man-made and artificial things within the natural setting, but it didn't seem to be destroying the setting as a whole in any way. It was a gentle nature to begin with, that one could expose himself to [and] didn't have to protect himself from. And it wasn't a nature that had to be dominated. We didn't feel that we had to tame it. It was something that didn't require taming. It was simply something to accommodate oneself to and to develop in what he built as a means of making more complete and general living possible.[29]

Because the California landscape he knew did not survive, it became something illusory and ephemeral—like almost all the other major influences on Harris's sensibility. The red-blooded reality of a specific moment or the unspeakably delicate mood of a place were made rarer and richer to him because of their temporality. He could let them go, but only after his receptive imagination had let them take him completely, after he knew he would be able to conjure them up again and again. What mattered most about his experience with nature, then, was that he confronted it alone and felt a personal, very direct connection with it.

Privacy attended all Harwell's discoveries to the point that it very early became a prerequisite for the truly moving events yet to come in his life. He once summed up this general attitude when he described his feelings about reading. "No book that I read," he wrote, "did I discuss with others. It remained a secret between the author and me. It was a more intense pleasure because it was solitary."[30] The pleasure of reading, shaped during the afternoons of waiting for his father in the El Centro library, rounded out his interest in nature (he became an avid fan of *Physical Culture Magazine*, for instance).[31] It also carried him into other areas, quite new and sometimes, it must have seemed, off limits to him. Here one sees him making the first marginal annotations—correcting, adjusting, sometimes rejecting the lessons of his parents.

I accepted my parents' moral standards. But from the age of twelve I did not accept their belief in a personal God. Possibly they suspected my disbelief; if they did, they were too wise to question me. And I could not bring myself to tell them for that would have hurt them. I did not need anyone to tell me why a personal God is an absurdity; the contradictions were so obvious. I was fifteen when I read a biography of Benjamin Franklin and discovered I was an agnostic. . . .

[It] wasn't the first book I had discovered on my own.[32]

Harwell Harris had the heart of a rebel but not the incumbent hostility. He intuitively felt, however, that he had to protect the integrity of his personal experiences with the world. Otherwise, he was in danger of accepting the ready-made, borrowed, respectable, but conventionally dull world he knew all too well. Because privacy had set Harwell's imagination free, he never got over his gratitude for it. Long after his fears of hurting his parents had subsided, he continued to value his time alone. The thoughtful, contemplative life was something he never took for granted. Believing that all people must feel the same way, he would later design houses that were not merely for sleeping or eating, for family life or for entertaining, not even for some abstract notion of beauty, but rather for the individual, alone and distinct. Nothing in his remarkably cohesive career of designing buildings is so consistent as the respect for privacy. It wasn't a question of tall fences or sandblasted glass windows. He wanted the house to speak to his clients the way authors had spoken to him, directly and exclusively—"invisible," he once wrote, "to all the others."[33] Certainly here was the sensibility of an incipient artist.

In his senior year at San Bernardino High School, Harris had the good fortune to find himself in a history class taught by Gideon Knopp, a retired professor from Clark University who had missed teaching too much to enjoy his retirement. What impressed Harris about Knopp was the way in which the teacher orchestrated his lectures so that, as he prepared students to understand an idea, he also built suspense and desire for understanding. During each class, Knopp would take the students on what Harris would later call a "journey of discovery." "We were detectives uncovering a plot," Harris has written. "Because he made it seem a first-time journey, it thrilled me with the feeling that I was his co-discoverer."[34]

Knopp's method of gradual disclosure offered Harris a way of revealing his ideas and emotions while heightening their mystery. More important, the approach had a formality, accompanied by a process of intellectual reasoning, with which Harris could feel comfortable. It is tempting to see Knopp as the critical link between the well-behaved, imaginative boy and the Modern architect who later persisted in using adjectives like "polite," "well-mannered," "graceful," and "elegant" for buildings. Harris, like Knopp, would see no need to shock others with his ideas. "The preparation for something is very desirable," he now says. "I like to be prepared. I like surprises, too, but they're more effective if they have some context. You make your way through something, finding things as they come along and making them a part of your picture and your understanding of it. The idea then comes at the climax of the trip of discovery."[35]

With Knopp as his inspiration Harris sought answers to the plethora of questions he encountered daily. He avidly read Spengler's *Decline of the West* and Alfred Russel Wallace's *Social Environment and Moral Progress* and found in them a common goal. Although they addressed different subjects, cultural history and evolution, respectively, what underlay each was a desire to uncover form. The nature and development of this mysterious quality intrigued Harris. It was something that cut across all media. Beethoven's Ninth Symphony had form and so did the seemingly formless "Leaves of Grass" by Walt Whitman. "Architecture," Harris would say later, "is the search for form."[36]

arwell Hamilton Harris in 1921,
ne year he graduated from high
chool.

Ourtesy of Harwell Hamilton Harris

After graduation from San Bernardino High School, Harris attended Pomona College in the nearby town of Claremont but found his teachers there disappointing after his year with Gideon Knopp. They seemed unable to grasp the presence of form in the subjects they taught. He complained that his English literature professor "talked *about* the work but did not *reveal* it" and that his biology professor "described the shape of the science but not its nature—omitting the puzzling, doubting, imagining, proposing and reconciling that continues to shape it."[37] Nevertheless, he pursued ideas in much the same way he always had and, in the process, became dimly aware that the end of World War I was allowing "long-delayed re-adjustments in every field of thought."[38] On his own he discovered Ibsen and, quite by accident, while in the library picking up another play by the Norwegian dramatist, bumped into a little book by George Bernard Shaw entitled *The Quintessence of Ibsenism.* It was a timely meeting and the susceptible Harris appreciated it for what it was worth. "Thru his eyes," Harris wrote about Shaw, "I saw the familiar in new light and what is so stimulating as the familiar in new light? Shaw freed me from many conventional ideas. The stimulation of that freedom was enormous."[39]

If Knopp had set Harris down at the beginning of the path of discovery and shown him how to proceed, then Shaw was the first clearing along the way, a place to air out second-hand ideas and shake off the shabby pretenses of the insecure. But the day was yet young, and one suspects that the intense but unfocused Harris may have found himself wondering where he was going.

2.
Form in Clay and Color, 1922–1925

There must be some one quality without which a work of art cannot exist; possessing which, in the least degree, no work is altogether worthless. What is this quality? What quality is shared by all objects that provoke our aesthetic emotions? What quality is common to Sta. Sophia and the windows at Chartres, Mexican sculpture, a Persian bowl, Chinese carpets, Giotto's frescoes at Padua, and the masterpieces of Poussin, Piero della Francesca, and Cezanne? Only one answer seems possible—significant form. In each, lines and colours combined in a particular way, certain forms and relations of forms, stir our aesthetic emotions. These relations and combinations of lines and colours, these aesthetically moving forms, I call "Significant Form"; and "Significant Form" is the one quality common to all works of visual art.

CLIVE BELL, *Art,* 1914

Sculptural form in plywood on a grand architectural scale, as it was shaped by Harwell Hamilton Harris for the interior staircase of the Weston Havens house, Berkeley, 1940–41.

© 1985 Henry Bowles

FRED HARRIS died of a heart attack in the spring of 1922 after a short bout with the flu that swept the country following the First World War.[1] Harwell was still in his first year of school at Pomona College and had not settled on a particular course of study. Toward the end of his second year, however, he had to drop out for reasons of illness. It is an event that stands out in the history of his almost ninety years of good health. What happened exactly is that he stopped eating and, already slight in stature, became quite thin and frail. He moved to San Diego to live for a few months with an older cousin, then to Los Angeles to be closer to his mother, who had returned to her former hometown after her husband's death. He enrolled at the Otis Art Institute but, still weak, soon afterward withdrew, this time for an extended visit with an aunt and uncle who lived in that most cherished place of his youth, the Imperial Valley.[2]

Harris was adrift. In the span of just one year he had been shaken by the premature death of his father and the growing realization that his intellectual energy had yet no direction. Without discounting the purely physical reasons for his wanderings, it is clear enough that the psychological aspects of the two situations alone could have proved enervating. He had never drawn or built imaginary houses or lingered over art books, as budding young artists are wont to do. A one-hour drawing course at Pomona had elicited only a tepid reaction from him.[3] Out of convenience, and because no exhausting study would be involved, he decided to give the Otis Art Institute a second try.[4] And it was a propitious moment to enter art school. The feeling he had begun to have at Pomona that the war had destroyed the surface of life and opened the way for great changes was already a *fait accompli* at the Otis Art Institute. "New expressions," Harris wrote, "were being proclaimed rather loudly . . . and we were glorying in what was new without feeling any necessity of having to destroy the old. We just left the old behind us."[5]

Harris knew "that what was emerging was something that had probably been developing underground for a good many years," but he didn't have a working acquaintance with the images of the new movement.[6] He found a woodcut of a Gauguin in the *Century Magazine* and read an article about Cezanne's use of color

15

Erich Mendelsohn, Industrial Building, 1917.
Courtesy of the Architectural Press, Ltd.

in the *Dial* but could find nothing but black-and-white reproductions to demonstrate it. When the *Dial* began to print one painting in color per issue he began his own collection of Modern art. To do this he added trips to old bookstores to his already frequent outings to the Los Angeles Public Library.[7] There he had already uncovered Clive Bell's *Art* with his description of "significant form" and Robert Henri's *The Art Spirit*, and, in a tiny little book, the expressionist, war-time drawings of the German architect Erich Mendelsohn.[8]

Mendelsohn's buildings interested him as shapes rather than as buildings, for which they seemed too arbitrary. Harris had ruled out architecture from his theory of what constituted a work of art because he felt that it "is for practical purposes [and] too impure to be an art."[9] Like sculpture, it contained the same possibilities for three-dimensional form, but it was, finally, "too much a mixture."[10] Mendelsohn had clearly not mixed in enough of the practical aspects of living to convince him otherwise.

Sculpture, on the other hand, did not pretend to be practical, yet it had a formal organization that appealed very strongly to Harris's desire to lose himself in art. During a first-semester course at Otis he learned to draw from plaster casts of sculptures and, outside of class, he made frequent trips to the Los Angeles Museum of History, Science and Art to sketch the Chinese sculptures of the General Munthe collection on long-term loan there.[11] On one such visit, he saw the virtuoso renditions of animals in bronze by the then-famous A. Phimister Proctor alongside the modest, abstract plaster works of an unknown, Harold Swartz. He did not think Swartz's pieces were great, but they possessed a presence and, he wrote later, "a form I felt instantly."[12] By happy coincidence Harold Swartz became the new clay modeling instructor at Otis, a course for which Harris had already registered.[13]

In the sculpture classes, he strove always to emote. "I learned to project myself into a form and so feel as the form felt," said Harris, who found himself modeling plaster cast details of Michelangelo's *David* for Swartz.[14] Other artists of the time, particularly American sculptor and painter Morgan Russell, had been captivated by Michelangelo's form.[15] His *Slaves*, embedded in their marble, were the grandest expressions of form struggling for freedom. While there were lessons to be learned from Michelangelo, the lines of primitive sculpture appealed to Harris more. They were in keeping with his emerging taste for the lean and simple. The ancient sculptures of Ajanta, Ellora, and Elephanta were the ones he "entered into with ease and sympathy."[16]

Michelangelo, 1527–28, *Crossed-leg Slave*, Accademia, Florence.
Photograph courtesy of Alinari/Art Resource

Sculpture class at the Otis Art Institute, 1924: instructor Harold Swartz in center; *continuing right:* Ruth Sowden, who encouraged Harris to discover Frank Lloyd Wright; Viola Kepler (model); George Stanley (future designer of the "Oscar"); Clive Delbridge (Harris's client for his first building, the Lowe house); and Harwell Hamilton Harris.
Courtesy of Harwell Hamilton Harris

Head of Clive Delbridge by Harris, 1925 or 1926.
Courtesy of Harwell Hamilton Harris

Harris learned that while sculpting entailed carving away unwanted material, modeling was quite different. In this process one added material to shape a form around the pencil-thin line of the armature. It was a critical difference for the young artist. "I built my forms with small bits of clay rolled between my fingers and added one at a time," Harris has written. "It was a slow process, but it enabled me to look ahead and keep the form in my mind ahead of the form in my hands. It even *invited* form to suggest itself and, seemingly, to realize itself."[17]

The same emphasis on emerging form characterized Harris's painting classes at the Art Students League of Los Angeles. The class was taught by Stanton Macdonald-Wright, who along with Morgan Russell and a number of other artists had in 1912 created the Synchromist Movement.[18] The Synchromists sought to define form in space by means of color principles. For example, in separate studies of Michelangelo's *Dying Slave*, Russell and Macdonald-Wright translated the forms of the *contrapposto* figure into a spiral of color that moved into and out of deep space.[19] In Germany, France, and later New York, Russell and Macdonald-Wright had caused minor sensations with exhibitions of the colorful paintings they called "synchromies."[20]

By 1925, when Harris took drawing and painting lessons from Macdonald-Wright, the painter had stopped painting synchromies, but he had not stopped theorizing about color.[21] *A Treatise on Color*, written for his students at the Art Students League in 1924, seems to have escaped Harris's attention, though the ideas expressed in it did not.[22] In it the artist discussed the analogies between color and music (Harris would always describe the colors he chose as "chords," some in major keys, others in minor keys), and he revealed how his own practice differed from Morgan Russell's. Russell's theory was based on light: yellow was the color of the "highest light" and violet contained the "deepest shadow." Macdonald-Wright's own theory used nature as its starting point: "As nature recedes from the eye it becomes blue-violet or violet, while as it advances it becomes warmer, or, in other words, more yellow or more orange."[23] Unlike Russell, Macdonald-Wright had always avoided total abstraction in his work because he feared that others, not understanding the theories behind the spiraling colors, would be inspired to use the patterns as mere decoration.[24]

In a tiny still life dated 1932, Harris played with the creation of depth through color, and it is probably no accident that the resulting crayon drawing looks like Macdonald-Wright's and Russell's early still lifes painted while they were under the influence of Cezanne.[25] This little drawing reveals how thoroughly Harris absorbed Macdonald-Wright's principles, but it seems rather incidental compared to the powerful expression he would give them later in his architecture.

Like Macdonald-Wright, Harris disdained the merely decorative, and his hues of color in buildings, as stunning and really audacious as they were, always had a basis in the *architectural* expression of the place as a whole. His walls were often yellow, the "color of light," and the window and door rails and mullions tended to be olive drab. The orange-red front door of a house would have the effect of making it advance toward the visitor; the turquoise blue of the window and door rails and mullions at a beach house would make them recede into the distance, blending, perhaps, with the sea itself. Harris's palette would never contain what Russell called "beautiful colors" but, rather, natural colors. To realize that Harris's cabinets at the Fellowship Park house (1935) were vermilion and alizarin crimson, the floors and cabinet tops were "deep blue tile made even deeper by a transparent glaze," and the ceiling was mustard, is to realize just how Modern and even Synchromist Harris's color sense was.[26]

Having learned from Macdonald-Wright that "color could be both harmony and structure," Harris was on his way to a more complete understanding of architectural form.[27] If an all-encompassing "total" form was to be the goal of his architecture, then color and, in time, materials were to be the integral parts, or handmaidens, of the form. Color would tie rooms together, creating subtle movements into and out of deep space, and materials, especially redwood boards and battens and three-foot Celotex panels, would rhythmically enliven those rooms without interrupting the flow of the whole form. Not surprisingly, Harris came to see that the choice of colors for upholstery or floors, the selection of materials for walls or furniture, could not be left to the discretion of an interior designer.[28] They were the critical devices that gave fullness, continuity, and depth to the entire architectural experience he was striving to create. Like the trunk and leaves of a tree, they were just different parts of the same living organism, and their development should seem just as natural.

In 1924, when Harris was starting his second year at Otis, the man who believed that architecture must have an intimate relationship with nature died in a dingy Chicago hotel.[29] Louis Sullivan had spent the final, desperate years of his life writing a book describing his belief that art must grow organically out of nature and, more fundamentally, that nature and man are one. To make this final point explicit, Sullivan had couched his philosophy in a story, the story of his own life, called *The Autobiography of an Idea*. The first edition of the book was published shortly before his death in 1924, and the architect made a gift of it to his former protégé and friend, Frank Lloyd Wright, at their last meeting.[30] Since Wright shared Sullivan's ideas about an organic architecture, the gesture might be seen as the passing of the torch.

Harris did not know about Sullivan's ideas at the time, nor had he seen his architecture. Soon after Sullivan's death, however, Karl Howenstein, the director of Otis, showed Harris a letter he had written to an architecture magazine in which he paid tribute to the Chicago architect who had once been his teacher.[31] Harris was impressed by Howenstein's respect for the man, and when he found a copy of *The Autobiography of an Idea* soon afterward, he quickly read it. The book did not entice him away from sculpture, but it captivated him and, along with the sculpture and painting instruction he had received, prepared him for his first encounter with the architecture of Frank Lloyd Wright.

Harris, sketch of project for
Neutra's class, 1929. This sketch
bears the inscription, "First house
by HHH designed for Ryland
Thomason." Thomason was
Harris's best boyhood friend.

3

Of Organisms, Machines, and the Illusion of Architecture, 1926–1931

Because we are organisms, all our actions develop in organic fashion, and our feelings as well as our physical acts have an essentially metabolic pattern. Systole, diastole; making, unmaking; crescendo, diminuendo. Sustaining, sometimes, but never for indefinite lengths; life, death.

Similarly, the human environment, which is the counterpart of any human life, holds the imprint of a functional pattern; it is the complementary organic form. Therefore any building that can create the illusion of an ethnic world, a "place" articulated by the imprint of human life, must seem organic, like a living form. . . . "Life" and "organism" and "growth" have no relevance to real estate or builders' supplies. They refer to virtual space, the created domain of human relations and activities. The place which a house occupies on the face of the earth—that is to say, its location in actual space—remains the same place if the house burns up or is wrecked and removed. But the place created by the architect is an illusion, begotten by the visible expression of a feeling, sometimes called an "atmosphere." This kind of place disappears if the house is destroyed, or changes radically if the building undergoes any violent alteration. The alteration need not even be very radical or extensive. Top-heavy added dormers, gingerbread porches, and other excrescences are very spectacular diseases; bad coloring and confused interior furnishing, though mild by comparison, may be enough to destroy the architectural illusion of an ethnic totality, or virtual "place."

SUSANNE K. LANGER,
Feeling and Form, 1953

The Organic

IN 1925, while Harris was still at Otis, he fell into an idle conversation with a fellow sculpture student that proved to have tremendous, life-changing consequences for him. Ruth Sowden, who had come to Los Angeles from the Midwest, proudly told him that Lloyd Wright was designing a house for her and her husband.[1] Harris didn't react. She then explained that Lloyd Wright was the son of the famous Frank Lloyd Wright. When his face betrayed no recognition the second time, she suggested that Harris visit the elder architect's home built for Aline Barnsdall, named the Hollyhock House for its sculptural decoration.

Stretched over Olive Hill in the midst of downtown, the massive Maya-influenced house and a handful of related subsidiary buildings (built between 1917 and 1921) represented the first of Wright's Los Angeles houses and the most ambitious.[2] Aline Barnsdall, an oil heiress from Oklahoma, hoped to create an arts center on the hill, with particular emphasis on theater, and she hoped Frank Lloyd Wright's prestige would contribute to the project. As it turned out, nothing lasting or cohesive came from her plans; one of the buildings functioned briefly as a kindergarten school, among other things, and the house, to which Barnsdall never warmed, became only an occasional residence for her.[3] She was still living there in 1925, however, when the trespasser Harwell Harris stumbled onto her grounds and, spellbound, saw for the first time the low walls of the house, its pool, and its ornament of abstracted hollyhocks. Even without access to the inside, he understood enough of the interlocking horizontal and vertical volumes to infer the interior plan and, more important, its spatial feeling. Later, he would see the house under more favorable circumstances, but this first encounter was the only one that really mattered. In his brief foray onto the Barnsdall property, Harris captured the

Frank Lloyd Wright, Hollyhock
House for Aline Barnsdall on
Olive Hill in Los Angeles,
1917–20.
Photograph by Julius Shulman

atmosphere of the building—what philosopher Susanne Langer would call "the illusion" of it. This he would never forget. Lodged firmly in the forefront of his mind, safe from all the destructive vicissitudes of life, his feelings have survived with their original freshness intact:

I took [a] Saturday to see the building, and I entered on the road that wound up from Vermont Avenue near Sunset. And as I came up I suddenly came on, I don't know whether it was called Cottage A or Cottage B. There were two guest cottages. And this really stopped me. I had never seen anything like it. It looked so very Japanese. Then I went on up and to the top of the hill, and there I could see bits of the main building through the hedge. I would stop, and look and go on, stop and look and go on. I was afraid to go through.

Well, here was a long, low building that I could only see bits of at a time, and I had to put the bits together. It was like a long animal for that matter. You get a part here and a part here, but you know it's the same animal. I finally came to a hole in a hedge where I could actually step through and see it. And I saw it under the most favorable circumstances. It was in the late afternoon, and the sun was getting low, and the walls—which were sort of a golden tan—were very gold in the light of the setting sun. And the building was very horizontal and had wings that came toward you and away from you, this way and that way, and the movement of these wings was paralleled with the movements of bands of repeated ornament. The horizontal bands were just above the window line, there was a ledge, and above the ledge the wall sloped slightly inward. And on this ledge was the hollyhock ornament. I didn't know what it was. It wasn't important that it resemble anything in particular . . .

. . . It was sculpture on a completely different scale, and I simply couldn't stand still. I just had to move. As the building moved, I moved. That was all. I had to follow its development. And the smooth walls of the building with the intricate cast ornament that . . . ap-

Harris with Charlotta Heythum at the Hollyhock House, undated photograph, ca. 1940.
Courtesy of Harwell Hamilton Harris

pears like locks of hair on a smooth brow. The ornament would follow around a wing, and then it would come back again on another wing. And then I suddenly saw the ornament on each side of the large opening in the wall of what turned out to be the living room. It opened the living room out to a rectangular pool. I could see this same pattern but now incised . . . and then I discovered it in the full round coming up out of the center of the building mass, from places you couldn't see from where I was, couldn't see what the ornament was part of, but the ornament was always in pairs. This building was something I had never been able to imagine before. And I was all alone, you see. That was the wonderful thing about it.[4]

The experience on Olive Hill was the supreme artistic epiphany it was because it made Harwell Harris feel understood, made him know that his own yearning for expression had been real and honest and right, if misplaced. Everything in his life was destined to take shape around this single event—the love of privacy, the drive toward sculptural form, the respect for nature. After the Hollyhock House it was just a matter of time before Harris switched from sculpture to architecture.

Harris soon followed up on his discovery with a trip to the Los Angeles Public Library. There he discovered the two-part folio of Wright's Wasmuth collection of drawings (published in Germany in 1910) and found his admiration for the architect broadened and deepened. The houses depicted in the drawings had the deep eaves, hipped roofs, ground-hugging horizontals of Wright's Prairie Style and were thus, superficially at least, at odds with the massive, inwardly turning Hollyhock House. While they merged into their midwestern sites, it dominated Olive Hill. Har-

Frank Lloyd Wright, Frank W. Thomas house, Oak Park, Illinois, 1901.
Courtesy of the Frank Lloyd Wright Archives

ris saw the differences, but he was more impressed by the force of what he knew was a single sensibility. These houses made him feel as though he were walking down a street in Oak Park, Illinois (something he would not do for eighteen more years), bringing to each new house along the way some feature admired in the previous houses. To him the cumulative effect was very great, and he likened the Prairie Style houses to a family in which "the buildings' apparent differences seemed natural and led one to believe any further differences he might encounter would be due to differences in situation or occasion." No, he decided finally, it wasn't like a family, "it was like a whole society."[5]

The Wasmuth folio in no way lessened his ardor for the Hollyhock House; on the contrary, he concluded, its power was such that it could accomplish alone something equivalent to the variety of the entire Wasmuth society. It is "large and rambling, stretching itself into the landscape, wrapping itself around the hill and enclosing gardens of its own—outdoor rooms becoming continuations of indoor rooms and indoor rooms using walls of the same material as the outside walls. What bowled me over on my first visit was the continuity."[6]

As with Hollyhock House, he was struck by the structural qualities of the Wasmuth houses: "I projected myself into these forms, and I couldn't help but move and stop and turn in rhythm with them."[7] When he realized that they ". . . spoke to me as forms that had nothing that would repel me or confuse me with other associations" he was beginning to transfer the Modern attitude that had been honed at Otis to architecture.[8] He no longer doubted that it, too, was art.

Plan, as form, was the next discovery and the most lasting. Projecting himself into the plan, he began to understand how rich and yet subtle interior form could be, how it was something separate and distinct from form as sculptural mass. "Certainly Wright has been the most continuing and strongest influence on me as far as plan goes," Harris has said.[9] In the Hollyhock House Harris felt Louis Sullivan's famous dictum "form follows function" come alive. In the Wasmuth folio houses he saw that "plan *is* form . . . everything grows out of [it]."[10] He embraced what his scrutiny told him was Wright's belief that a plan was "the very beginning and essence of all form."[11] Later, a Harris plan, like a DNA protein, would be the source of form, the essential kernel of information concerning the building's development. But the impact of Wright on Harris went way beyond the theoretical allure. "I have never escaped the influence of the Wasmuth Folio plans," he has lately admitted, ". . . wings, one-room-and-a-corridor wide, all walls and floors in unit dimensions rather than feet and inches."[12]

In the wake of his discovery of the Wasmuth folio, Harris also came across the Dutch architectural magazine *Wendingen*, which had published *The Life and Work of Frank Lloyd Wright*. However fascinating Wright was to him, however, Harris was having a hard time pulling himself away from sculpture. It still had a hold on his imagination, this is clear. He was to spend the two years following his completion of Otis in 1926 as a sculptor. But one suspects that he wavered because he didn't quite know how to begin a career as an architect. He took the step of registering in the architectural program at the University of California at Berkeley, but he knew no one who was an architect, at least not as he now understood the profession to be, and, at twenty-three, he worried that he was too old to start something new.[13] He needed a push, and in 1928, before he was to begin school, he got one.

After the Hollyhock House experience, it had become his habit to look closely at the new structures going up in Los Angeles, and one day he saw a building under construction that was unlike any building he had ever seen. The general feeling he picked up on in the building reminded him of the expressionism he had seen years earlier in the little book of Erich Mendelsohn's drawings.[14] But this time he was intrigued by the shapes as they performed as architecture. "It's not Wright," he said to himself, "but it is a Modern thing."[15] In fact, the Jardinette Apartments, as they were called, had a reinforced concrete frame, continuous ribbon windows, and cantilevered balconies that spoke clearly of the Modern Movement. Harris had to know who had designed it. When he was told the name Rudolph M. Schindler, he quickly went to a phone book, looked up Schindler's address, and drove to see him. Eventually, he would learn that the expressionism he had seen in the apartments came from Schindler's partner, Richard Neutra, who had worked two years in Erich Mendelsohn's office.[16] That realization struck him, however, only after he had assimilated two more immediate demands on his impressionable nature—the organic beauty of Schindler's house on Kings Road in Hollywood and the eagerness of Neutra, whom he met there, to hire him.

Schindler and Neutra, both Viennese, had had their own rather dramatic encounters with Wright when the Wasmuth folio toured Europe in 1910.[17] So taken, in fact, was Schindler that he came to America in 1914, eventually finding work with the American architect in 1917. Neutra, who stayed in Vienna to finish school, got caught in World War I and had to delay his own trip until 1923. In the meantime, Schindler was living in Los Angeles, where, in 1920, Wright had sent him to supervise the construction of the Hollyhock House. By the time Neutra arrived in this country, Schindler had left Wright and built his own home on Kings Road in

R. M. Schindler and Richard Neutra, the Jardinette Apartments, Los Angeles, 1926.
Courtesy of Harwell Hamilton Harris

Left to right, seated: Dion and Dione Neutra; *standing:* Richard Neutra and R. M. Schindler, in the Schindler patio, Kings Road, 1928.
Photograph courtesy of Friends of the Schindler Home, gift of Dione Neutra

Hollywood. After working for Wright three months in 1924, Neutra also went to Los Angeles. Because part of Schindler's house—a duplex for two couples with studio space enough for each of the four inhabitants—had recently been vacated, it was a logical place for Neutra, his wife, Dione, and their child to settle temporarily.[18]

When Harris arrived at Kings Road in 1928, it was Schindler who opened the door and showed him in. Harris explained why he was there and Schindler took him into the living room, brought him some photographs, and invited him to make himself at home. But Harris was too amazed by his surroundings to concentrate on the photographs. Kings Road, he would write later, was "an organism of spaces, a structure of rhythms, an air of unreality, enchantment."[19] What he was seeing was Wright's organic architecture but filtered through a very different, though equally authentic, sensibility.

From the outside of the house he had noticed that the walls were slabs of raw concrete, and he was struck by the simplicity of the construction as well as its visual effect. Now on the inside he observed the cement again:

I was looking at the room that I was in. It had a cement floor. The walls were partly slabs of cement, uncolored like the floor, but with a little bit of texture from the casting still on them. They were in panels about four feet wide, and between each pair of panels was a strip of glass about two or three inches wide. And outside light fell on the floor through these. Outside the glass there was ivy growing up it in many places. Walls on opposite sides of the building were tied together overhead at intervals by doubled beams of redwood. The slabs formed the outside walls, not the partition walls. Above the level of the tie beams there were small windows about sixteen inches high by four feet wide that let light in high up. Opposite, a slab wall would usually be a wall into a court. There were several courts in the building. This opposite wall was made up, usually, of sliding panels filled with cheese-cloth or some very inexpensive, but translucent material. The whole thing was a very inexpensive building done with many temporary materials, some of which, like the cloth, was replaced later by glass. Outside—because I looked through the glass into the garden—there was simply Bermuda grass and hedges of castor bean plants and bamboo. Everything was extremely common, and I was amazed at the total effect and decided it must be magic.[20]

At one point, while Harris was still lost in his musings, Dione Neutra walked through the room barefoot and clad in a toga, adding an even stronger note of idyllic unreality to the place.[21] The mystical mood was broken, however, and another equally interesting one begun when Richard Neutra hurried in and introduced himself to Harris. With enthusiasm he picked up the photographs and talked to Harris about them. Neutra had arrived in Los Angeles with an agenda to write a book, get important jobs, and alter the way Americans lived. He needed help and Harris had arrived just in time. When he suggested that Harris join him, the inexperienced sculptor decided to accept. After all, he thought, "[Neutra] was present and Wright was not. Though Neutra represented something different from Wright that something was exciting and real. When he told me I could learn more working for him and taking technical courses at night school than I would in an architecture school, I cancelled my plans to enter Berkeley and started working on a drawing board resting on a trunk in the corner of Schindler's and Neutra's drafting room."[22]

R. M. Schindler, Kings Road house interior, 1922, Pauline Schindler's studio.
Architectural Drawing Collection, University Art Museum, University of California at Santa Barbara

R. M. Schindler, Kings Road house, 1987 view of the roof rebuilding with "sleeping baskets" temporarily removed.
Photograph by Julius Shulman

The Machine

As was evident in the Jardinette Apartments, Wright's influence on Neutra had weakened considerably. From the beginning, Neutra's work in Los Angeles seemed to follow a course that had more to do with the contemporaneous Modern Movement in Europe. Although Schindler had broken with Wright over work at the Hollyhock House, it was too late for him to extricate himself from the ideas, both structural and philosophical, of his American mentor. His own transformations, in the years Harris was getting to know him, were of a very personal sort, affected but certainly not overwhelmed by his knowledge (through magazines) of European design.[23] This difference in attitude would eventually become critical for the two Viennese. Harris alluded to it when he wrote many years later that "Schindler represented the unique and Neutra represented the typical."[24]

While Schindler was getting to know Louis Sullivan and Wright, Neutra was being exposed to the early works of Le Corbusier and the Bauhaus architects as well as Mendelsohn. Far from his war-torn homeland, Schindler discovered the American West and, on a camping trip to Yosemite Park, fell in love not only with nature but with the tent as an appropriate form, capable of defining architectural space.[25] Neutra's impressions of America, shaped by the war experience, were completely different. To him it was the land of powerful machines and amazing technical innovations. When at last Neutra found himself in America, he had no intention of taking the machine for granted. He not only wanted his buildings to resemble machines (going so far, on several occasions, as to paint wood with metallic paint) but he also wanted them to result from simple, efficient, machinelike construction. *Sweets Catalogue*, from which architects could order all parts for an entire building, fascinated Neutra, and the standardization and interchangeability of machine parts were, to him, breakthroughs with incredible implications for future architecture.[26]

That Harris should encounter the machine-oriented ideas of Neutra during the very time when his passion for Wright's naturalism was at its most intense is one of those odd accidents of fate that can force artists to develop their own points of view. In Harris's case, particularly, contact with Neutra preempted the possibility of his falling too blindly into the already-swollen ranks of Wright's disciples. Neutra's worship of Henry Ford might never inspire anything more than quiet bemusement in Harris, but his obsession with Modernity, with materials and means that could change the world, would find a welcome in Harris's developing sensibility. However Modern Sullivan and Wright seemed to Harris, the underpinnings

Richard Neutra, the Lovell Health House, 1927–29.
Photograph by Julius Shulman

of their naturalistic architecture lay in the nineteenth century. If Henry Ford was Neutra's symbol of America, then Wright's and Sullivan's was Walt Whitman.[27] Harris's upbringing in the paradisiacal Southern California, where his experience with nature was direct and personal, enabled him to make the spiritual leap backwards to Sullivan and Wright that would so influence his architecture. And later, like his fellow Americans, he would also quote Whitman. But in 1927 he was yet young and willing to test new ideas. The sudden encounter with Neutra would hit him like a much-needed and very bracing blast of pure twentieth-century air.

It is doubtful that Harris could have found a building anywhere, before or after 1928, that was as evocative of twentieth-century Modernism as the house on which Neutra put him to work. The Lovell Health House, designed for Dr. Philip Lovell, a popular local authority on the healthful benefits of fresh air and exercise and an advocate of natural healing, made use of all the modern technological advantages. A steel frame of four-inch H columns and twelve-inch open web beams held together a three-story house of stucco and glass and allowed it to hover dramatically over a steep Los Angeles hillside. Its relationship to the site accentuated the house's verticality, but the horizontality of the three floors was also given expression in the wide spans of stucco sheathing and ribbons of glass composed of standard-size windows.

Because of his use of steel and the abundance of glass Neutra further demonstrated that Modern building could do without mass. In this way, more than any other, the Lovell Health House was a clear departure from what Harris had seen

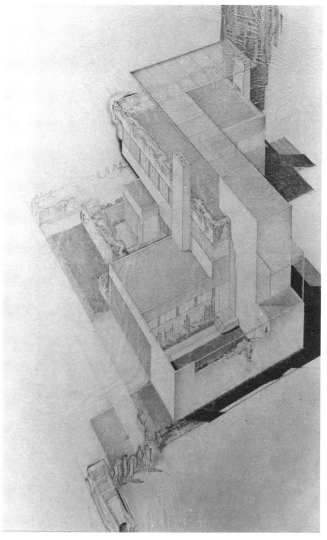

Harris, house project for Richard
Neutra's class, 1929.

(and felt) in Wright's Hollyhock House and to a lesser extent in Schindler's concrete, Kings Road house, where mass was heavier and more sculptural. Wright was doubtless behind the asymmetrical composition of solids and voids across the surface of the Lovell house, as Kenneth Frampton has noted in a comparison of it with Wright's textile block houses of the same decade.[28] Indeed, as early as 1914, after seeing the Wasmuth folio, Neutra had written that he marveled at Wright's "ability to be both serious and monumental without stressing symmetry."[29] But in 1927, it was he who was serious and monumental and the Wasmuth houses, if not also the textile block houses, were beginning to seem quaint.

In only five days the working drawings were out of the Kings Road studio and Harris was out of a job. He took a short summer course in architectural drawing at Southern Branch University of California (later U.C.L.A.), and for a while he only saw Neutra when he ran into him on the construction site of the Lovell house, but before long the contact became more frequent.[30] Harris took an architectural drawings class and, while attending some lectures that Neutra gave at the Academy of Art, met Gregory Ain, who also had aspirations of becoming an architect. When a class grew out of Neutra's lectures, Ain and Harris enrolled. Thus, Harris was free to travel from the final touches of the Lovell house to the fantasies of his own imagination. As it turned out, his fantasies, manifested in the house he designed for the class, bore a strong resemblance to the Lovell house with a little of the Jardinette Apartments mixed in. Like the apartments, it was a concrete frame construction, but like the Lovell house, it had a dramatic vertical appearance that Harris accentuated in his drawing. Harris now admits his sources candidly: "The flat roof, smooth walls and ribbon windows belong to the 1920s manner of the Central European Modernists. The secondary form growing out of the box (pushed out by the developing space form originating at the core), belong more to Frank Lloyd Wright."[31] Although the plan of this house does not survive, Harris makes it clear with these words that it was organic, a "form," growing out of a "core," in the manner of Wright. The sleeping porches for each bedroom are an outgrowth of the indigenous California climate and life-style. He had seen them all his life, but the concrete nature of his porches perhaps owes something of its inspiration to the Hollyhock House and, particularly, Schindler's home with its concrete-enclosed patios and rooftop sleeping baskets.

Clearly, Harris was taken by the romance of Modern ideas as they were expressed in the Lovell Health House. In the long run, however, the Lovell house, monument of Modernism that it was, did not sustain Harris's interest. Never in Harris's writings and conversations about it is there any feeling for what the house felt like to be in and move through and around. These omissions may suggest that its pristine edges and nuts-and-bolts spirit were less capable of moving him than the cruder but infinitely more sensuous mood at Kings Road. But the Lovell house did have form, that ingredient Harris demanded of every work of art—had it, indeed, in a way that was destined to impress him very deeply. Form existed in the Lovell house without the need for heavy massing. He saw that it was comprised of doors and windows and the intervals of space between steel piers. Form could be shaped with Neutra's standardized parts, the typical materials that the Machine

Age had produced. The units of space (or modules) created by the materials became the cells of Harris's organic architecture.

A module was the basic unit of measurement, usually four feet, in which a variety of building materials came, including wall panels and concrete forms. Designing on a four-foot grid with these modules in mind was economical and straightforward; although they were generally used for warehouses, architects like Schindler and Neutra, who wanted to exploit technology, made a point of using them. Wright, too, had demonstrated the value of the module, particularly in his fenestration. Harris had noticed, in fact, that the windows in Wright's houses were of a standard size and arranged in a regular rhythm, but not until he saw the Jardinette Apartments and the plans of the Lovell Health House marked A-B-C-1-2-3 did he truly understand the modular system. "You could immediately tell what size everything was, whether it was an opening or a piece of wall. Each part had the same dimensioning unit every other part had," Harris recalled.[32]

Neutra impressed upon Harris that modular design was especially efficient for additions one day when the two of them were at the Los Angeles Wholesale Produce Market. He pointed out that all the warehouses had reinforcing bars protruding at the end to ease the attachment of an addition. "Everything was designed," says Harris of those structures, "with the idea that it might be expanded and the most economical way was to build in regular units."[33]

With warehouses, of course, there was no thought of aesthetics, but Harris quickly translated the module into his own artistic scheme. In time he would notice a connection between the architectural module and the pieces of rolled clay he had used previously in building his sculptural forms. He realized that architecture, like sculpture, could also be a "matter of building up rather than carving out." The module did not have to be as predictable as it was in warehouse design. It would become his entrée into form, that was all, and using it he would be able to put together architectural plans that were enigmatic. His own choice of units for small houses would be three feet rather than four, and he would delight in breaking the unit into smaller components, carefully planning rhythmical variations—how many floor tiles might fit within a three-foot-wide Celotex panel, how many bricks might span a double-unit fireplace.[34]

When the class was over and Neutra still had no work, he suggested that Harris and Gregory Ain join him to work on projects. He had already begun the plans for his vision of an ideal city of the future, what he called "Rush City Reformed," and he had prevailed upon Schindler to call their partnership the Architectural

Group for Industry and Commerce.[35] Harris would come to admire the large view that Neutra inevitably took with every project, but the names he chose, intended to convey that vision, always embarrassed him a little. Perhaps "Rush City," based on Neutra's attitude toward Los Angeles, was a name and an idea a bit at odds with Harris's more familiar, hometown experience of the city. (After all, his Uncle Arthur had an orange grove on Sunset Boulevard and his mother's house occupied the future site of the University of Southern California campus.) The Architectural Group for Industry and Commerce was something else. It was a name that, in its anonymity, showed how much Neutra savored connections with European Modernism. (Philip Johnson's and Henry Russell-Hitchcock's book *The International Style* would soon tout such anonymity at the expense of the individuality of Wright and others.) Harris was suspicious of the anonymity and otherwise found it self-conscious and self-defeating. He explained:

Anonymity has been glorified in fields other than architecture and usually by persons with *no* passion for their *own* obscurity. Neutra was no exception. However, he did sign some projects of this early period with the name "Architectural Group for Industry and Commerce." On my first day in his office Neutra told me that if the telephone rang while he was out I was to answer it with "Architectural Group for Industry and Commerce." It did ring and because I had it all plainly written in front of me and had done a little rehearsing, I answered correctly. For a moment there was no reply; then, "Oh! I thought I was calling an architect's office," followed by the click of the receiver.[36]

In 1929 the Lehigh Portland Cement Company announced a national competition for the design of an ideal airport and Neutra invited Ain and Harris to work with him on an entry. They accepted and for Harris it became an intense learning opportunity. Because of Neutra's penchant for seeing the larger picture, because of his sincere hope and belief that Modern architecture would affect what Harris has called "the coming shape of man's organized life," he proposed that they design not simply an air terminal but an air transfer.[37] In his Rush City work he had seen that in the future, the critical problem facing a traveler would not reside so much in the design of an airport as it would in the interconnections the airport had with other modes of travel—buses, trains, cabs, and so on. Necessarily the AGIC entry, affecting the design of the city and the region as it did, was immensely more complex than a scheme for a simple airport would have been, and it was thrilling to Harris. "Of all the lessons I learned from Neutra," Harris recalled when his former teacher won the American Institute of Architects' Gold Medal posthumously in 1977, "integration is the most important, and I learned it working on our entry in this competition. How one thing calls for another, how one thing excludes another, how two things produce another—it was all there."[38]

Neutra was the perfect teacher for Harris and Ain because he let them in on the issues that required tough decisions. He asked them to weigh the possible design choices with him. "The marvelous thing," Harris has said about those years, "was that Neutra was doing his thinking, his musing, his proposing, his adopting, his rejecting with me and Ain as ringside watchers."[39]

After work on the competition was finished in 1929, Neutra decided that his small office should become the first American chapter of the CIAM (Congrès Internationaux d'Architecture Modern), an international organization dedicated to the unification and promotion of the forces for Modern architecture. According to an early document, the first Congrès had been convened in 1928 "with the aim of establishing a programme of action to drag architecture from the academic impasse and to place it in its proper social and economic milieu."[40] Neutra invited three architects from the East Coast to join them and appointed Harris secretary, responsible for collecting the dues and sending them to Sigfried Giedion, the general secretary, in Zurich. Because low-cost housing was a preoccupation of the Europeans, Neutra was eager for the American chapter to compare its proposals with theirs. Harris recalls, "At Neutra's suggestion I prepared a chart with which we could compare designs based on size of family, building area, cubage, unit cost and total cost. Neutra named it 'The Minimum Existence Correlation Chart,' the name reducing somewhat my enthusiasm for it."[41]

Harris has recalled how active their office became when the CIAM later called a Congrès that focused on the idea of the functional city. Neutra pulled out his Rush City Reformed schemes, to which he had already added the air transfer from the airport competition, and the small office got busy. From the Southern California Automobile Club Harris got a print of a large map of Los Angeles. The territory their project was to cover was enormous—from the San Pedro Harbor thirty-five miles to the south and north into the San Fernando Valley—and the drawings produced were also enormous. Harris's part included the throughways and overpasses as they came into Los Angeles.[42]

In 1930, having received his fee for the Lovell house, Neutra left for Europe, with a stopover in Japan. In addition to photographs of the Lovell house, he took the Rush City Reformed sketches to present them at the 1930 Congrès (CIAM III), held in Brussels. There he would meet Le Corbusier, Walter Gropius, and Mies van der Rohe, who invited him to teach for a month at the Bauhaus.[43]

Richard Neutra's Rush City
Reformed, 1926–27, a vision of
Los Angeles in the future, which
Harris could not share with his
teacher.
*Courtesy Dion Neutra, AIA Son and
Partner*

In Neutra's absence Ain and Harris continued to work on projects at home.
Not since the work on the Lovell house, which was done at Schindler's Kings Road
studio, had Harris worked in an office. Everything else—the Rush City Reformed
project, the Lehigh Portland Airport competition, the CIAM housing work—Ain
and Harris had done separately and at home. They had access to an empty room
at the Academy of Modern Art and there they showed Neutra what they had done
and received his criticisms.[44] If it was a fairly makeshift arrangement—working at
home and for free—still it was a time of learning and experimenting. Even without
Neutra's supervision, Harris managed to illustrate the stamp of his teacher. His
proposed multifamily dwelling for Arthur Jensen bore a striking resemblance to
the Jardinette Apartments with its ribbon windows and the interrelationships of
its flat, concrete planes. And that wasn't all. At the bottom of the drawing he wrote,
"Harwell Harris—Architectural Group for Industry and Commerce."

In spite of his attachment to Neutra, Harris had not forgotten about Wright or,
for that matter, about Schindler. For instance, once, while working with Neutra on
the airport commission, Harris's conviction that they were sure to win was be-
sieged by doubt: "I wondered out loud if Frank Lloyd Wright had entered the competition. Neutra felt sure he hadn't. My fear of Wright's entering and winning
shows my high regard for Wright (he topped all architects) and my ignorance of
Wright's habits."[45] The latter years of the 1920s were rich for anyone interested in
the Wisconsin architect. The *Architectural Record* was publishing his famous series of articles "In the Cause of Architecture" during 1927 and 1928 and his textile
block houses—the Storer (1923), the Ennis (1924)—dotted the hillsides of Los Angeles while the Millard (1923) graced a shady ravine in nearby Pasadena. Wright
gave a lecture in the Los Angeles Philharmonic Auditorium that Harris attended in
January 1930, the same month, Harris recalled, that the *Architectural Record* pub-

lished a perspective drawing in colored crayon of Saint Marks in the Bowery. Harris recalls, "Wright talked in a very easy way . . . He had on a dinner jacket and glasses on a black ribbon and it was all a very easy thing and it was very impressive, but I still avoided [him] . . . I didn't go up to meet him afterwards."[46] Seeing Wright in person only added to Harris's belief that he was a kind of god; refusing to meet him was a way of keeping him on his lofty throne.

The Illusion of Architecture

Harris never plied Neutra or Schindler with questions about Wright. Because their work seemed so different from his, as well as different from each other's, he tended to forget that they had worked for Wright. He took it for granted that they admired him. "The only personal remark I heard in those first days was when Schindler shoved a book aside (I believe it must have been the Wendingen *The Life and Work of Frank Lloyd Wright*) and a photograph of Olgivana fell out. In picking it up Schindler remarked that Wright seemed happy with her. That was all. Of course I later learned that Schindler had had close relations with Wright over several years . . . and that Wright had treated him very unfairly."[47]

Most of Harris's impressions of Schindler were of this fleeting, snapshot nature. He did not know that the open, very genial Schindler was, at the time of their meeting, going through a period of trial almost Job-like in proportion.[48] After opening his home to Neutra's family and introducing him to his many friends, including the Lovells, their own friendship began to sour. Neutra managed to capitalize on the Lovells' frustration about cost overruns in the beach house Schindler had designed for them, to the end that their prized commission—for a townhouse—went to him. When the Neutra-Schindler League of Nations entry toured Europe, Neutra's father-in-law, who was acting as an agent for the architects, removed Schindler's name. In the meantime, Wright had become incensed because he had heard that Schindler had claimed to have originated some of the ideas at work in the Hollyhock House, a claim which, if made, may have had some justification.[49] On June 19, 1931, Schindler received a letter from Wright in a tone so vituperative and with language so strong as to bring their relationship, personal and professional, to a sudden and permanent halt.[50] He was hit hard by the news that Neutra was to be represented in the Museum of Modern Art's epoch-making exhibition, "The International Style," but that he had been passed over. (His passionate plea to Philip Johnson to consider the Lovell beach house was answered by a firm, cool refusal.)[51] Finally, and not least, during these same years Schindler's wife, Pauline,

an ardent, intelligent champion of his work and of Modern ideas generally, left him.

It is little wonder, then, that the next glimpse of Schindler that emerges from Harris's memory of the time shows him bitter, without the high spirits Harris had seen before. Harris had picked Neutra up at the station following his return from Europe and had made a stop at Kings Road to get something. When Schindler drove up a few minutes later, Harris excitedly told him that Neutra was inside and, not knowing the situation, was confused when Schindler turned away without responding and walked off Neutra and his family were not invited back to Kings Road. Harris found them a house on Douglas Street very near Elysian Park, which was large, undeveloped, hilly, and close to downtown Los Angeles.[52]

The pathos of Schindler's position (his best work, the Newport Beach house and his own Kings Road duplex, was behind him by the early 1930s when Neutra's star was on the rise) adds to the difficulty of assessing his influence on Harris, though it does not obscure the overlooked but very obvious connections between them. From the beginning Harris was taken with Schindler's rendering technique, which was very painterly and evocative.[53] Even such early drawings (1932) as his houses for Mr. and Mrs. Barney Rudd and Lewis Gaffney suggest Schindler more than they do Neutra. The bird's-eye perspective of the house dramatizes its cliff-hanging aspect, the colors—purples and oranges and blue-grays—and the vision of the landscape itself (taking up almost half the foreground) are some of the artistic qualities that speak of Schindler's graphic skills. The concrete frame with cantilevered balconies and porches pushing out of the central volume of space, the organic unity achieved out of a fusion of the bold, sculptural protrusions—these elements are more than a little suggestive of Schindler. Clearly, Harris had been looking at Schindler's Lovell beach house on Newport Beach with its expressed concrete frame and *De Stijl* composition of surfaces and volumes.[54]

Harris, house for Mr. and Mrs. Barney Rudd, 1933.

One need only consider the profound impact of Wright's Hollyhock House on Harris to appreciate the subtlety of Schindler's influence on him. Harris has confirmed that the first building that so arrested his attention on Olive Hill was Cottage A, and Cottage A, sometimes known as the Director's House, bore the stamp of Wright's superintendent of the Barnsdall commission, Rudolph Schindler.[55] Indeed, Schindler authorities August Sarnitz and David Gebhard attribute it to the Viennese architect outright. Although there is debate over the point, it is worth noting in the context of Harris's reaction to Olive Hill. Significantly, Harris did not want to believe that anyone but Wright had been involved in the design, but he found himself admitting the possibility of Schindler's considerable input. "Once in stopping by Olive Hill, I came across Schindler directing some changes in Cottage A. Perhaps Schindler had himself designed Cottage A; if so, altering it was not as sacrilegious an act as I naturally thot it to be."[56] At another time, speaking of the encounter, he recalls being shocked at the way Schindler changed things:

[They were] things that he designed and that Wright had designed, although he designed more of the detail of all of the Olive Hill houses than I realized at the time. The larger aspects of it were very much Wright, but the smaller ones, many of the details, I've since discovered were very much Schindler.

And Schindler did them in the most sympathetic and the most imaginative way. It was his ability to drop one idea and pick up another fresh one and develop it in a way that one would think that he had been thinking about it for years and years and this was not his first try. This was very surprising to me. And his use of unconventional materials, the cheapest of materials, and extracting design possibilities from them. All of this had a very strong influence on me at the time.[57]

As with his first encounter with Schindler's designs at Kings Road, Harris's shock gave way quickly to genuine admiration.

Harris realized it wasn't only the little details that Schindler had designed but some of the characteristics that had most profoundly affected him: "I believe it was Schindler [who] told me he had designed for Miss Barnsdall the remarkable pergola with playful pool in which a child could wade or walk along the length edge, trailing a toy boat. For the free-standing walls supporting the pergola (and also for

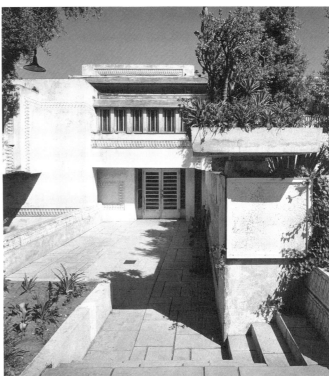

stepping stones) he used the concrete blocks (F.Ll.W.'s 'textile blocks') that had
been made for some other use, later abandoned."[58]

Harris responded strongly to Schindler's sense of structure as it was expressed in concrete. Aside from the Lovell beach house with its monumental concrete piers, he admired the Pueblo Ribera Court in La Jolla, which was built of concrete poured into movable forms built of two-by-sixteen boards. Always interested
in rhythmical patterns, Harris admired the vertical unit created by the molds. In
Schindler's buildings, he said later, "it was the directness with which results were
achieved and the simplest of processes suggested the form."[59] This logic, Harris
believed, was so unexpected that it surprised and delighted, and became the tool
of Schindler's sense of humor.

But in the end, what Harris took from Schindler was more amorphous. At the
parties that the Bohemians Rudolph and Pauline Schindler hosted in the late
1920s, Harris had an opportunity to observe Kings Road at its most alive and functional.[60] At these times he tried to seize upon the components of the architecture
that made the atmosphere so rich and conducive to interesting experiences and
conversations. Indeed, Kings Road was notorious for the ways in which it inspired
a sense of freedom in its guests. He noted that there was a strongly marked Japanese feeling in spite of the concrete walls and surmised that the rhythm created by
the joints of the wall modules was responsible. Natural colors and finishes contributed: gray cement, unstained redwood, unfinished fiberboard, weathered copper,

boughs of gray-green eucalyptus. The furniture line was kept low, and Harris was taken by the elegant and seemingly improvisational way Pauline Schindler served meals—trays of food and drink that became tabletops when placed on redwood stools. Because of Schindler's handling of materials, particularly the concrete walls, inside and outside became one continuous space. The nature that came so freely indoors at the Kings Road house was the same nature that had moved the child Harwell so much—"the gentle nature . . . that one didn't have to protect himself from."

And there was one final detail of Schindler's poetry at Kings Road—light. Harris wrote, "Fixtures were concealed. Sometimes the sources were too, as when a reflecting wall or ceiling seemed to make its own light. Other times the source was a cluster of eucalyptus leaves, still attached to their branch and drooping as in nature but now from the tie-beam that concealed the lamp. Light from many such sources produced an overall glow and points of direct light, as the several fires (one in each room, another in each patio) added sparkle. With a fire indoors beckoning to another in the garden, indoors and outdoors became even more one."[61]

Schindler—exuberant, long-haired, joking, in white duck trousers and open-collar shirt—and Harris—shy, exceedingly polite, and dapper—were far more alike than the differences in their personal styles suggest. Both reacted to and synthesized the same elements—Wright's organic form, European Modernism, and nature, of the sort found especially in California. Their struggles to make something original out of these forces rarely caused their buildings to look alike, but they did partake of the same feeling. The Kings Road house, like the Hollyhock House and the California landscape, was fated to become a memory, albeit a memory of a particularly vivid sort. When, in 1974, Harris wrote Pauline Schindler about his recollections of the place, his descriptions became almost a definition of Susanne Langer's "illusion of architecture" idea. Kings Road had undergone severe changes, but Harris's remembrance of its "visible expression of feeling" (or "atmosphere") brings the ghosts of those who understood it to life again. He wrote: "Even though the livers and thinkers are gone, evidences of living and thinking remain. So, in the drafting room are drawings and drawing boards and drawing tools. As in the other rooms, it seems that the occupant will be back shortly and activity will resume. It is the pattern of particulars that makes the form—building-form as much as use-form. It is this rather than the dictations of the abstract that creates living form and gives universal significance. No other building says this more clearly."[62]

4.

Rubbing Aladdin's Lamp, 1932–1934

Douglas Haskell had been sent out by the Record—*he was just a freelance writer—to interview Wright for the 1928 series called "In the Nature of Materials." One of the stories he told me that I remember so well was that he was walking around the garden there at Taliesin with Wright. There were some visitors coming, hopefully a client, later in the day. He remarked that Wright reached up and pulled some flowers off of a tree and took them out and scattered them over the water in the pool there, and then he turned to Haskell, smiled and said, "Rubbing Aladdin's Lamp."*

HARWELL HARRIS to Judy Stonefield,
UCLA Oral History Series,
August 22, 1979

It WAS IN 1932, soon after Neutra's return from Europe, that Clive Delbridge, an old friend from sculpture class at the Otis Art Institute, handed Harris his first commission, a home for himself and his new bride, Pauline Lowe. The plan Harris developed—a simple L with a courtyard held in the crook of its perpendicular arms by a street-facing garage—drew its inspiration from the organic forms of Frank Lloyd Wright's architecture. A walkway past the garage and through the court placed a person at the juncture of the arms and thus at the center of the house, a quality that became a characteristic of all later Harris buildings.[1] It was a Wrightian beginning, but the development bore all the blandishments of Modernism—a steel frame, a sheathing of bubble stone wall panels, and a flat roof.[2] Although he had been absent, Neutra's influence on Harris had certainly not weakened. In this first house, he was clearly present in the form of a muse. As it happened, however, this was not the Lowe design destined to introduce the singular vision of Harwell Harris to the public.

After his return from Europe, an enthusiastic Neutra had put Harris to work on a scheme to bring the Museum of Modern Art exhibition, "The International Style," to Los Angeles. The show had to have monied local sponsors, so Neutra assigned Harris and Ain the task of calling businessmen. Harris called John G. Bullock, the president of Bullock's Wilshire, who had already shown a taste for Modern art in commissioning the stunning Jacques Peters interiors of his own store. In their conversation, Harris's tact betrayed sensitivity to Bullock's previous patronage while it also revealed his genuine excitement about the show. "Over the telephone I told him that this exhibition would revolutionize architecture in the same way the 1925 Paris Exposition had revolutionized the decorative arts. I knew he must be familiar with the decorative arts."[3] He was right. Bullock became one of the directors of institutions subscribing to the exhibition and the show opened in Los Angeles on the fifth floor of his store in July 1932 and ran until August 20.

From every indication, Harris was delighted by the show and the ideas expressed in it. Although he has no memory of reading the Philip Johnson, Henry Russell-Hitchcock book *The International Style*, he was certainly familiar through Neutra with its major themes—concrete or steel structures, eliminating the need

Ludwig Mies van der Rohe, German Pavilion for the International Exhibition in Barcelona, Spain, 1929.
Courtesy of the Mies van der Rohe Archive, Museum of Modern Art, New York

for load-bearing walls and thus lightening the mass, the visual regularity of window and door openings of standard sizes grouped together, and a horizontality emphasized by broad expanses of white stucco, lacking any ornamentation. Even though he had not built anything himself, he couldn't help the overwhelming feeling that he was caught up in a movement. Predictably, at the opening he was taken by the model of Frank Lloyd Wright's House on the Mesa. Not so predictably he became "an instant admirer" of Mies van der Rohe's Barcelona Pavilion.[4] With his enthusiastic reaction to the simple glass and steel building (what William Jordy has described as "light planes modulating a continuous space"), Harris hinted at the direction his architecture would follow.[5]

To some extent Harris would always be interested in articulating Wright's organic form inside a lighter, more modern mass. Neutra had taught him how to take the heft out of form through the use of steel and concrete structures, and it is possible that what stirred Harris about Mies's Barcelona Pavilion was the way in which a powerful formal statement was made without compromising the overall delicacy of the building's spirit. The solutions of Neutra and Mies notwithstanding, Harris was about to be forced by circumstances to develop his own way of keeping mass lean and immaterial without the aid of either steel or concrete.

Pauline Lowe was denied a loan for the house Harris designed. The loan company had objected to the steel frame, the prefabricated bubble stone panels, and the flat roof. Although she had a good job as a buyer for the French Room at

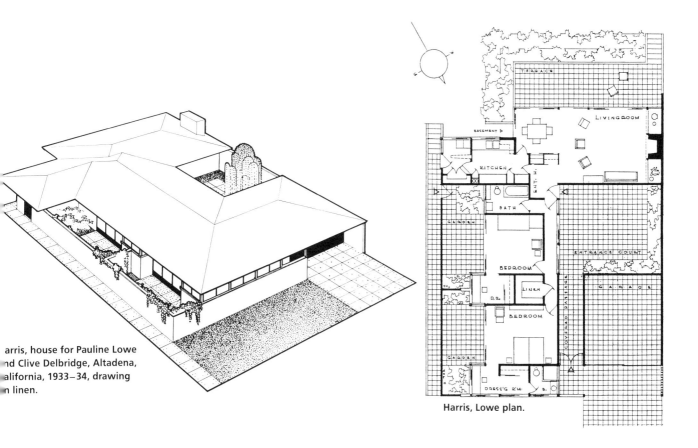

Harris, house for Pauline Lowe and Clive Delbridge, Altadena, California, 1933–34, drawing on linen.

Harris, Lowe plan.

Bullock's Wilshire, she and Delbridge, a sculptor who worked part-time at a nursery, did not have the prerogative (open to some early patrons of Modern architecture) of paying for the house outright. They had to get a loan and that meant Harris had to redesign the house. The house that came off his drawing board in 1933 kept the L-shaped plan but substituted a wooden frame for the steel one, board and batten walls for the bubble stone panels, and a hipped roof for the flat roof. With these changes, Harris had precociously arrived at a mature, original variation of Modern architecture.

Radical changes are rarely as abrupt as they seem, and Harris's alternative Lowe house was no exception. Each of the three areas of change—the framing material, the sheathing, and the roof shape—had an evolution that can be loosely traced through Harris's experiences. For instance, before and during the design and development stage of the Lowe house, Harris was a frequent visitor in the home of Carl Anderson, a furniture designer who had become a friend when they were each studying painting with Stanton Macdonald-Wright. Anderson lived in a house he had remodeled on a hillside in a rather wild, undeveloped inner city area called Fellowship Park (where Harris would later build his own house). Anderson's house was stone and wood, but his remodeling was very strongly influenced by Japanese designs. Harris had long been interested in Japanese art (indeed, he shared this interest particularly with Clive Delbridge), but this house sparked his enthusiasm for Japanese architecture.[6]

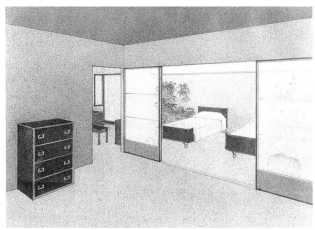

The form of the Japanese structure, as Harris experienced it in Carl Anderson's house and observed it in the books he had begun to study, had a strong appeal.[7] In a 1975 letter to Jan Strand, a friend in California, who had inquired about the influence of the Orient on him, Harris wrote:

I liked the clear shapes and clean spaces of the Japanese house. I enjoyed its equal concern with indoors and outdoors. I applauded its harmonizing of natural and geometric forms, playing up the superficial similarities. Stone sculpture most satisfied my liking for mass. The Japanese house most satisfied my liking for immaterial form—space. It did not displace space; it marked space, it shaped space. And the materials of the Japanese building—hardly more than thin lines and flat planes—were arranged to effect rhythm, rhythm without mass. My first architectural love, as you know, was Wright's Hollyhock House. This is rhythm with mass and with arabesque. It was something I had admired in early Greek sculpture and even more in Chinese stone sculpture. But the Japanese building eschewed mass and made me want to be an architect more than a sculptor. I still love mass but never find it as satisfying in a building as in stone sculpture.[8]

As he makes clear, the attraction was not simply the lighter mass but also the increased opportunity for creating a rhythmic unfolding of form. It was the rhythm of Hollyhock House and Kings Road that had made him think of Japanese design, but he now realized that with a wooden construction the rhythmic play could be much stronger. Wooden framing members marked off bays that could then be broken into smaller shapes by sliding doors and window panels. Grass mats added their own design to the composition.

Harris, Lowe house interior.
Photograph by Fred R. Dapprich

Having been schooled by Neutra, Harris was eager to develop rhythmic patterns in a modular way, and it was at the Lowe house that he arrived at three feet as his preferred porportioning unit. The combination living and dining room, only twelve feet wide, was, he felt, too small to accommodate the more standard four-foot module. By manipulating patterns of three-foot spaces Harris saw that he could enlarge the feeling of the room: "If the same 12 foot wide glass wall were in 4 units, the wall not only looked wider, but if I used a pair of doors in the center, I could get a 6 foot wide opening for passage and the two flanking single doors could be screened and used for light and ventilation. So, the unit was scaled to the wall and the room. Since I used plaster (or redwood boards) for walls and ceilings, there was no greater economy in the 4 foot unit."[9]

Harris, Lowe house drawings on linen: *left,* bedroom and sleeping porch with beds rolled out on the porch; *right,* fireplace and flanking tokonomas.

Gypsum board, plywood, and his preferred panel material, Celotex, came in four-foot widths, but Harris could always use the extra one foot on upper walls. (They were particularly handy for the intersection of the four-inch fascia and the

Louis B. Easton, C. C. Curtis ranch, Pasadena, ca. 1909.
California Arts & Architecture,
May 1939

ceiling.) Redwood boards, along with their battens, marked off intervals of one foot each. Likewise, but seemingly only by coincidence, the customary Japanese sliding panel was also three feet wide.[10]

Harris copied the homemade sliding panels he had seen in Anderson's house (for which favor he would always credit the furniture designer as "associate") and put them to work in the Lowe plans. Using butter paper and pencil he experimented with the range of possibilities for breaking the doors and window panels into panes. Finally, the sliding doors were given three horizontal panes of glass each above a wooden support. Wall panels on either side (made to look like rice paper because Harris used cotton cloth impregnated with parafin, a material usually reserved for chicken houses and sold for one cent a square foot) were divided into eleven pairs of horizontal panes. Grass matting, another feature of Anderson's influence, required no adjustments by Harris. The blocks were exactly one foot square, the perfect size with which to mark the rhythm of Harris's interior space. Seeing them against the door panels, there could be no question that the time signature of the Lowe house was three beats to a measure.

The board and batten exterior walls that replaced the bubble stone of the original Lowe design had an equally logical derivation. Harris had seen them all his life, as they were an indigenous, inexpensive form of construction in California. Their thinness—they were usually only one inch by twelve inches—did not connote cheapness to him but rather gentle nature and the simple means by which man could separate himself from it if necessary. Left unpainted, they became even stronger evocations of Japanese architecture. Moreover, Harris admired the way the battens marked off regular intervals, becoming "the thin lines and flat planes . . . arranged to effect rhythm, rhythm without mass."

Around the turn of the century, the Pasadena architects Greene and Greene had used boards and battens unapologetically and with graceful sympathy in such houses as the Bandini house of 1903. But in 1933 Harris had not heard of the architect brothers. If there was a direct influence, it came from a house he passed every

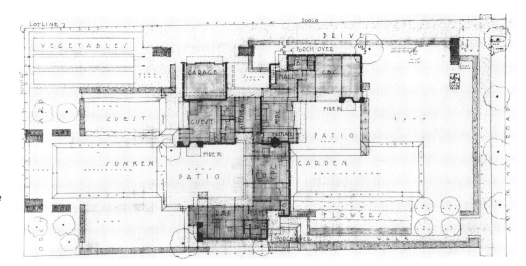

R. M. Schindler, Kings Road house plan, 1922.

Architectural Drawing Collection, University Art Museum, University of California at Santa Barbara

day on his way to the Lowe site in Altadena. He had found himself admiring it because of its low, one-story shape and the redwood boards and battens. He would later learn that it was known as the Curtis ranch and that it had been designed and built by an Arts and Crafts devotee, Louis B. Easton.[11] In 1933, confronted with a major conceptual change for the Lowe project, it was enough that the Easton house and a few other anonymous structures appealed to Harris's subconscious with an obvious solution.

At one point in the evolution of the house's development Harris must have believed that the change to wood frame and redwood boards and battens might be enough to satisfy the loan company. Among the drawings in the University of Texas collection is a colored rendering of the Lowe house—changes in material made— but a flat roof persisting (see photo page C-3). If Harris was reluctant to give up the flat roof, this is the only indication. The hipped roof he eventually gave the Lowe house was inspired by the roofs he had seen in the Wasmuth edition of Frank Lloyd Wright's work. Declaring a special regard for the sheltering image of the roof shape, Harris would return to the hip throughout his career.[12]

As the second Lowe concept came together, it became clear that Harris had not thrown off the influences of European Modernism as he knew it through Neutra, but rather that he had taken them beyond the superficial expression of his first attempt to something deeper and more personal. Everything was still there (Neutra's sense of mass and modular development, a Wrightian plan and roof shape); they were just a little less obvious and a little more refined due to the intervention of Japanese architecture. The change in Harris that the Lowe house reflects cannot, however, be credited to Japanese architecture alone.

The Lowe house exhibited certain traces of Schindler. The plan, no doubt because of its connections with Wright's organic plans, evokes comparisons with Schindler's Kings Road house. Both houses are approached by a walkway through nature to the center of an L-shaped form (Kings Road is the fusion of two such plans).[13] In both, all rooms open onto courtyards, or patios, through sliding doors.

Neither Schindler nor Harris considered a patio to be lower in the hierarchy of a building than an interior room. Indeed, Schindler considered the roof porches at Kings Road with the sleeping baskets he provided to be the bedrooms. Harris, too, fully expected his clients to sleep in the outdoor garden section of their rooms, as his drawing showing beds with wheels (already pushed outside to the porch) demonstrates.[14] Lighting was indirect and hidden in sections of the ceiling that were dropped even with an interior cornice molding that ran smoothly through the house, connecting all windows and doors in its reach.

Finally, Harris's attitude toward architecture as it was expressed in the Lowe house demands one last comparison with Schindler. To begin with, he shared with Schindler a similar approach to European Modernism. When he was told that his stucco and steel had been rejected, he simply dropped them. He did not attempt a gestalt of the look by tampering with his materials, using paint on his wood, for instance. He had liked the International Style exhibition but he certainly did not see it as prescriptive.[15] Second, and of equal importance, was his very unmonumental approach to the Lowe house. Indeed, he rather liked the liberating mood of places that felt temporary. Nothing, he would come to feel, was as deadly as an architect's attempt at permanence.

From his earliest childhood he had believed that architecture was little more than a necessity and that most practitioners (with, granted, varying degrees of ingenuity) were merely involved in the task of keeping rain off their clients' heads. Wright had helped him overcome the prejudice that architecture had to be stifling, that it had to be a kind of straitjacket for the soul, but he still balked when he thought about how this very powerful medium was used to inhibit people. His response to a new architecture building on the University of Southern California campus is quintessential Harris and helps explain his attitude toward the Lowe house and almost all his other buildings:

In 1929 the University of Southern California was ready to dedicate its new architecture building. The old architecture building there . . . was a World War I temporary building. It was made up of panels and it was on a cement slab floor and at the ground plates it was bolted. It had a flat roof. And it was an ideal School of Architecture building because when they had special things that students would want to do—an exhibition or something else of the kind—they would pull out walls and move them out and change things around so that the Bermuda grass court would become a part of it. It was ideal that way. But finally they were going to be given an architecture building [in keeping with the other buildings on campus]. Well, all the buildings at that time were Romanesque, brick Romanesque with limestone lintels and other things of this kind. The building [when it was finished] looked alright, but suddenly they [the students] were moved into a building that was a prison to them. *It was a prison.* That's exactly it. It was a prison. And I can remember the remark, "Well, maybe it wouldn't seem so bad after it got all marked up with graffiti and things." The perfection and permanency about it were the things that just frightened them.[16]

Among the Modern architects Harris knew, there was no one who understood and appreciated the appeal of the temporary, or ephemeral, as well as Schindler, who had raised it to a kind of high art. During these early years in Los Angeles, Harris admired what he called Schindler's "architectural flowers," engaging evidence that architecture could be a momentary experience, that it could have wit and fancy.[17] Schindler took on the design of temporary buildings with enthusiasm, applying his imagination to everything no matter how small the problem. With budgets that were impossibly low, Schindler seemed inspired. His inventiveness allowed him to use materials with no prior history as building materials in novel and, Harris believed, "spectacular" ways. The Braxton Gallery on Vine Street became dramatic when Schindler designed a striking canvas awning whose steel supports could be manipulated to block the sun while adding a functional, contemporary look. In the foreword to Esther McCoy's book *Vienna to Los Angeles: Two Journeys*, Harris recalled that many of Schindler's flowers "were not made to endure. They charmed," he wrote, *"as nothing permanent could."* [18]

This element of charm (a word Schindler himself used to differentiate artistic expression from machine production) seems closely aligned with the basic principle of organic design.[19] In a world characterized by rapid changes almost any building shaped by Louis Sullivan's maxim—form follows function—was destined to be a temporary building. New clients begot new functions; even altered landscapes could undermine the original organic form. This was no less true of houses than it was of the small businesses—restaurants and galleries—that Schindler designed—perhaps more true. Frank Lloyd Wright's mythic stature might serve to protect some of his organic buildings against the incursions of time and change. Schindler's flowers were, by contrast, egoless and, as he well knew, bound for obscurity. Nevertheless, Harris wrote, these temporary buildings "occupy permanent places in my memory."[20]

Harris not only took note of Schindler's attitude, he intuitively understood and appreciated it. Schindler, Harris would later write, "was the first to point out in the connection of a frame, or a method of flashing, a theme sufficient to regulate an entire composition. It led me to look at each new job as a new set of circumstances, and to expect new forms to emerge naturally from it."[21] And herein lies Schindler's primary contribution to Harris's developing sensibility. Like Schindler, Harris would always be interested in taking on specific design challenges, using his imagination to create a feeling of intimacy and immediacy. He might use standardized parts, but he could never think in terms of standardized people. This attitude would make Harris's later work for Dallas developer Trammell Crow—shopping centers, high-rise apartment buildings, and commercial office space—more difficult and out of character. His discomfort with the ponderous expression of permanency would make his Greenwood Mausoleum of 1956–57 almost a *non sequitur* in the gradual evolution of his career. In the 1950s monumentality was the mannerist outcome of an aging Modernism. But it was still the 1930s, the movement was just stirring, and the delicacy of the Lowe house could easily be read as the full flowering of something new, and that something was quickly and accurately labeled Modern.

The Lowe house, which cost its young owners only $3,900, hit a nerve. In some ways, it is possible to measure the effect of it in the 1930s by how familiar, and even how commonplace, it appears in the 1990s. The boxlike exterior form of the house, with low, overhanging roof, high redwood fence enclosing private gardens, and a garage incorporated into the overall composition, was copied all over America in the 1940s and 1950s. Like the Gamble and Blacker houses by Greene and Greene, which spawned hundred of bungalows, it can hardly be held accountable for the adulterations and indiscretions perpetrated under its influence. What was more important, perhaps, from the standpoint of Harris's career is that two unknown architects in Chicago appeared to have copied not just the spirit of the house but the letter.

Soon after its completion in 1934, the Lowe house received national attention because Chicago architects R. Paul Schweikher and Theodore W. Lamb won the $2,500 grand prize in the General Electric small house competition with a virtual duplicate of it. *California Arts & Architecture*, which had originally published it, now responded by reprinting the plan alongside the Chicago plan. The *Architectural Forum* and *Apéritif* did the same. A scandal ensued at the suggestion of plagiarism, but Schweikher and Lamb, who admitted that they had seen the Harris plan, denied the charges and kept the money.[22] Their reaction was almost inconsequential, however, compared to the overwhelmingly favorable publicity Harris received. Years later, architects he met in New York would tell him that the Lowe house debacle was what had brought him to their attention.

Schweikher and Lamb, the prize-winning plan for the General Electric small house competition, which provoked accusations that Harris's Lowe house plan had been copied.
Architectural Forum, *June 1935*

5.

Jean Murray Bangs and a Career Takes Shape, 1934–1937

1919–1921: New York City.
Came with the idea of working in every industry in which women were employed as preliminary to Ph.D. in "Women in Industry." Abandoned this for attempt to save suffering humanity and uplift the poor and oppressed. Gave this up as bad job and returned to home in Los Angeles.

JEAN MURRAY BANGS, résumé entry

IN THE TEN YEARS since Harris's move to Los Angeles to attend the Otis Art Institute he had not only found his calling and his own architectural voice, he had begun to feel that he was one of a larger community of artists in Los Angeles. He counted as his friends the sculptors and painters and furniture designers from his experiences at Otis and the Art Students League as well as the architects—Neutra, Ain, and the more bohemian Schindler. Through them he was beginning to realize and appreciate California's growth and the ways in which settlers to the state underlined opportunities there and made the setting even more conducive to artistic thinking. "Their minds," Harris has said, ". . . were more on the new things they could do as a consequence of all these new things they discovered, and not so much upon reproducing or holding on to the older things."[1] A new world was clearly taking shape in Los Angeles, one that was less reliant on the traditions of Europe and the eastern United States and one that was willing to take on the task of defining America for Americans.

Meanwhile, and in the midst of this intellectual ferment, Harris's personal life was largely unchanged. He had started to eat and had long since regained his health, but, he said, "living at home with my mother in my Aunt and Uncle Harper's house, 1128 West 28th Street, during the time I was at Otis and immediately after, and earning no money, except during summer while I was at Pomona, I had developed no independence either financial or psychological."[2] Caught between two worlds and without the impetus to quit the former, Harris's nature, so prone to privacy already, may have become intensely serious and a bit cynical. In 1940 he recalled for the *Architectural Forum* his feelings about the Lowe house commission: "When I left school, building was at a low ebb and there were no jobs for beginning draftsmen. After a year-and-a-half's work on design projects, I found a friend who wanted to build. To my mind at that time the decline of the West had already reached an advanced stage and I doubted that I would ever build another building. This would be my first and my last executed project."[3]

He was heartened by the small Lowe fee he received, but, in these days before the house was built, he was to find a sense of confidence and independence not just in architectural design but in a person, Jean Murray Bangs. This woman, who was by nature lively, intelligent, and outspoken, would become a strong force in his life. She would facilitate his move from home, set into motion the design of the

Fellowship Park house, acquire an interior designer's license to help his clients purchase furniture at a cheaper rate. In short, she would expand Harris's world and foster his success in any way that she could. And she was a woman of considerable resourcefulness. In 1937 she would become Mrs. Harwell Hamilton Harris.

They met at a party in 1931, while Neutra was still away. It was a rather unusual party, progressing from the house of one hostess to the house of a second—down a hill and through a ravine—as the night wore on. Jean Bangs and Harris were the first two guests to arrive and, as the hostesses were busy with preparations, they fell into a conversation. Later, at the second house, they were the only guests who were sober. "When the party was over," Harris recalled, "we walked back through the ravine to where we had left our cars. It was a hilly district which was a part of the same hills as Fellowship Park (which I had not even heard of at that time). Jean took my arm. We parted with the understanding we would see one another again. I believe that was rather soon and at Jean's house and probably for dinner."[4]

Jean Bangs, born in Calgary, Canada, on August 25, 1894, was nine years Harris's senior. A graduate in economics from Berkeley, she had gone to New York with the intention of working in all the major labor unions in preparation for her larger goal of becoming the first woman secretary of labor. In New York she came to know Emma Goldman, Max Eastman, John Reed, and other intellectuals, among them Katherine Anne Porter.[5] In 1921 she had married a labor leader there, Abe Plotkin, with whom (wearing World War I leggings) she had hitchhiked from New York City to Los Angeles. By the time she met Harris, she was a social worker for the Los Angeles County Welfare Department and divorced from Plotkin, who had returned to the East. She was friendly with Pauline Schindler and had attended many of the Kings Road parties before the Schindlers separated. Coincidentally, the only architects she knew were Richard Neutra, whom she had met soon after his arrival, and Schindler.[6]

There were no more parties at Kings Road when the couple was getting to know each other so they spent their time together talking. Harris recalls that their conversation was mostly about architecture, and it is true that Jean began to record some of his comments in a notebook she would later call *Portrait of an Architect*. And yet there is evidence enough to indicate that their times together were punctuated by the humorous comments Jean could make—the limerick she wrote after meeting a female reporter who had interviewed Pancho Villa, the mischievous description of a black dress (held together with a single button) she had

Jean Murray Bangs in 1937, the year of her marriage to Harwell Hamilton Harris.

Courtesy of Jean Murray Bangs Harris

purchased at a studio lot in Hollywood.[7] One begins to see Jean and Harris as a couple, stepping out to Chinatown for Chinese food, spending the night at the beach on army cots in tents on the sand, Jean writing an occasional article for *California Arts & Architecture*, or getting Harris to model a sculpture of Clarence Muse, a black actor she had met at a meeting of the California Art Club in the Hollyhock House.[8] It is a picture of Los Angeles as a small town, where everyone knew almost everyone else and the settings, both architectural and natural, were animated by those for whom they had actually been intended.

Harris has recalled that his business was slow at this time, but in looking at the years 1935 and 1936 it is possible to see his young office beginning to take shape. It was at this time that a writer by the name of John Entenza stopped by to meet him, intrigued by the Lowe house he had seen while reading about the General Electric small house scandal in *California Arts & Architecture*.[9] It was soon after the Lowe house, too, that a young woman told Harris she wanted him to design her a house and, moreover, that she believed herself possessed of a "Gothic soul." This piece of information from Helene Kershner was destined to encourage a particular kind of Modern response in Harris. He finished the working drawings quickly, but because Kershner also possessed an empty pocketbook, the project stalled. And Jean Murray Bangs, who had a small savings, quit her job to become Harris's full-time assistant.[10] In the worst part of the Great Depression it was a token of faith and love that was not lost on Harris.

Meanwhile, Jean had moved to a house very near the Fellowship Park area where Carl Anderson lived.[11] It was then that she and Harris became aware that their favorite lot in the neighborhood was for sale. Jean bought it for very little money. Soon afterwards Pauline Lowe asked Harris to remove the Japanese sliding doors from her house (complaining that they rattled in the wind) and replace them with conventional hinged doors. Harris decided to buy them from the contractor (for $1.00 apiece) and have them delivered to the small wooded lot in Fellowship Park that was becoming more and more the place he and Jean planned to call home.

Out of this period of starts and stops there was, nevertheless, one project that emerged as a *bona fide* second commission, free of delays and interruptions. It was a home in Pasadena for Graham Laing, an economics professor at Cal Tech, and his wife. The Laings were friends of Neutra's who had elected not to hire him because of his dominant personality.[12] They hired Harris, a Neutra student, believing that they were more likely to get what they wanted. If they were expecting a

Harris, house for Mr. and Mrs.
Graham Laing, Pasadena, 1935.
Photograph by Fred R. Dapprich

Harris, Laing living room with
eggplant-colored linoleum and
white couch selected by Harwell
Harris.
Photograph by Fred R. Dapprich

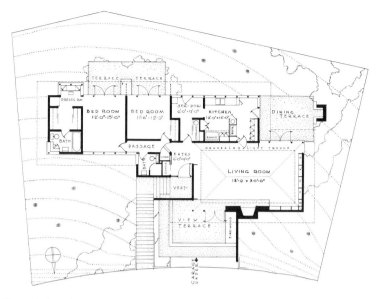

Harris, Laing plan.

somewhat diluted Neutra house, they may have been surprised. Harris had been the ideal student employee for Neutra. "I gave myself over completely with him," Harris has said. "I never thought of trying to introduce anything that I didn't consider was his. And then when I was away from him, then I was completely free."[13]

If in the Laing house Harris, the student, had broken away from Neutra, the teacher, he was also demonstrating that "completely free" was a relative idea. For the moment, it meant that he felt free to express the deeper influence of Frank Lloyd Wright. With its stucco walls, broad eaves, ribbon windows, and boxed-in balcony, Harris's Laing house showed that Harris's romance with the Wasmuth folio houses had not let up. To some small extent, because the Wright influence was pronounced, the Laing house, like the later De Steiguer home, is a reminder of how young and inexperienced he still was.

Harris later internalized Wright's architecture, taking liberties with ideas he had observed in the master's buildings so that they emerged in a uniquely Harris fashion and with a deeper resonance. In the Laing and De Steiguer houses, however, he was still acquainting himself with the language, getting to know the forms more intimately. For this reason it is useful to consider the Laing house together with the De Steiguer house of the next year. It, too, was in Wright's Prairie Style idiom—stucco, deep overhanging eaves, ribbon windows, and boxed-in balcony. It also happened to be in Pasadena.

Although neither house was large, Harris created the impression of space by opening one room into another—a living room into a garden, a bedroom into a bedroom. The most ingenious use of such an open plan would come later in Harris's house for the George Bauer family (1938), where the slanting of walls obviated the need for hallways.[14] But in the Laing and De Steiguer houses the method was also effective. The living rooms of both houses opened onto second-story balconies, and the Laing bedrooms on ground level had access to bricked patios.

The plans of the houses demonstrate very simply how Harris enlisted the module for the creation of his form. In each, the unfolding of space is more dramatic and sculptural than in the earlier Lowe plan. The kind of slow disclosure of form that would later make his work difficult to photograph can be seen in the foyer of the Laing house. There, visitors must make a ninety-degree right turn to a living room that presents itself through a six-foot (two-unit-wide) opening or take three steps to a one-unit-wide opening leading to the left down a private hallway to the bedrooms beyond. In the De Steiguer house a straightforward entrance into the living room, on axis with the front door, is made more interesting through Harris's use of a built-in sofa that crosses the visitor's path, thereby forcing movement around it and thus acknowledgment of the little alcove it has created.

Both the Laing and the De Steiguer houses posed specific problems—the Laings wanted 150 feet of bookshelves and room to accommodate Professor Laing's seminars; the De Steiguers wanted a shop connected to yet discrete from their house for the purpose of selling imports from Majorca. Harris dispatched the problems easily enough. The Laings got a large living room surrounded by bookshelves, and the room could be made still larger by opening the doors to the balcony. The De Steiguers got a gift shop that faced Colorado Boulevard, the main thoroughfare between Los Angeles and Pasadena, but was also accessible to their home via a courtyard.[15]

Photographs, contemporary with the houses, illustrate Harris's solutions, but they do not capture the nuances of his Modern design that were beginning to make it so original and poetic. In the Laing house, for instance, interior color was rich and unusual.[16] Stucco walls were a sand color and window rails and mullions were deep coral red. The linoleum floors were eggplant purple. The landscaping also broke from the traditional mold of formal and somewhat pretentious domestic lawns of suburbia. Wanting a more natural planting schedule, Harris contacted Theodore Paine, a leading authority on California's native plants, who recommended eucalyptus, Catalina cherry, wild coffee, wild lilac, and lemonade berry, all of which were readily accessible, inexpensive, and appropriate.[17]

The emphasis on natural materials was more obvious in the De Steiguer house, where walls were covered with grass wallpaper and floors were wood. Color emerged in the De Steiguers' furnishing which, somewhat to Harris's chagrin, they selected themselves. Nevertheless, in the De Steiguer house, even more than in the Laing house, Harris countered the overall heaviness of the Wrightian idiom with a lightness that was entirely his own. For example, on the balconies he

Harris, house for Mr. and Mrs.
Edward De Steiguer, Pasadena,
1936.
Photograph by Fred R. Dapprich

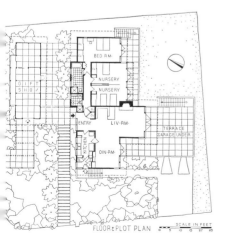

Harris,
De Steiguer plan
and
children's rooms.
*Photograph by
Fred R. Dapprich*

Harris, house for Mr. and Mrs.
George Bauer, Glendale, 1938.
Photograph by Fred R. Dapprich

Harris, George Bauer house at
night, view from the patio.
Photograph by Fred R. Dapprich

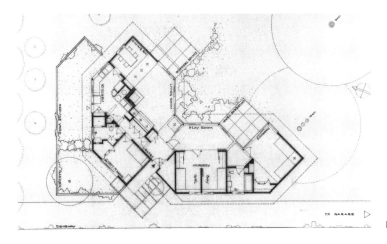

Harris, Bauer plan.

extended the eaves three feet by using corrugated iron. The iron not only could support itself for that distance, but it overlapped conveniently and, most important, it looked light. Although it had a more industrial connotation, its appearance was as natural on the terrace as the De Steiguers' bamboo and net screens.

It was the little shop for imported rugs and baskets, however, that most caught Harris's imagination. Although the De Steiguer house was photographed almost exclusively from the front, Harris made two colored renderings of the side where the shop faced the thoroughfare. The shop was wooden with board-and-batten construction throughout, and Harris gave it a trellised, ground-level terrace covered over with a pergola. The wooden boards of the pergola could support and thus display the primitive Majorcan rugs while contributing an overall lightness and natural simplicity to the entire shop. Also, Harris's desire to shield the shop from the street led to his first use of an ingenious roof design. Based on a hip, this roof called for raising and extending one side, so that instead of meeting the other three sides at the top it passed beyond them, creating an area for high, clerestory windows along the ridge. By creating what he called a "fold" in the roof, he had figured out a way to get natural light into the blind (usually street) sides of his buildings.

The shop is the best part of the De Steiguer house and it is quite possible that its success is due primarily to its relatively low priority in the overall scheme. That is not to say it was unimportant to the clients, but rather that the house itself was the focus of their time and money. Harris, however, was a little more himself playing with the cheaper forms and materials of the shop. "I always do better work on a poor piece of paper or a discarded piece," Harris once explained in talking about his drawing, "because I never think of it as being final. I'm more daring when the paper is worthless. . . . What starts out pretty temporary then becomes final."[18] Contained within these words was the key that was beginning to unlock the best of Harris's sensibility.

The Helene Kershner house of 1935 was wood, in spite of the fact that at their first meeting she had told Harris she wanted a house of stone. Stone, she felt, was more evocative of the Gothic. "There was a lapse of time in our consultations," Harris has written, "and in my tricky way, I got around to suggesting the use of the expensive stone in the fireplace and chimney whose back would form one wall of an alcove behind the fireplace. She fell for the proposal of having this small room in which she could be 'gothic.'"[19] As it turned out, Kershner was so happy with the house that she chose never to build the alcove.

**Harris, house for Helene
Kershner, Los Angeles, 1935.**
Photograph by Fred R. Dapprich

Rising above a steep, corner site, the redwood house showed a series of volumetric boxlike spaces to the street. Because of its corner location on a lot with few trees, the Kershner house had a quality of exposure that was almost urban in feeling. Harris protected the privacy of his client by sheathing upstairs porches as well as downstairs rooms and fences in redwood boards and battens. A hipped roof spread itself protectively across the top. In such a buttoned-up manner, the L-shaped plan followed the L of the intersecting streets, but on the opposite side the house embraced the outdoors. The lap of the L was opened to the interior through glass. Indeed, Harris stressed the outdoor-indoor relationship by bringing the redwood paneling into the living, dining, and music rooms as well as the entry vestibule. Along these same lines he called for a stone (slate) path to run through and around the perimeters of the public rooms, which were concrete covered with carpet. Harris gave the stone fireplace a ribbed copper hood and flanked it with niches, or Japanese tokonomas, whose dropped ceilings of translucent glass hid the electric lighting fixtures above them. As a result, the fireplace wall became the immediate focus of the room.

A combination of factors gave the Kershner house a striking appearance. In spirit it was not so different from the Lowe house. It had the same redwood boards and battens, the same hipped roof—even the tokonomas had counterparts in the earlier house. But while the Lowe house was on a relatively flat piece of property, the Kershner house was on a steep site. Here, in contrast to the Laing house, Harris designed a hillside residence that departed from Frank Lloyd Wright's Prairie

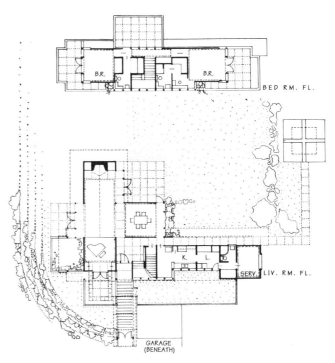

Harris, Kershner house detail of
ribbed copper fireplace hood
with flanking tokonomas.

Photograph by Fred R. Dapprich

Harris, Kershner plan.

Harris, Kershner house detail of
wooden struts.

Photograph by Fred R. Dapprich

Style. Indeed, the dramatic entrance with wooden struts emerging out of the house framework and down to the ground suggests Schindler and the kinds of visual compositions he made to connect light, wooden sections of houses—porches and balconies—with heavier stucco and concrete elements. That Kershner had such a combination of elements (chiefly, a three-tiered stone retaining wall) was a function, Harris recalls, of her irresistible way with people. She had talked a team of WPA workers, building a similar wall for a public park bordering Riverside Drive, into coming to her lot and doing the same work.[20]

Jean didn't find Kershner as charming as Harris found her.[21] Rather, she was frustrated that this client, who had so little money, bought a piano and had it delivered before the house was roofed, that she bought an antique wicker baby carriage even though she didn't have a baby (or a husband). And once when Kershner bought a new pair of shoes, Jean ordered her back to the store, saying, "Every penny must go to finish this house." Perhaps Jean felt a small amount of jealousy toward this attractive young woman, but it is more likely that Kershner, with her winning ways and her conventional and amusingly inappropriate pretenses, was simply at odds with Jean's more individualistic, hard-won worldview. Jean, for instance, did not care to have children, she would never purchase a piano she couldn't play, and under no circumstances would she frivolously spend money on her wardrobe. Like Harris, Jean was a truly Modern spirit, sensitive to the ways in which conventional thinking could weaken the kind of life she wanted to live. She later confessed to a friend, "One could easily think I don't like people [but that is because] I have to

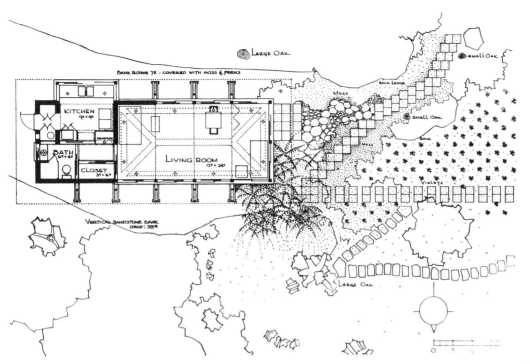

Harris, Fellowship Park plan, 1935.

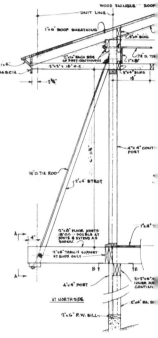

Fellowship Park, drawing of buttresses.

protect my own inner life or I wouldn't ever have an idea."[22] Modern architecture held out the kind of protection and nourishment she wanted. It is little wonder that she was to live so well, so simply and elegantly, in the very hidden, unfurnished, and, for a time, closetless and plumbingless Fellowship Park house that Harris began designing after the Kershner construction was over.

When the doors from the Pauline Lowe house were delivered, there was nothing on the steeply sloping lot but a small shed, so Harris stored them in it. Several months later, however, he discovered that the rails of the doors were beginning to warp. Realizing he would have to do something soon, he decided to dismantle the small shed and frame out a structure that could hold the sliding doors. When he ran out of doors, as he did for two bays, he simply made a solid section that helped to brace the structure.

The pavilion, which began as one large room, twelve by twenty-four feet, did not interrupt the hillside but rather worked with it to create a dramatic effect. The entrance at the back of the house was accessible beyond a series of steps that led down the hillside. Once inside, however, only twelve feet (the equivalent of two six-foot bays or four three-foot units) separated the visitor from the opposite exposure, which hovered dramatically above the drop-off of land. Here Harris planted a gift from Ed and Margaret De Steiguer, three or four little boxes of baby tears that spread rapidly. He also planted asparagus fern and mint he got from an aunt. "When expecting visitors," Harris has recalled, "I would hose it off and so fill the air with the mint odor (very fresh)."[23] It was his own version of "rubbing Aladdin's lamp."

So extraordinarily simple was the idea of a platform on a hillside that even the structural precautions and adjustments necessary to make it secure heightened the overall effect. This is particularly true of the outriggers that occurred at each bay on the horizontal lengths of the pavilion. Here, a pair of floor joists, one on each side of the post, are cantilevered three feet to receive an angled wood brace and a steel rod that together form a compression-tension buttress.

Opposite, Fellowship Park.
Photographs by Fred R. Dapprich

When the walls of the Fellowship Park house were closed in Jean Bangs and Harris moved into it, though it still lacked plumbing. Down the hill was a cesspool and the WC left from the rotten, half-wood, half-canvas shack that Harris had torn down for its materials. "We erected an enclosure around it and went down a steep, winding path with stone steps when we needed to use it. We took cold showers with a hose on the pebbled entrance to the house, one of us clothed and standing on the public path above to warn the other if anyone was approaching on the path."[24]

Although there was no electricity, Harris had dropped a three-foot shelf beneath the hipped ceiling and around the interior perimeter of the room for indirect light (in the manner of Frank Lloyd Wright). Neither Jean nor Harris had or wanted furniture. The grass matting on the floor and a small bed that served as a low couch were almost enough. With the addition of a small Chinese table that Harris gave to Jean as an early birthday present and a large black ceramic vase, which had belonged to his paternal grandmother, Fellowship Park was finished and ready to be photographed.[25] Both the table and the vase, whose lines he admired, would appear in photographs of almost all of Harris's early houses.

The Fellowship Park house was an immediate success. It won the 1937 *House Beautiful* Small House Competition and first prize in the Pittsburgh Glass Institute Competition for a house under $12,000 (outdoing two houses by Richard Neutra). Delighted, Harris's mother gave him the $2,000 needed to make the house true to the sketches he had made showing the proposed kitchen and bath.[26]

Harris was neither a registered architect nor a member of the American Institute of Architects when he won the honor award of the Southern California chapter of the American Institute of Architects in 1938.[27] Such acknowledgment from the architectural profession certainly suggests the impact the Fellowship Park house made at the time. Perhaps more intriguing, however, is the Pittsburgh Glass award.

By stressing as it did the use of glass, it reminded the public that the little

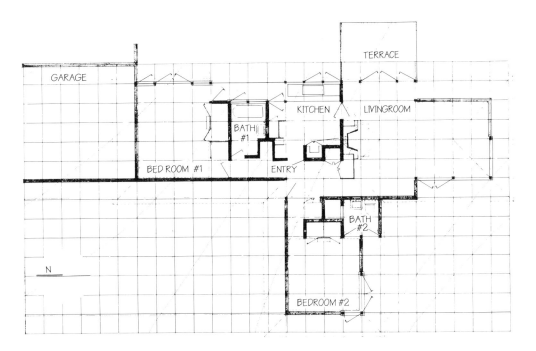

Harris, Clark plan.

pavilion, often shown in photographs as open-air, was really a glass house. In this light the Fellowship Park house invites comparisons with the famous Modern glass houses that came later—Mies van der Rohe's Farnsworth house in Fox River, Illinois (1945–1950) and Philip Johnson's Glass House in New Canaan, Connecticut (ca. 1949).[28] These houses sat in the landscape to be seen as objects and to be understood as architectural statements. By contrast, Harris's Fellowship Park house was meant to slip rather inconspicuously into nature and merge with it. Behind these different attitudes lay the essence of the dichotomy that would later split the Modern Movement—the seeds, too, of Harris's eventual decline in popularity. In the moment after its completion, however, it signaled a surge in Harris's modest but constant rise in commissions.

Jean helped Harris get his next job, a beach house for Marion Clark, because Clark's sister was a close friend she had known at Berkeley. Clark, an unmarried schoolteacher from Oakland, presented Harris with two adjoining lots near Point Lobos, just out of reach of the waves that crash onto the beach at Carmel. His job was to design a small house for holiday and weekend retreats.

The house he designed turned a quiet side to the street (with only a few openings) and, except for one back bedroom, turned all its rooms toward the sea. The three-foot grid was adhered to in the house and was particularly noticeable in the dropped lighting, the door and window widths, and the exterior eaves. Although the house was stuccoed inside and out with sand from the Carmel beach to make it blend with the landscape and the white roof recalled the whitecaps of the ocean, color—bright color—also played an important role in defining the forms of the Clark house. Turquoise posts and window rails disappeared in the view of the ocean. Exterior soffits were natural-color redwood, as were bookshelves and cabinet work. Rugs were patterned with crimson, yellow-green, and red-violet. In the kitchen the plastic laminate and backsplash trim were crimson and the floor was turquoise-blue jasper linoleum.[29]

Harris, Entenza house steel staircase.
Photograph by Fred R. Dapprich

Although most of his work throughout his career would be done for couples and families, it is worth noting that a number of single women came to Harris for residential design. His hipped roofs (which kept a house looking like a house) and his natural materials and colors tended to be androgynous, appealing to men and women alike. Harris had as much dislike for the bric-a-brac pretenses, silk-skirted vanities, floral wallpaper, and period frou-frou as the next Modern designer, but his antidote tended to be less extreme than the machine esthetic of the European Moderns. His next client was to make it clear that he considered this form of Modernism to be decidedly more masculine.

John Entenza, who had been so impressed by the competition scandal involving the Lowe house, finally came back a year and a half later. He told Harris he wanted a masculine-looking house and said that he had seen Fellowship Park and wanted to emphasize that that was the kind of house he *didn't* want, but, "because you could design this house, I know you can design the house I do want."[30] The house Harris designed sent him back to the lessons of Neutra and the forms of the International Style. As at the Laing house, however, one sees the trademarks of an influential idiom at work—in this case not Prairie Style but International Style—at the expense of Harris's own nascent and very authentic architectural sensibility. If Entenza misunderstood his architect's strengths, Harris nevertheless gave him an elegant, organized home, managing to avoid compromise with his own feelings about form and particularly color.

The house was wood frame covered with stucco, and the interlocking arcs of a driveway and a porte cochere (as well as another arc for the bedroom on the opposite side of the house) gave the house sculptural qualities that were uncommon in Harris's work where form was to be felt and not seen, except in the subtle patterns created by the materials. From a practical standpoint, however, the drive and porte cochere, which perfectly accommodated Entenza's 1925 Ford, provided a thoughtful solution to the problem of orienting a driveway on a hillside where backing out could be dangerous. It became a favorite answer to a common Los Angeles challenge.

The simple plan, with a horizontal living room and a kitchen and bathroom, was dramatized by the arc of the bedroom wall, which glided into the trees like a space-age observation deck. Harris made two twelve-foot-wide sliding glass doors extremely inexpensive by placing them on a barn-door track. Rails for the living room balcony, onto which they opened, and for the rooftop deck were steel pipe, and the exterior staircase, which led upward to the deck, was also steel. Harris

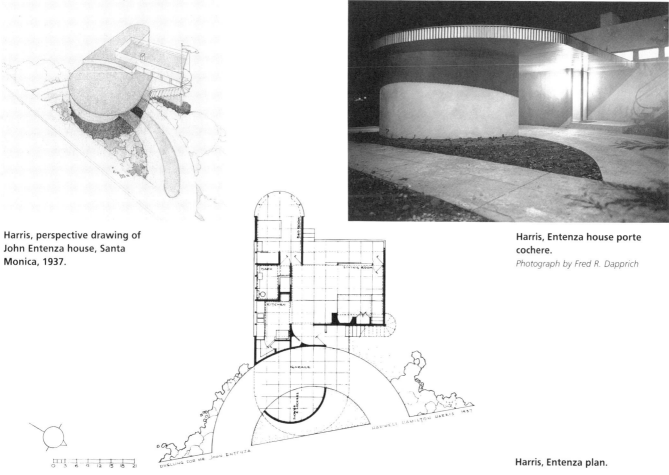

Harris, perspective drawing of
John Entenza house, Santa
Monica, 1937.

Harris, Entenza house porte
cochere.
Photograph by Fred R. Dapprich

Harris, Entenza plan.

suggested the staircase after one of Entenza's friends offered him a gift of steel from his fabrication plant.[31] (By making a feature of the steel, silhouetting the stairs in front of the stucco instead of a part of the building's fabric, Harris may have been expressing his admiration for a similar staircase on Neutra's entry—a stucco and steel "bungalow"—in the Austrian Werkbund Exhibition held in Vienna in 1932). In one of his most inspired touches at the Entenza house, Harris finished the curving edge of the porte cochere roof in corrugated iron. It may have been an abbreviated homage to the steel-faced arc of Neutra's 1935 house for movie director Josef von Sternberg.

Richard Neutra, house for the Austrian Werkbund Exhibition, Vienna, 1932.
Museum of Modern Art, New York

For all this cool, lean Modernism, some of the features Harris included in his earlier houses appeared in the Entenza house as well. For instance, the continuous wooden cornice line was adhered to throughout the interior of the house, as was the indirect lighting hidden behind dropped ceiling panels that Harris called light soffits. The ceiling was white and the walls were sand color. Tile was crimson. Fabrics were crimson, chartreuse, and natural color pongee silk. Doors and rails were gray green.[32] And Harris's skill with small budgets was the final defining feature of the Entenza house. The six-hundred-square-foot building cost a mere $2,700.

When *California Arts & Architecture* published the house in 1938, the anonymous writer announced, "So here it is, as smartly turned out as the season's new cars, and a man's house every inch of it."[33] Harris, unburdened by concerns for what seemed masculine or feminine in architecture, could hardly have been moved by the praise. In later patronage both personally and professionally, as publisher of *California Arts & Architecture*, Entenza's taste in architecture would follow even more the direction in which he urged Harris. His own later house in Santa Monica Canyon was designed by Charles Eames and Eero Saarinen, and the Case Study houses, sponsored by the magazine, celebrated a more skeletal, high-tech taste.

The minimalism that Entenza would come to favor was the Modernism of thin black structural steel and the wide expanses of plate glass it made possible. Before the overwhelming influence of Mies in California, this aesthetic was most commonly found in Neutra's buildings.[34] As Los Angeles neighborhoods, like Silver Lake, developed in the 1930s, it was possible to see houses that demonstrated diverging attitudes toward Modernism go up almost side by side. David Gebhard and Robert Winter have pointed out in their description of Silverwood Terrace that "it is interesting to see the different design philosophies of Neutra—the dwelling as an art-object-machine (Koblick House, 1937)—and Harris (the Walter Joel House, 1937)—the dwelling as a romantic shelter—on the same street."[35]

Harris's Joel House, with its daring plate glass wall section next to a fireplace, certainly indicated that Modern construction, of the sort he had learned from Neutra, had lost none of its thrill. And while Harris never wanted wood to look like metal, he frequently did paint (or, as he would say, "dye") it black to effect a more Japanese appearance. This he had done in the Lowe and Fellowship Park houses and in the very elegant George Bauer house. When this latter house with its Wrightian angles and Japanese-inspired details was published *California Arts & Architecture* stated, "Out of the ranks of modern houses, so serious in their demeanor, steps this one—simple, light and frankly playful." It is thus somewhat surprising that this house, more than any of Harris's early works, brings Neutra to mind.[36] It does not show the influence of Neutra on Harris so much as it anticipates an Americanized Neutra, a Neutra closer to nature, a Neutra that in any case did not yet exist in 1938. Still a devotee of the International Style, Neutra would not soften his pristine white Lovell house aesthetic until the following year, when he built the McIntosh house, the first of his redwood houses in Southern California.[37]

As for Harris, the fascination with European Modernism, never really fervent, was decidedly on the wane in the late 1930s. Gradually the trappings of that movement and even of Wright's powerful forms were evaporating from his architectural vocabulary. Although what remained—a lightness of mass, a sense of organic structure, of Modern, machine-made materials—seemed as evanescent as the aroma of fresh mint at Fellowship Park, it was this that would last.

Harris, Greta Granstedt house with uninterrupted view of Hollywood hills, 1938.
Photograph by Fred R. Dapprich

Harris, Granstedt plan.

6.   Houses with Good Manners, 1938–1942

Charles Cruze's car, on which he lavished such care and for which he felt compelled to dress properly, was an MG,—an early one, small, and with fine features, reminding me of Elinor Wylie's "These to me are beautiful people. . . . They wear small bones in wrists and ankles . . ." (I hope I've got that correct. I haven't read it since about 1924 when I contemplated making drawings to go with her verse.) Maybe I would come closer in describing it by comparing it to a faun. Just looking at it made one gentle, even as he hand-cranked the motor. (The sound of an electric starter would have seemed raucous.) Bending down in front of the radiator to lift the crank from its sling, and later restoring the crank to its sling after the motor had started, was almost a ritual. Refusing to let anyone else wash it, polish it, fix it, or adjust it was just to protect it. And to attend to it was to learn good manners.

HARWELL HARRIS,
letter to the author, 1986

Harris was becoming well known, and a steady stream of clients would soon give support to the *Architectural Forum*'s claim in 1940 that "by avoiding the cliches of the moment—whether 'modern' or 'traditional' —he has succeeded in establishing an idiom of his own." [1] For *California Arts & Architecture* he compiled a nine-point list of dos and don'ts with the title "In Designing the Small House." [2] Although it was not written in the breathless, intense style of a manifesto, it served him well as one. It is particularly instructive in light of its early date, 1935, and the faithfulness with which he adhered to its principles throughout his career, even, in fact, in designing the large house:

1. Don't make rooms serve as halls. To do so reduces the proper use of the floor area, disrupts the grouping, destroys the privacy, and so suggests crowdedness. Confine the main traffic stream to its proper channels and let rooms become quiet bays easily accessible to the main current but undisturbed by it.

2. Accept the fact that light attracts, and give every room a sunny exposure. Deserted space is waste space.

3. Don't crowd too many activities into one room. If necessary, reduce the size of the main room and provide alcoves off it for related activities. Minor activities, if unconfined, have a tendency to spread over more area than the major ones; and one often finds himself sleeping in a dressing room instead of dressing in a sleeping room as the consequence of someone's mistaken notion of how to save space.

4. Group the openings. If possible get all the windows together and all the solid wall together. Grouping the two makes a sizeable representation of each and gives scale to the room. Small holes punched here and there look piddling and make furniture arrangement difficult. Decide what walls should be glass, and leave the rest intact for "back."

5. Plan the walls of a room in scale with its floor. That is, in a small or narrow room reduce the height of the openings and lower the ceiling.

6. Keep the same finishes throughout. Cover every inch of the floor of the room with the same carpeting material, and use the same carpeting in every room. The constant repetition of a shape or a material creates the feeling of endlessness. Furthermore, sheer quantity of one plain material best displays the quality inherent in it.

7. Make one whole wall of the room of glass and open the room into a garden. With the solid material that the glass replaces, build a wall around the garden. Pave the floor of the garden next to the glass, making the outer floor only an inch or two lower than the inner

floor. The garden then becomes the outer portion of the room, separated from the inner portion by a removable glass screen. If possible, project the roof three feet or more beyond the screen and bring the eaves down to the very top of the opening. Board-in the under side of the eaves so that there is a low, horizontal ceiling just outside the opening. This extends the shelter of the interior to a portion of the exterior, and in an overlapping fashion links the outside with the inside.

8. Keep the furniture line low and the pieces of furniture few, light, and movable. Avoid fixed grouping. Avoid accessories. Let the floor show. Rooms are for people, not for furniture.

9. Plan the building not as a hollow box cut up into cells, but as a series of partially enclosed spaces opening into one another. By partial screening create the feeling of space beyond.

Harris's rules were given clear expression in the very small house he designed in Hollywood's Laurel Canyon for Greta Granstedt and her husband, Max de Vega.[3] This house, which cost its owners an even $5,000, was more ambitious than many of his previous homes and Harris would return to it for a variety of reasons later on. Like the Entenza house, the Granstedt house had a circular drive and a porte cochere, but it worked more easily with the landscape. Resting on a ridge, it seemed to ride the rise to the summit before making a partial descent.

Although all of the important rooms of the Granstedt house were arranged along the south side of a straight corridor running laterally through it, the plan did offer the kind of gradual unfolding of space that Harris admired. To begin with, the corridor broadened to two units, or six feet, at the entranceway to become a gallery space that denied the visitor immediate access to the living room. To reach it, one had to walk around the partition wall. Once there, another partial wall, containing the fireplace, obscured the dining room from view. Harris had a way of encouraging the visitor to move on, as in the case of these partial walls, or to change directions (or moods), as in the case of the bedroom hallway. When the entrance gallery narrowed from six feet to three feet to lead down into the bedroom wing, as it had also done in the Laing house, Harris was suggesting privacy.

As in all Harris houses, space was enlivened by the rhythm of window and floor modules and their reflection in the trellis above. The roof of the Granstedt house became a unifying presence as it had not been before in Harris houses. Instead of making it shingled, Harris wanted to use a standing-seam metal roof. When the Granstedts couldn't afford one, he devised his own by using a cap sheet covered with marble chips and wooden boards to cover the hips. Then he formed a gutter by turning up the lower edges of the roofing.

Harris, Granstedt house.
Photographs by Fred R. Dapprich

The roof became one of the most interesting aspects of the Granstedt house. From the street it gave the house a simple, low profile lightened with a touch of angular trellis. On the cliff side of the house another trellis outlined the drama of the crowning gable. But most important, it was a full-blown development of his first, somewhat experimental De Steiguer shop roof. A line of clerestory windows spaced at three-foot intervals zigzagged above the living room, bathroom, and kitchen spaces below, providing them with northern light. The device of the clerestory freed Harris to concentrate on exposing the interior of the house to the dramatic view of a still-undeveloped Hollywood Hills. Afterward, he preferred to design for sites, like the Granstedt lot, that had a view to the north and a southern entrance, believing that one should never be hit by light in the eyes but should, instead, be guided to see the light side of an object "whether it is a piece of furniture or a mountain."[4] Thus, it was possible for him to give the Granstedt house generous exposure to the outdoors. With their simple, spare furniture and the floor matting running continuously throughout the house, Harris ably demonstrated how a small house could appear much larger and more open.

As can be seen in the Granstedt house, Harris's suggestions were practical, flat-footed, clear enough for any builder or homemaker to follow. They did not cater to the intellectual's love of abstractions or the aristocrat's love of pretense and exclusion. Obfuscation of any kind was abhorrent to him. What he valued in successful architecture was the way in which it cut through the haziness and confusion of Modern times to the place in Everyman's soul that desired sanctuary, delight, and freedom. When he chose to speak of his own work he found words that evoked the organic aspects of life or he drew upon his Victorian upbringing and spoke rather quaintly of good manners in buildings. Sometimes he did both: "I came more and more to see architectural form, not simply as plastic form, but as something that grows up around the form of an activity, and the activity has to have form of its own or you can't have architectural form. This is why you can have manners in building—because you have manners in people."[5]

In his description of Charles Cruze's car Harris illustrated how a design could have good manners. "Just looking at it made one gentle, even as he hand-cranked the motor," he wrote. Appearance and function complemented each other and the effect was gentleness. "Just looking" was not enough for an organic architect. As with Cruze's car, Harris preferred a small scale. He liked "small bones" and he felt that delicacy of an image fostered genteel conduct. In a similar vein, he was to write this of Fellowship Park: "Sometimes the slighter the construction the better, the simpler the materials the more harmonious, the quieter the shapes the more satisfying."[6] Of course, there was nothing intrinsically quiet about the shape of a rectangle, but Harris could make it quiet by adjusting the textures, rhythms, and colors and, by so doing, encourage a soft-spoken, respectful attitude toward it as a living form. Good manners made a Harris house poised, marked not by stiff codes of behavior but by its ability to encourage an easy, balanced composure. Much later, while a visiting professor at Yale, Harris assigned his students the task of designing a house for a playwright. His own solution for such a house together with his description sharpens the focus on his vision of architecture. Here client and building reflect each other's good manners. This interaction was Harris's ideal.

Our client is a bachelor. He is a playwright. He works at home. His work requires periods of solitude and freedom from all distraction. These periods of work must be relieved with periods of relaxation, including one of a social nature. He has two distinct lives: one solitary and the other social. The house is a tool to keep these two lives separate and to enable each to operate as smoothly and as effectively as possible. Our client's solitary life revolves around his work. Grouped together will be his workroom, his bedroom, his bathroom and an anteroom serving as a buffer between these rooms and the other parts of the house. In the anteroom a meal can be served without interrupting his work. The bedroom is for sleeping only. The workroom is for work only and both must offer as little distraction from work as possible. Furniture in the workroom will include a desk, filing cabinets, typewriter, Dictaphone, shelves for books and a couch.

Let's try to put ourselves in the place of the client, still speaking of him in the third person.

It is morning. Our playwright is still in bed but awake. His mind is fresh and he is reviewing the outlines of the play on which he is working. Rest, and the long interval since he put the work aside, have now enabled him to see yesterday's stint in truer relation to the framework of the play.

His bedroom is small. It is free of books, dressing-furniture, pictures and objects that focus attention on themselves or recall labor done or to be done. The window is low and provides a cheerful glow of light and a suggestion of openness, without, however, letting the outdoors exert a strong attraction upon the room's occupant; he must not be tempted to spend the morning out of doors rather than at work.

After a quiet breakfast the client passes on to his workroom.

The workroom is long, with wall-space for books and maps and floor-space in which to pace. One side of the room opens on an enclosed garden. The floor of the garden is paved. There is a tree for shade and a small pool for water plants. The garden provides the only view from the workroom. Its walls are high so only the sky shows beyond. The pool is still so there is no sound to distract. The floor of the room is carpeted. Our client wears loose fitting clothes and slippers. He works sometimes at a desk, sometimes on a sofa, sometimes pacing up and down the room. Occasionally he goes into the garden, but only to let the sun fall on him for a moment, to take a breath of fresh air and then return to work. The garden is for pause but not for distraction. It is the other half of the workroom—seldom the working half.

Shortly before lunch the playwright takes a walk outdoors.

He walks across the garden and through a gate in the outside wall. On the other side of the wall is a loggia. On the right it runs toward the main block of the house; on the left it runs through a garden much larger than the one opening off the workroom and filled with trees, flowers, grass and water. The naturalism of this garden is in contrast to the formalism of the other. Closing the gate behind him he follows the walk to the left.

So far his thoughts have been running back over the morning's work. But now, with each step that he takes, he leaves the morning's work further behind him. His consciousness is filled with the smell of plants, the sound of water, the movement of air, the pattern of sunlight on the ground, and the sensations of his new-found muscular action.

The soft and yielding carpet on which he earlier walked, when he walked at all, is replaced by stone paving that resists his weight; the shoes he now wears brace his feet and add spring to his step. The sight, sounds, odors of the garden, and the sensation of his own regular movements, form patterns in his consciousness. He finds his thoughts following the patterns as they form, dissolve and reform. It is like a melody releasing his mind and his energies, a path he travels with ease and pleasure. . . .

It is unnecessary for our present purpose to follow our playwright through the entire day or the entire house. The other half of the house is designed with as much attention to its social uses as the solitary half was for its work uses. The rooms differ in character as they differ in size, shape, openness, outlook and the mood necessary to their particular use. Transition from one to another is by means of vestibules, passages, or sections of garden, and with changes in ceiling height, flooring materials, lighting and outlook to emphasize the change. . . .

The day's path, along which he is conducted, is a series of planned wants and succeeding satisfactions: the need of companionship after solitary work, of physical action after physical restraint, of freedom after confinement,—to walk, breathe deeply, see far, think different thoughts.

The figure that emerges is not the figure of the playwright alone; it is the figure of his house as well. The complexity and richness of the architectural figures are in direct proportion to the complexity and richness of the owner's life and his capacity to sense and respond.

For example, I have used the design of a house for a playwright, but the design of a building for any other person might illustrate equally well the approach I consider proper to architecture as an expressive art. Fine art is expressive art, and in architecture the materials for that expression are more various than in any other art.[7]

Clearly "manners" for Harris had to do with simple, tranquil living. Buildings might not have ideas, but an organic building with manners helped people have ideas. As was evident in the playwright's house, however, Harris's theory had very little to do with an artificially applied code of conduct. Everyone knew what manners were, and he could thus avoid the confusion that Neutra's more technological words implied. Fortunately, Harris was never characterized as an Architect of Good Manners, for such a tag would have greatly subverted the real meaning of the concept for his work. Like "good taste," "good manners" would have suggested safe, tried and true designs. Nothing could have been further from his intent.

To Harris, every aspect of a house ought to reflect its good manners—the garage no less than the living room or dining room. It followed, then, that Harris would be among the first architects in Los Angeles to place this necessary appendage in front of a house. There were practical reasons for the arrangement that Harris appreciated, but the reason for his complete acceptance of it had more to do with his natural sense of refinement.

Alleys were not a common feature in subdivisions after 1920, and a driveway leading to a garage behind the house robbed the house of space for a side garden. I, at least, disliked entering the house thru a kitchen door and taking a guest thru the kitchen. I disliked looking past the open door of the garage, especially at a collection of tools and trash. Whenever possible I turned a side of the garage toward the street so the open end didn't hit one full face. A wide overhang over the garage entrance could usually be continued on to the house entrance providing rain-proof cover.[8]

One did not drive by a Harris house and get interested in his architecture. Clients came to him because his work was published in a wide array of home magazines and because he had shown a special facility with small budgets. But this certainly wasn't all. The same claims could have been made of Schindler, Neutra, Ain, and any number of other Modern architects in Los Angeles at the time.

There was a subtlety that bound together Harris's early clients. It might be described as a complete absence of pretense, for not only did they want to be liberated from the symbols of the status quo, they did not even care to show the world that they were up to date, avant-garde—and thus Modern. After World War II, clients would come to him for his name and prestige, but earlier there was a different motivation: It was a desire to lose oneself in a house that was itself lost in nature. Such an intense yearning for seclusion and repose, for a private house whose secrets were vouchsafed only to the dwellers, was a Modern phenomenon of a particular American sort. European modern homes spoke of different strivings—participation in the artistic intelligentsia, for instance, as well as a familiarity with machine-inspired efficiency and its outward appearance. They stood out on the landscape, in plain view, and one tended to read them, as Bruno Zevi sadly observed in *Towards an Organic Architecture*, as two-dimensional pictures.[9]

And it was on such basic issues that Harris's opinion of the International Style was beginning to turn. For him, the buildings of Walter Gropius and Le Corbusier were like abstract sculptures, but not sculptures in the way the Hollyhock House was a sculpture. There, it had been easy to see the generative principle, the stimulation of a life to be lived in the setting. The International Style forms were, by contrast, arbitrary and he felt that they weren't truly abstractions (as there was nothing to be abstracted). They were merely nonrepresentational. He found nothing "that began to compare with what I saw in Schindler and especially of course in Wright," he wrote. "These things were not alive."[10] To Harris they lacked the spatial qualities that were so critical to organic architects. Architecture that was alive allowed for continual discoveries. By contrast "an abstraction," he would say, "is a creation and therefore an end in itself—not a means."

He was both hindered and helped in this opinion by the medium of architectural photography. While he actually knew the houses of Wright and Schindler and had experienced their spatial qualities, he had to rely on photographs for his exposure to works by Gropius and Le Corbusier, and photographs emphasized the two-dimensional, diagrammatic aspects of these International Style houses. Although this means of viewing their architecture revealed little about interior space, it was a method that was not necessarily at odds with the International Style. Indeed, the very surface quality of such buildings had recommended them to Hitchcock and Johnson, who treated it specifically in their book. Chapters with titles like "Surfacing Material," "Concerning Regularity," and "The Avoidance of Applied Decoration" underscored their fascination with a flat exterior image.

The way photography was used by architects began to say a great deal about their sensibilities. Most of Harris's California colleagues tried to capture in photographs the spatial qualities of their buildings, an element of dynamism. Neutra, Ain, and Soriano had a penchant for hiring photographers with a strong linear style who tended to make bold forms in contrasts of black and white. Harris's choice of Fred Dapprich's soft, very painterly, sepia-toned prints spoke of very different concerns. They were as romantic as the International Style photographs were classical.[11] They were never frontal and symmetrical; rather, the camera's eye looked in and around angles, pushing its way into the depths of space. In their rich gradations of tone, one might also feel the presence of color. And Dapprich, whom Harris met through Carl Anderson, not only strove to weave the setting into the organic, spatial life of a Harris house, he also conveyed the tactile, natural materials of which it was made. "Architecture can express ideas," Harris once said, "but it is not made of ideas."[12] In the late 1930s, Dapprich's photographs of Harris's houses were capturing an architecture that was ever more frankly and lovingly made of wood.

In May 1939 *California Arts & Architecture* published an essay by Harris on wood in which he addressed the issue of permanency. "Wood," he said, "swells, burns and rots. It is as variable, unpredictable and unreliable as the human creature it shelters or warms. . . . [It is] not so permanent as stone perhaps, yet permanent enough as human lives go." And, as if to clear up any doubts that he was soft or careless on the issue of durability and life of buildings, he pointed out that wood was "lasting" and that it aged "gracefully." With special protection wood could resist fire and even rotting. Paint, he cautioned, was not the way, for wood "must be allowed a margin for movement. It is for this that we have the lap and the batten."[13]

Harris was rhapsodic on the beauty of wood. Because it was "warmer and therefore more intimate than stone," he commented that it "invited the close contact of a small room." Steel, terra cotta, and plaster which lacked natural patterns were capable of "living" only as they reflected the stamp of the human imagination, while wood "lives in natural patterns of infinite variety." Illustrating the article

Harris, house for Mr. and Mrs. Lee Blair, Los Angeles, 1939.
Photograph by Fred R. Dapprich

were photographs not of the Lowe house or the Fellowship Park house, but of the board and batten Curtis ranch by Louis B. Easton that Harris had passed every day on his way through Altadena. Having discovered that her husband admired the house, Jean Harris arranged for him to see it through a close childhood friend, Honor Easton, the architect's daughter.[14]

The Easton house was such a fine embodiment of Harris's feelings about wood that he was moved by it all over again. He had actually strayed from the kind of abundant use of wood that had set the Lowe and Fellowship Park houses apart from the designs of his contemporaries. The Laing, De Steiguer, Entenza, Clark, Bauer, and Granstedt houses were all built out of the less expensive stucco. They were embellished with wooden details, but the predominant material was stucco, that material so "lacking in natural pattern." Thus in 1939 Harris set his mind to thinking again about wood, and the next wave of commissions reflected a revived passion that was deeper due to the variety of experience he had had. His enormous success with the material, separate from but concurrent with the success of Bay Area architects like William Wurster and Gardner Dailey, would persuade Neutra and Schindler to experiment with the material. In time, labels like "Redwood school" or "woodsy," "cozy," or "human" would be used to categorize and (depending on who used it) denigrate the California Modernists generally. To Harris, who had in the early 1930s accidentally come upon the Easton house as an example of fine wooden architecture, this eventuality would have seemed absurd.

Mr. and Mrs. Lee Blair were directors for the Walt Disney Studios who had been interested in a house by Harwell Harris since 1937. He had, in fact, designed a house at that time that was canceled due to an uncertainty regarding their work. (Of the five Disney clients Harris had during these years only two would see their houses reach the construction stage.) In 1939 they returned with a new lot and he started over again. This lot was extremely steep and Harris designed the tiny, one-bedroom house with three stories sheathed in horizontal redwood siding.[15] Each of the three blocks of the house rose another step up the hill. At its rear, each floor rested on the natural level of the ground and at its front it rested on the rear edge of the block below it. Thus, the second story used the roof of the first story for a roof terrace; and the third story used the roof of the second story for its roof terrace. So high, in fact, was the studio that the clients had a spectacular view of Los Angeles and even of the cowboy and Indian movies being filmed at Fox Studios.

The Blair house followed all the rules of Harris's nine-point plan. The same finishes—grass matting, plywood walls, and Celotex ceilings—were used through-

**Harris, house for Mr. and Mrs.
Lee Blair, Los Angeles, 1939.**
Photograph by Fred R. Dapprich

Harris, Blair house bedroom.
Photograph by Fred R. Dapprich

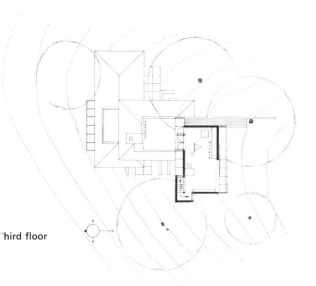

third floor

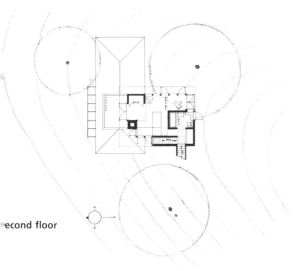

second floor

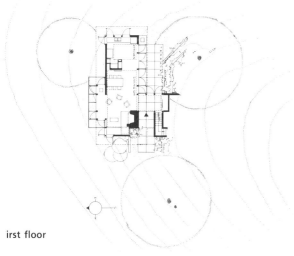

first floor

Harris, Blair plan.

Harris, Blair house: *above right,*
entrance elevation and,
right, studio.
Photographs by Fred R. Dapprich

Harris, house for Edwin (Stan) Hawk, Los Angeles, 1939.
Photograph by Fred R. Dapprich

out, and each room had one wall of glass opening into a garden or terrace. The furniture line was low and the pieces were few and far between. This allowed not only for a more generous display of the floor but also showed the Alvar Aalto chairs and Harris-designed couch and dressing table to their full advantage.

In the Edwin Hawk, Jr., house, built the same year against another Los Angeles hillside, Harris reversed the order, making the entrance level living room the top floor and two bedrooms one floor lower. The Hawk house, to which the Blair house is often compared, shared with its predecessor not only its redwood siding but its emphasis on the unfolding of the interior forms. To look at the exteriors of these houses is to see how dedicated Harris was to the idea that an architect worked from the inside out. Gone were the houses that "looked like houses" (even though he did use hipped roofs in sections of each house). The Hawk and Blair houses were compositions of boxlike masses, abutting each other in unexpected ways. They were completely different from Neutra's very orderly hillside houses, where a unified exterior idea prevailed and where interior plans could be inferred from the outside. Harris, in a spirit much closer to Schindler, was looser, more like a sculptor feeling his way around the form of the interior, draping it and articulating it with wood.

David Gebhard has mentioned that Schindler was drawn to wood after an early rejection of it not only because of the popularity of Harris's houses and those of the Bay Area architects but also because Frank Lloyd Wright's Usonian houses, mostly wood, were beginning to appear.[16] Harris also continued to be influenced

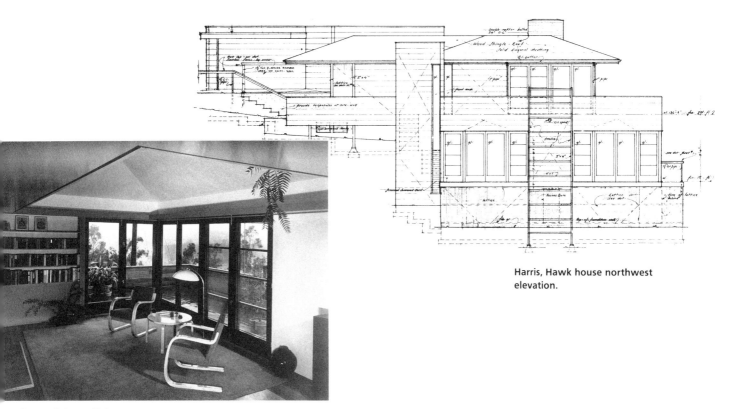

Harris, Hawk house northwest elevation.

Harris, Hawk house living room and balcony.
Photograph by Fred R. Dapprich

by Wright, but it wasn't wood that kept the connection with the master alive (wood was too much Harris's own medium). The Usonian houses nevertheless reiterated ideas that Harris had first seen in the Hollyhock House, ideas about the integration of building and landscape. In the stuccoed Fred Harris house of this period, overlooking a small, idyllic pond in Pasadena, Harris introduced a garden between the garage and entrance to balance the dramatic view on the opposite side of the house. Like the architect's imaginary playwright, the Fred Harrises could have an active, busy experience with a landscape that came in through an abundant exposure of glazed doors or they could have a quiet, contemplative contact with a more private patch of nature. I found a color photograph of this house by Fred Dapprich illustrating Harris's palette of crimsons, purples, and yellows.

David Gebhard and Robert Winter have commented that Harris's small house for Dr. and Mrs. Herbert Alexander in Silver Lake showed him working with the compositions of Wright's Usonian houses, the hipped roofs, the simple walls, and so on, but other houses of the period show how much more sophisticated Harris could be with a Wrightian idea. His dwelling for Mr. and Mrs. J. E. Powers in La Cañada shows him using the thirty- and sixty-degree angles that so appealed to Wright. An ingenious back-to-back fireplace for the living room and study exploited these angles. And here, too, Harris's love of delicacy of form boldly asserted itself. Translucent panes of glass, with overtones of Japanese rice paper, let light into the hallways of the Powers house without disturbing the privacy of the inhabitants. Like the Paul Frankl chair that Harris placed in the living room when he and

Harris, Powers house interior showing living room side of fireplace that backs onto a small similarly angled study.
Photograph by Fred R. Dapprich

Harris, northwest elevation and plan of the house for Mr. and Mrs. J. E. Powers, La Cañada, California, 1939.

Jean rented the house from the Powerses from 1942 to 1943, the interior was a study in contrasting textures. A pinkish tan wall plaster was juxtaposed against the dyed black redwood trim of the windows and doors. The exterior redwood of shiplap construction was interrupted at rhythmic intervals with smooth sections of glass.

Harris has admitted that his very dramatic Byron Pumphrey house of 1940 bears the influence of Wright's Sturges house of 1938. The Pumphrey balcony of beveled wooden studs is an unusually direct reference at a time when Harris's own sensibility was asserting itself. Even so, Harris had already arrived at wood without the aid of any of his mentors, and his use of it, particularly in buildings like his Grandview Gardens restaurant in Chinatown, was clearly an outgrowth of a more indigenous approach. By making walls of a single thickness of vertical one-by-fourteen redwood boards lapped (one in front, the next behind), by using crumpled aluminum foil for the ceiling's finish as well as the insulation, and by designing the furniture, Harris made it possible for two Chinese brothers, ages twenty-one and twenty-four, to move their restaurant from the old to the new sector of Chinatown. Harris's decorations for the restaurant were characteristic. The roof was mustard yellow with deep olive-green trim, tabletops were crimson, upholstery was vermilion, interior plywood was pale olive green, and all exposed framework was black. When the brothers could not afford a sign of the elaborate sort their competitors owned, Harris's solution (which, regrettably, they never used) may have betrayed, in a rather offbeat way, that Wright was still an adored mentor. His presentation drawing shows gas-filled colored ballons, tied from within a tall plant box and lighted by a hidden lamp, that bubble up in a fanciful, exaggerated fashion and beckon to passersby. As it happens, Wright had thought of decorating the Midway Gardens of 1914 with gas-filled balloons tied to the roof.[17]

It was about this time that Harris met Wright for the first time. Designer Paul Frankl and his wife invited Harris, the Wrights, Charles Laughton, and Elsa Lanchester for dinner. They offered him the opportunity to pick the Wrights and their daughter up at the airport, but Harris refused, worried that the trick door on the

Harris, perspective drawing of
Pumphrey house.

Harwell Hamilton Harris at his
Byron Pumphrey house, Santa
Monica Canyon, 1939.
Photograph by Kellett-Imandt

passenger side of his car might spring open and spill the great man out onto the freeway. Finally, Wright arrived at the dinner party, having been fetched by Frankl's secretary, and Harris could forestall their meeting no longer. When they were introduced, Wright responded robustly (to Harris's everlasting surprise and delight), "I know Harwell Harris," adding, "Harwell, you're a great artist and when your hair is as gray as mine, you'll be a great architect." [18]

It was a cryptic statement in many ways, not the least of which in its implication that architecture transcended art and that such transcendence was a perquisite of age. Wright, the artist/architect of the era, who had begun his career as a precocious youngster, was an unlikely person to lend credence to either idea. What is important about the comment is that he clearly knew Harris's work and he had observed, quite rightly, that Harris approached design as an artist. At the Hollyhock House on Olive Hill Wright had taught Harris that it took an artist to make architecture inspiring, to make it alive; fifteen or so years later, it was the highest compliment that the elder architect understood Harris's work as art.

Wright was undoubtedly aware of the Weston Havens house, then under way in Berkeley. In this wooden house against a hillside, Harris was the consummate artist, indulging the passion he felt immediately for the site without forsaking his commitment to his client's needs. This house, on the one hand so spectacular and on the other so simple, became an instant masterpiece.

It is fitting that the house that sent Weston Havens to Harris was the Fellowship Park house he had seen in a photograph on exhibit in the Museum of Modern Art. He wanted a house that was only "bookshelves and glass," but after returning to New York from Europe, where he had interviewed Modern architects, he had almost given up finding anyone who seemed right.[19] A bachelor, Havens was also the sole heir to a land fortune in the Bay Area and to the antique furnishings of three grand houses. In his search for a Modern architect Havens seemed to be searching for himself, searching for an expression that suited him. The sensibility behind the Fellowship Park house struck him as exactly right, and when he got back to California he went to Los Angeles instead of directly home to Berkeley.

Through a mutual friend he met Harris. They talked about Lewis Mumford's new book *Sticks and Stones*, which they both admired, and about architecture generally, but Havens didn't mention he was thinking of building a house.[20] He waited until he got home and then he called Harris and invited him to come see the lot in Berkeley.

Harris was taken not only with the view from the top of the hill—to the west encompassing the San Francisco Bay, the Bay Bridge, and the Golden Gate Bridge—but also with the broad expanse of sky above it.[21] While he knew that the house would have to be built below his eye level as he stood on the brink of the slope, he also knew that he wanted the view to be upward toward the sky. In the plan that developed, only subsidiary buildings—a garage, a servant's room and bath—actually skirted the edge of the land. In effect, the house floated above the hillside, accessible only by means of a bridge a few steps down from the street-level garage. The first rooms encountered were those that did not necessarily need to take advantage of the fantastic westward view; that is, the kitchen, stairway, and guest bedroom. Finally, beyond these rooms, came the living and dining areas with their staggering exposures to the bay.

Harris's most ingenious feat with the Havens house was perhaps his use of the structural solution to heighten the drama. What appeared on the outside as inverted gables appeared on the inside as ceilings that angled out from low interior walls to high balcony eaves, rising from seven feet at the rear and moving outward to fifteen feet at the balcony's edge. Like broad hat brims tilted upward, these ceilings exposed the view without disrupting the sheltering effect of the interiors (though Harris was careful to bring eastern light into these rooms through clerestory windows). Structurally these ceilings became trusses and capable of support; the middle inverted gable served as both the floor of the first public level and the ceiling of the lower, more private area. In addition, Harris's triangular roof shapes created spaces that became plenum chambers, thus enabling the ceilings to radiate heat.

The narrow lot had necessitated putting rooms on another level, one flight of stairs down the hill. While they had a slightly less exciting view of the bay, they had the advantage of large terraces on the street side of the house, albeit far beneath street level. Protected from the wind as it was, this area became the location for Havens's badminton games and thus the fulfillment of one of his few requirements for the house. Harris, ever vigilant where matters of privacy were concerned, made sure that the court was out of sight of visitors crossing the bridge. Through the

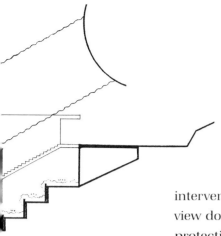

Harris, drawing showing how morning light could enter the Havens house through a system of clerestory windows and interior skylights.

intervention of louvers on the angled sides of the bridge, visitors were denied a view down below. A massive plant box near the street served a similar function— protecting the court from curious passersby.

Harris's use of redwood in the house demonstrated just how sympathetic he was to its properties. He played down the vertical structural elements in the house by sheathing them with boards of vertical grain redwood, well seasoned to further minimize shrinkage and connected by an unusually deep tongue and groove to insure the nailing remained blind. The inverted gables became the featured elements when he emphasized their shapes by mitering the end wood facings into increasingly diminutive concentric triangles. The bridge into the house appeared on the outside as a decorative feature—a kind of trough of horizontal redwood boards held in place by double two-by-fours turned edgeways. As the trough narrowed toward the bottom, the horizontal redwood sides were eliminated and only the framework of studs could be seen coming together at sharp angles at three-foot intervals across the distance of a single supportive redwood beam. The lower section of the planter box repeated the pattern of horizontal boards battened at three-foot intervals with double studs. Harris's battening here was an outgrowth of his knowledge that wood would shrink and change and the simple logic that horizontal boards could be held in place with the same strategy used on vertical boards. This idea was developed most fully in his next major commission, the Cecil Birtcher house of 1941–42.

It is a measure of Harris's reputation at the time that the principal photographer for both the Havens and the Birtcher houses (as well as the Byron Pumphrey house in Santa Monica of 1939) was the surrealist artist Man Ray, who had left Paris after the outbreak of war in Europe.[22] When they met, Harris asked him if he had ever photographed a house, and when Man Ray said no, Harris responded, "Then you're just the man I need." He had earlier hired a local San Francisco photographer to shoot the Havens house, but with disappointing results. Using the rising front on his camera, a feature that prevented vertical lines from converging and thus dramatized the Modern houses he was used to photographing, he had created a picture of the house that looked like it was exploding at the sides. Accustomed to architects who liked to capture bold contrasts of black and white with the darkest of shadows, he had also made the mistake (in Harris's view) of shooting the house against the light.

Man Ray, possessing a fresher, more artistic eye, seized the elements that Harris wanted to emphasize immediately and without any coaching. He realized

Facing pages: Harris, Weston Havens house, Berkeley, 1940–41, dubbed "Havens Above" by Jean Harris. Photograph below by Man Ray shows the striking inverted roof lines, while the one at the bottom is of the deceptively uneventful street view.

Opposite, clockwise from top right badminton court protected from the wind and the views of visitors, view of the San Francisco bay from the balcony at night, master bedroom, and main-level living room.
Photographs by Maynard Parker except bottom right by Roger Sturtevant

Lower level

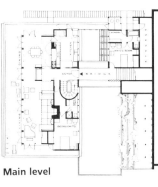

Main level

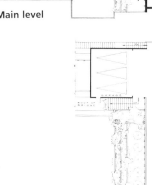

Street level

Harris, Havens plan.

The photographic outing: *from left to right, sitting:* Charlotta Heythum, Juliet (the future Mrs. Man Ray), Man Ray, and Jean Harris; *kneeling from left:* Antonin Heythum, a Czech artist who designed his country's pavilion for the 1939 World's Fair, and Harwell Hamilton Harris.

Courtesy of Harwell Hamilton Harris

Harris, house for Cecil Birtcher
with Man Ray's car, Los Angeles,
1941–42.
Photograph by Man Ray

that the light covered a broad surface of the house, and so he simply used it for his own purposes to give the house a weightless, atmospheric quality. Furthermore, he captured the rush of excitement the house inspired by including in his view a piece of the ordinary looking house next door, whose vertical lines were even more distorted and so made the Havens house angles look natural. So bold and dramatic was the image he caught, so close and overpowering, that the Havens house seemed to soar above the observer's head. Here was a photograph that seemed capable of causing a crick in the neck of even the most casual viewer. Man Ray captured how it felt to be underneath this house that Harwell called a "sky house" and Jean had playfully dubbed "Havens Above." His was the image that would come readily to mind as the house became more widely celebrated. And it was celebrated. Today it may not be as well known as Wright's Falling Water or Neutra's Lovell Health House, but in 1956 when the American Institute of Architects selected the best buildings from the one hundred years of the organization's existence, the Havens house appeared alongside these monuments. Out of the only fourteen houses selected, it had tied with Neutra's Lovell Health House for ninth place.

If the Havens house was a "sky house," then the Birtcher house was a land house. Here Man Ray could afford to be more straightforward in his approach. Cecil Birtcher, a designer of diathermic equipment, came to Harris when Charles Cruze recommended him. (Cruze should be remembered not simply as the one who approached his car with good manners but as a graphic designer for whom Harris designed an office near downtown Los Angeles.)[23]

The plan of the Birtcher house was meant to unwind slowly as one moved through it. Like a lecture in Gideon Knopp's high school class, the states of disclosure were calibrated carefully for the greatest effect. From a motor court, past the garage and down an outdoor corridor, the visitor reached the entrance at the center of the house. There the turning began that would eventually open up the house that, at first glance, seemed so uncommunicative. A sharp left out of the entranceway led into a library separated from the living room by a built-in couch. The living room, exposed to the outdoors through broad expanses of glass, invited another turn into the dining area, and from there it required only one more rotation into the sequestered but central kitchen to come full circle.

Harris had been able to utilize seasoned redwood in the Havens house, but at the Birtcher house, begun in 1941, and under construction in 1942, he had to get by with untreated boards (war production claimed the sturdiest materials).[24] Once again concerned about shrinkage, he used very narrow horizontal boards, only three and a half inches wide. They would have less across-grain shrinkage, and with more boards the shrinkage could be distributed among more joints. Vertical battens, thirty-six inches apart, covered end joints in the boards and the face nails at their ends. Battens at three-foot intervals enlivened the rhythm, and a smooth, uninterrupted fascia of three boards (because they were lapped there was a slight battered effect) tied together the wings of the house. To protect the broad expanses of glass from the harsh sun, Harris cut holes three feet square in the cantilevered roof section that extended out over the terrace.[25] The holes were deep

Harris, Birtcher house living room.
Photograph by Maynard Parker

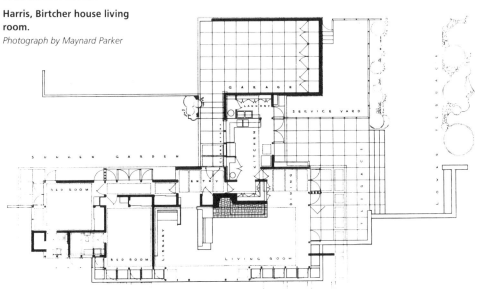

Harris, Birtcher plan.

Harris, Birtcher house entrance way.
Photograph by Fred R. Dapprich

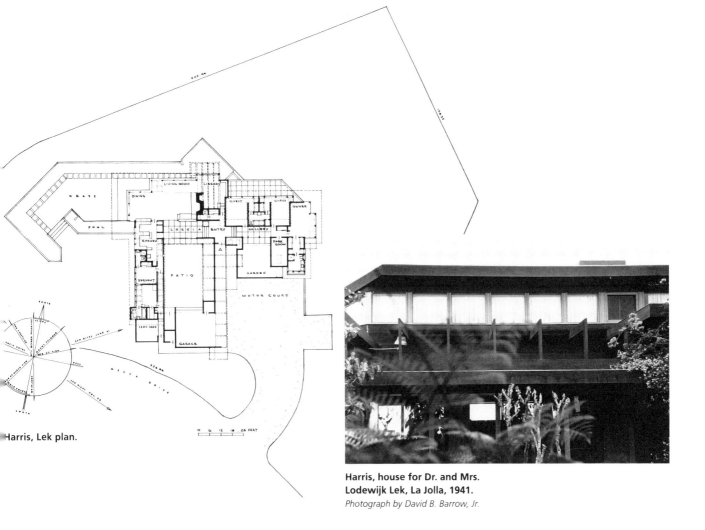

Harris, Lek plan.

Harris, house for Dr. and Mrs.
Lodewijk Lek, La Jolla, 1941.
Photograph by David B. Barrow, Jr.

and had the ability to protect the inside from light coming in at sharp angles. Because of his similar use of a sunscreen and three-board fascia in the small John Comstock mountain cottage of 1940, it is tempting to see it as a precursor of the Birtcher house, a place where Harris tried out some of his new ideas with wood.

In the early 1940s Harris's commissions were getting larger. The Sox house, essentially two houses (a public wing and a bedroom wing) connected by a loggia, and the Lek house, three bedrooms, a study, and large living and dining area shaped around two gardens, were ambitious. Horizontal redwood with no battens was the sheathing material on both houses. The Lek house shed roof gave Harris a chance to bring light into a living room from its blind side. Once again, a clerestory on one elevation opened up another with a broad exposure to the outdoors, in this case through plate glass. Beneath the clerestory, on the unit lines outside, wooden braces emerged like tentacles and bolted into the structural members of a pergola below. Something of the strength of the image, almost a brutality, was a bit reminiscent of Schindler, but the joining of wood was all Harris, and though he had always shown a predilection for junctures of wood, this house was prophetic of a return.

Harris was so busy during the late 1930s and early 1940s that Jere Johnson, owner and publisher of *California Arts & Architecture*, persuaded a retired architect, Walter Webber, to help him supervise construction.[26] With the Sox house in Palo Alto, the Havens house, and, just down the hill from it, the residence for Mr.

Harris, Birtcher house hallway
leading into study and living
room.
Photograph by Fred R. Dapprich

and Mrs. Linden Naylor under construction in Berkeley, Jean and Harris had decided to lease a house in Berkeley. Harris's commute back and forth from Los Angeles to Berkeley may have shaped the design of his "Highway Hotel" of 1940, designed for the *Architectural Forum*'s "Design Decade." He was interested in making accommodations that were more convenient than an ordinary hotel. "It was an effort to provide something that had the influence of the automobile," he has remarked, "and I almost brought it into the living quarters." The concept of the motel was beginning to take shape. But Harris also liked the way a hotel outside a city was closer to nature. The overall form made up of separate living quarters with flat roofs "jagged and jogged, opened and closed, in the landscape."[27]

At home again briefly in her beloved college town, Berkeley, Jean spent her time getting to know Bernard Maybeck, whom she had met through Harris's supervisor on the Havens house, Walter Steilberg. (Steilberg had also supervised many of Julia Morgan's homes in the Bay Area.) Since her student days, when she had first become familiar with Maybeck's Hearst Hall on the campus of the University of California (destroyed by fire in 1922), Jean had greatly admired the architect. She now found him at home, a bit cynical but still lively and inventive. One imagines that Jean was the perfect interviewer, equipped as she was with a quick, unorthodox wit and a shrewd intelligence. Maybeck's response was to entrust her with a vast amount of materials, drawings and personal photographs.[28]

Jean interested Harris in Maybeck (he would discover that the elderly architect had pioneered bubble stone, the material Harris had tried to use at the Lowe house), and she told him that Walter Webber had mentioned Greene and Greene to her.[29] Neither of them knew exactly what the architect brothers had done, which is a reason why one of Webber's comments would haunt Jean until several years later when she began to understand that in creating a style that could so readily be imitated, Greene and Greene had temporarily, at least, designed themselves into oblivion. Referring to the way homebuilders had diluted the power of their early Craftsman masterpieces by excessive copying, Webber had said, "They got Greene and Greene and they'll get your husband too." Harris knew he must have seen and admired some of their houses without learning or remembering the architects' names. He was too busy with his own work to think very much about them. He certainly knew what a California bungalow was like, admired, in fact, many of its characteristics, but presumed that those Greene and Greene had designed must be just better examples of the same. That, he would discover, was how they "got" Greene and Greene.

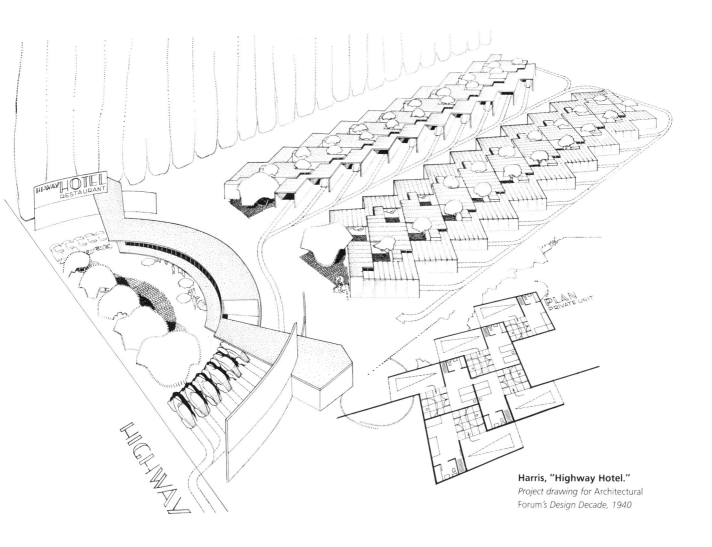

Harris, "Highway Hotel."
Project drawing for Architectural
Forum's *Design Decade, 1940*

Webber's presence, as well as the help of an increasingly distinguished coterie of young draftsmen, freed Harris to think more carefully about what he most loved and to express it with the greatest economy; to work, in other words, like a poet.[30] He accomplished such an aim in the showroom he designed with Carl Anderson for the 1939 New York World's Fair exhibition entitled "America at Home," receiving a rave review in *Pencil Points* by Talbot Hamlin. The critic admitted his own inability to describe the subtle feeling a Harris room inspired, though he made a most valiant effort: "the furniture, wall surfaces, colors, and materials have a character almost musical, a feeling which results only when the functional solution of a problem is seen not as the final end but merely as a statement of a program on which the creative imagination plays (see photo page C-10)."[31]

But things were changing. A week after the Havens house was completely finished, the Japanese attacked Pearl Harbor. Very soon the kind of young Americans that elicited such delicacy of feeling from Harris in the World's Fair exhibition were, in fact, not at home. They were at war.

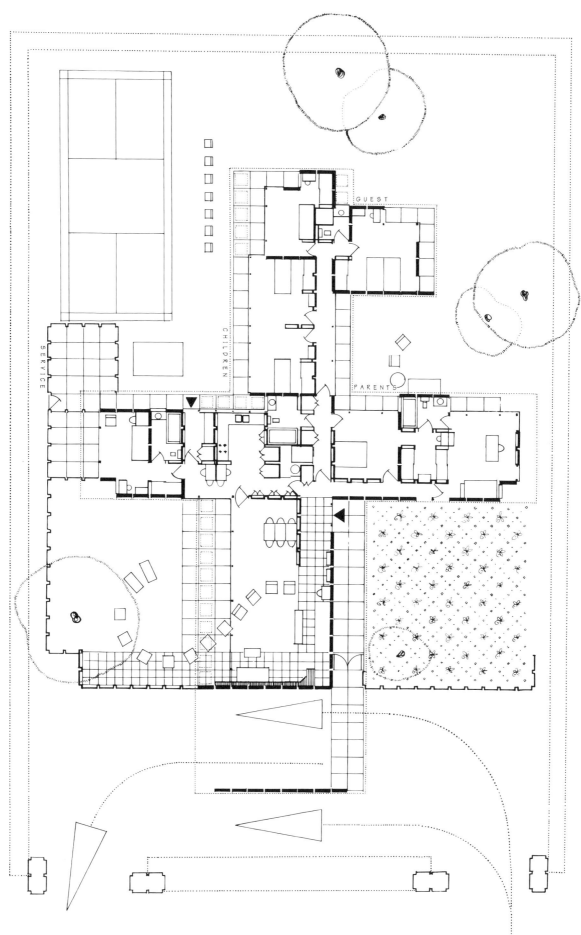

GUEST

CHILDREN

SERVICE

PARENTS

7.

New York: Glamour and Dissension, 1943–1944

or Jean and Harwell
who know how to think and how to build—from the
heart. But above all for Jean and Harwell because
Pissarro and I love them for their fighting answer to
the "men of genius" and magic. With much much love.

Gibby

October 3, 1947

Inscription found by author on the inside cover page
of the Harrises' copy of Mona Lisa's Mustache, *written*
by T. H. Robsjohn-Gibbings

Harris, Segmental House, project
for the Revere Copper and Brass
Company, 1942, which takes a
small house with one bedroom
and one bath and gradually adds
a garage, a second bedroom, a
third bedroom, a private master
bath, a bedroom with a bath for
housekeeper, a study, a
playroom, a guest bedroom, and
walls to screen the garden and
the service yard.
Courtesy of David B. Barrow, Jr.

UNDER THE SHADOW OF WAR Harris had fared well, managing to complete the largest and most ambitious houses of his career. But there were disappointments. For instance, a house he had begun to discuss with Arnold Schönberg fell through when a bank reneged on a promotional offer of land to the famous composer.[1] It was a direct result of wartime sentiment and a harbinger of the increasingly difficult times ahead. By 1942 World War II had brought almost all residential building to a halt. Harris again had the kind of days he had known as a very young architect, days in which to sketch and indulge his fascination with floor plans, to anticipate the return of young soldiers and their need for post-war houses.

He was not alone in this. Since there was no new construction, American home magazines focused optimistically on small, inexpensive plans for imaginary houses that might be built when the war was over. Harris's projects appeared in articles like "The Browns Build a War Time House with Peace Aims" for the *Ladies Home Journal*, "Blue Prints of Tomorrow: Western House of the Future with Bathing Lounge" for *Sunset Magazine*, "How the Shumways Can Build Their House" for *Woman's Home Companion*, and, as the decade wore on, others for *Mademoiselle* and *House & Garden*. Companies also patronized the American architect as an optimistic form of advertising during the war. And it was as a result of one such commission, for the Revere Copper and Brass Company, that Harris was able to tap into his loosely formed but very genuine interest in a house that could grow as the family and income grew.[2]

This house, called the Segmental House, was published in *Architectural Forum* in an article called "For a Quicker Start in 194X." (No one could predict when the war would end, hence the "X.")[3] In ten steps Harris took a house from a simple one-bedroom, one-bathroom plan to a plan with six bedrooms, a library, large living and dining rooms, and four baths. The appeal of such a project for Harris was that he could work not only with the various segments of the plan but with the smaller pieces that came naturally with construction, the constituent parts (floor tiles, glass panes, wall panels, and so on) that became the rhythm of this three-foot modular unit. Their sizes and shapes were determined, Harris wrote, "partly by material-manufacturing-erection considerations and partly by

Harris, Segmental House
perspective.

Harris, patio of the Segmental
House.

another consideration; the size of the human unit." And, as always, prefabricated modular units became the tools of organic architecture in his hands. "Segments alone do not make an organism. But an organism is formed with parts, and the parts with other parts,—each with an affinity for the others."

Harris's Segmental House was never built, even though twelve servicemen wrote him from overseas expressing interest in it. The early 1940s were years of ideas more than action in architecture, and when Harris and his wife decided to go to New York City to wait out the war, they were to find themselves face to face with current architectural issues. It was the first trip away from the West Coast that Harris at forty had ever taken, and it was to have a decisive influence on his subsequent architecture. More than this, however, the intellectual climate in New York would force him to articulate his theories and ideas in architecture. It might also be said that it pushed him to take sides.

When Jean and Harris arrived in the city Howard Myers, the editor of the *Architectural Forum*, hosted a party for them at the Rainbow Room, the top floor of Rockefeller Center.[4] There they met Hugh Ferriss and Russel Wright and a crowd of other Modern designers. Harris was deeply impressed by Rockefeller Center and soon afterwards was delighted to work part-time in the International Building there, walking each morning past the Lee Lawrie sculpture of Atlas in the forecourt.[5]

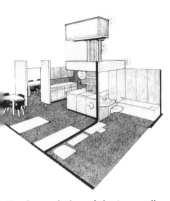

Harris, rendering of the Ingersoll Utility Unit, designed while working with Donald Deskey in New York; produced by the Borg-Warner Corporation, Chicago, in 1945 and introduced in 1946.

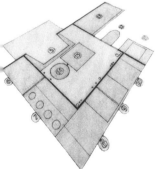

Rendering of the Ingersoll Utility Unit.

Myers had gotten Harris a job with industrial designer Donald Deskey, who was just then trying to develop a utility core, a factory-made plumbing, wiring, and heating package, or unit, that placed bath, kitchen, and laundry facilities in the center of a house.[6] Since these facilities usually amounted to 40 percent of a building's cost, as Sigfried Giedion observed in his 1948 *Mechanization Takes Command*, a prefabricated unit was deemed a necessity to bring postwar housing down to an affordable price.[7] Buckminster Fuller had demonstrated such a core in his Dymaxion House of 1927, but it did not catch on as an idea until the war galvanized the steel industries and designers at home started to wonder how the plants and resources could be best used when airplanes and weaponry were no longer needed.

Harris knew how critical such an idea was if architects were to be able to furnish returning veterans with affordable homes. (After all, his Fellowship Park house had only cost $430 until the cost of plumbing and electricity brought it up to $2,430.) When Harris started to work in Deskey's office Lawrence Kocher, former managing editor of the *Architectural Record* whose work with Albert Frey Harris knew, was attempting to add a circulating, wood-burning metal fireplace to the core. Harris immediately sat down and began sketching the floor plan possibilities around such a core. Later, as work developed, he devised a way of raising the ceiling in the central rooms of the house affected by the core so that he could illuminate the activities around it—cooking, bathing, washing clothes, etc.—with natural light from a skylight. (Harris very much disliked the necessity, inherent in the core idea, of turning one's back to the outdoors.)[8] When the core was finished it was nine and a half feet square and could be divided into several sections for easy installation.[9]

Two weeks after Harris had returned to Los Angeles, he got a call from Deskey asking him to join him in Chicago to interest Roy C. Ingersoll, president of the Ingersoll Steel and Disc Division of the Borg-Warner Corporation, in production of the core. He was impressed by Ingersoll's questions about the social uses the core might have. The businessman agreed to manufacture it and Deskey did a little streamlining of Harris's scheme.[10] The project was announced in 1945, though not exhibited until a year later.

Ingersoll had left publicity for the project to Deskey, who struck upon the idea of asking prominent architects to design houses around the core, houses that would actually be built in Kalamazoo, Michigan. There were eight architects in all. Aside from Harwell Harris, Alden Dow, George Fred Keck, J. Fletcher Lankton (who had earlier developed his own core and was a consultant to Deskey), Edward D.

Stone, Hugh Stubbins, Jr., Royal Barry Wills, and L. Morgan Yost were chosen.[11] "Because I had designed it to begin with," Harris recalled, "they insisted on my taking the bigger house. I didn't *want* the bigger house because it would have to have three bedrooms and I thought this [utility core] is not for three bedrooms. We only had one bath on this. Well, anyway, I had to take it. Ed Stone was given the smallest one and [he] put his up on stilts and after they had got it well along he said, 'Look, it's a waste. Let's fill it in.' So his actually turned out to be the biggest."[12]

Harris's house looked a great deal like his Birtcher house, completed not long before his departure to New York. Fine redwood boards, horizontally placed, were again braced by battens at the three-foot unit lines. Wooden trellises followed the shape of the gable roof to give interest to a patio. *Interiors* magazine used a "scalped model" of Harris's house (the most expensive) for the opening spread of their feature story, "Eight Men on a Unit."[13] This cutaway dramatized how invisible the core could be after installation. As expected, of course, Harris placed it in the center of his house so that one face of the unit became a wall of the kitchen, a second face became a wall of the laundry, a third face became a wall of the bathroom, and the fourth became the fireplace wall of the living room. As the plumbing pipes occupied very little space, enough remained to house the water heater and furnace. Daylight entered through clerestories in the part of the unit projecting above the roof and reached the kitchen, laundry, and bathroom through translucent ceilings above the workstations. With his back to the windows, the cook was never in his/her own light.

Harris was kept busy working on the utility core at Rockefeller Center, but he also found time to jury architectural competitions, teach at Columbia, and socialize with his architectural colleagues, among them Frank Lloyd Wright. Jean began to do research at the New York Public Library. On her résumé she made the following entry for the year 1943–44: "In New York City. Devoted time to serious study of origins of Modern architecture. Wrote 'New England Keeps it Dark,' with T. H. Robsjohn-Gibbings. This was published in *Town and Country* and later reprinted in *The Reader's Digest*."[14] Jean Murray Bangs, the economist who had worked as a labor union organizer, a social worker, and an interior decorator, was becoming a historian of the Modern Movement and a journalist.

From the earliest days of their romance, Jean Bangs had listened closely to Harris's comments about architecture (later she would admit, "He wooed me with a cantilever") and her curiosity had been aroused.[15] In New York Jean found herself in a front-row seat at the spectacle of American Modernism. She was tempera-

Harris, scalped model of Harris-designed house exposing the Ingersoll Utility Unit in center, Kalamazoo County, Michigan, 1945.
Photograph by Ezra Stoller

Jury for a competition sponsored by *House & Garden*, March 7, 1948: *from left,* Marcel Breuer, Fred MacKie, Eero Saarinen, Harwell Hamilton Harris, Katherine Ford, and Joseph Hudnut.
Condé Nast Publications, Inc.

mentally disposed to analyze, form opinions, and speak out, and it was an intellectually stimulating moment for her. Her best friend in New York, quick-witted, irreverent, and well-connected interior designer T. H. Robsjohn-Gibbings, surely added to the enjoyment of this new pastime.

Robsjohn-Gibbings had made a reputation with a best-selling book, *Good-Bye, Mr. Chippendale,* that argued that Americans, blessed with a democratic society, should seek out and encourage native architects who were in the best position to mirror their society. In the August 1944 issue of *House Beautiful* Robsjohn-Gibbings put his case before the American people again as he described the choices they would soon encounter: "In the postwar world, . . . supposedly there will be three groups offering their wares to a war-bond-rich public. The prefabricated tycoon–industrial designer group; the interior decorator–period architect–antique dealer group; and the organdy curtains–Victorian knick-knack–Grand Rapids reproduction–women's magazine–department store group. You cash your war bonds and you take your choice"[16]

It seems at first that his complaint with American consumers was their dependence on European reproductions and miscellany, on the one hand, and what he calls the self-conscious "modernistic" industrial design, on the other. As he continues, however, his language becomes less hyphenated and hyperbolic and a genuine, persuasive tone takes over:

This is the way I see the fourth choice: For a long time now (it might be eighty years—it might be more), there has been slowly evolving in America a new type of architecture—a new type of house—a new conception of the relationship of man and the buildings in which he works and lives. Historians of this new conception have placed its exact origins in America because the very nature of this new approach to architecture could *only* be evolved by a democratic people.

He discusses the democratic values of Louis Sullivan and Frank Lloyd Wright and then points to their rich legacy, contemporary houses going up in Texas, California, and the Middle West that suggest the end of an era of imported architecture.

It was not until the work of Sullivan and Wright was taken up in Holland and Germany and France, caricatured, distorted, and served back across the Atlantic, that America became aware of so-called "modern" architecture. It is from these European sources that all the grotesque "modernistic" rubbish in America has come, and this is the final folly that America has had to pay for in its worship of the myth of European culture.

Finally, in closing he makes it clear that the opportunity for Americans to show they understand and appreciate their own heritage will come after the war.

Following his polemic, the magazine featured a building that they considered to be emblematic of the democratic American architecture of which he spoke. Indeed, the editor's note before Robsjohn-Gibbings's essay made the connection explicit. "The editors of *House Beautiful* deem this article by Mr. Gibbings a fitting preface to the next nine pages, where we present one of the most perfect examples of contemporary American architecture. We invite you to read both with unusual care."[17] The building chosen was the Weston Havens house by Harwell Hamilton Harris.

Gibbings had sought the architect out much earlier while the couple was still in Los Angeles, but Jean, imagining that she wouldn't like the interior designer–turned–writer, had always begged off chances to meet him. When it finally happened in New York, the pair hit it off immediately, remaining close friends until his death in 1976. Their friendship was undoubtedly strengthened by their feelings about American design, a feeling they shared with *House Beautiful* editor Elizabeth Gordon. Gordon, whom the Harrises had met through James Marston Fitch, was turning the magazine into one of the most influential shelter magazines of the time and, because of her very strong American bias, also one of the most controversial.

What was happening was this: the forces for Modernism in America were becoming polarized. Largely as a result of the much-publicized arrival of the Bauhaus architects in New York from Germany, there began to be set in motion the idea that they had brought Modernism to this country. In much the same spirit as Henry Russell-Hitchcock and Philip Johnson's book *The International Style* of several years earlier, the Museum of Modern Art and prestigious universities heralded them as having saved American architecture from languishing any longer in the dark period of eclecticism.[18] To many architects, critics, and historians who had been here observing the years preceding the Bauhaus architects' arrival, the claim was greatly overstated and even erroneous. As a result of their dissatisfaction with the emerging mythology, the mid-1940s through the 1950s would see a great flurry of magazine articles and books from those who wished to redress the issue. Among the most disturbing, albeit witty, was T. H. Robsjohn-Gibbing's *Mona Lisa's Mustache*, which traced the lineage of the Bauhaus back to the fascism of the Italian Futurists and attacked the elite fashion mongering of the Museum of Modern Art. This book, in which the so-called men of genius were depicted as magicians, was being researched and written in the mid-1940s, at the time the Harrises were in New York; when it appeared in 1947, it was dedicated to Jean Murray Bangs.

As Neutra's student and associate Harris had developed a great respect for the basic tenets expressed in the architecture of the European architects. It is true that he found the buildings of Gropius and Le Corbusier without the organic life of those by Wright and Schindler, but he still felt a kind of solidarity with what the men had accomplished. In 1943, soon after their arrival in New York, Jean and Harris traveled to Boston for a few days and were invited to tea in the house Gropius had designed for Professor and Mrs. Ford in Lexington, Massachusetts. The following day Marcel Breuer and his wife had them to tea at the house he had designed on a lot they shared with Gropius. Still another invitation for tea came on the next day from Walter and Mrs. Gropius.[19] The gatherings were friendly, but oddly and somewhat noticeably void of architectural exchanges. Harris is silent on his impressions of their homes.

Soon afterward, Harris had another and rather fatal encounter with the European architects in New York:

[Sigfried] Giedion and [José] Sert were also there, both having come over to lecture at Harvard and now found themselves unable to get home on account of the War. Because I had been secretary of the American branch of the CIAM, Giedion remembered me. He and Sert, whom I had recently met in another connection, invited me to lunch and announced their wish to found a CIAM group for Relief and Postwar Planning. They wanted me to join them in this. I quickly discovered I was being used. They needed a native American for the job they had in mind. Wanting to learn more about their scheme, I went along with them. After 6 or 8 luncheon meetings, at which we discussed many things, including who should be president of the proposed group (they considered Le Corbusier, but agreed he would not be acceptable because he had never publicly repudiated the Nazis; this made my hair stand on end). It was decided to call a meeting of all CIAM members then in the U.S. (mostly in Washington and New York). I sent invitations to them (and a few Americans we wanted to make members) to attend a meeting on a Sunday morning in June in the New School for Social Research, to consider the formation of this new chapter of CIAM. I had listened to so many stories of their delightful conferences held once on a Greek island and another time on a cruise ship in the Mediterranean, that I expected this meeting to be a joyful reunion of old comrades in arms. But even before I called the meeting to order I could feel the room was full of tensions. Besides Giedion and Sert, the only ones there I already knew were

Gropius and Breuer. In this setting, Breuer seemed almost American. Breuer said that CIAM had once been very valuable and had accomplished important things but he believed that that time had passed and it would be a mistake to try to revive it. Gropius talked but said very little; was pussyfooting, I believe. Soon everyone was talking and disputing one another. German was the native tongue of most of them but they were trying hard not to speak it here. In the heat of argument, a speaker would start suddenly in German but quickly switch to French when he discovered what he was doing, and couldn't say it in English. I couldn't see we were getting anywhere. After about 2 hours it came to an end. In my mind the meeting had been a flop. Then I saw Giedion hurrying toward me, smiling and almost dancing. He declared the meeting had been a success and gave me credit for it. Apparently he had been expecting a fight and thought I had had something to do in preventing it. I then decided my strength in the situation had been my utter and obvious innocence, and the disputants stopped short in their expressions in order to save me embarrassment. For a time I remembered the names of some of them but no longer.[20]

For Harris, who had once said of the Modern Movement, "we weren't rejecting the old, we were just moving beyond it," Harris, who disliked argument intensely, the CIAM incident was an unfortunate experience.[21] He *did* forget many of the people who attended, convinced for the first time that the unity of purpose he presumed was nonexistent. He had been too close to Neutra and Ain not to appreciate the social goals of the Europeans and believe them to be sincere, but he was beginning to doubt this sincerity. He now saw the émigrés as "salesmen" who "had to portray a new product to sell and take credit for."[22]

When he first arrived in New York he seems to have taken for granted the socialism of his European colleagues and to have been more or less comfortable with it. Indeed, one of his earliest memories from the time there was his dislike of Ayn Rand's *The Fountainhead* because of the way she glorified the individual. (Rand, who had spent her early life in Russia, hated the Soviets and wrote her novel to dramatize the nobility and power of an individual, in this case, an architect based on Frank Lloyd Wright.) Harris recalls that Talbot Hamlin, the architecture critic of *Pencil Points*, had loaned him his copy of the book to read:

For the first month of our stay in New York we lived in an apartment on the corner of Fifth Avenue and 10th Street, and one Sunday morning we walked over to the edge of the East River, taking *The Fountainhead* with us. As I looked at the river, Jean started to read aloud from it. I stood it as long as I could and then told Jean to stop; that I might believe in Zarathustra but not in Roark. I was amazed that Hamlin liked it. Many years later I found myself watching it as a movie. I still didn't like it but in the movie Roark was represented with a flesh and blood actor and this made him halfway believable.[23]

Harris at the Museum of Modern Art, 1945.
Photograph by Yousuf Karsh

By the time the Harrises left New York in 1944 they had begun to resent what they saw as the European "attack on the individual."[24] The following year, after their return to Los Angeles, Elizabeth Gordon would publish a special editorial on Harris entitled "Meet Harwell Hamilton Harris" with a debonair photograph of the architect taken by Yousuf Karsh at the Museum of Modern Art. In it she conjured up the spirits of Emerson and Whitman and spoke of the "great tradition of American architecture." She said that Harris believed "American culture . . . is based on a belief in the supreme importance of the individual man."[25] She also made a point of contrasting him with the European architects:

Harris looks upon the free-standing, individually owned house as one of the brightest flowers of American culture. He will go to any extreme to avoid sacrificing it to the European design formula of building row or group housing as a means of meeting rising costs. This has called for skillful planning on his part and has resulted in houses often almost diminutive in size yet possessing the dignity, privacy, and other amenities of houses many times as large.[26]

The very apolitical, nonconfrontational, nonideological Harris had become part of a camp, if rather unwittingly. The internecine struggle between Modernists had only just begun. After New York, Harris would begin to speak more about his American roots, about democracy, about the individual. In time he would have the opportunities to demonstrate the depth of his devotion to Louis Sullivan and Frank Lloyd Wright, whose buildings in Chicago and Oak Park he was just getting to see on his return trip to Los Angeles. And Jean Harris, still haunted by Webber's comment on Greene and Greene and her own fascination with Maybeck, would interest her husband in them. After all, they were not only Americans but fellow Californians as well. While they were still in New York, Jean and Harris resolved to look for Greene and Greene houses when they returned home and to learn if the architects were still alive.

Harris, house for Clarence H. Wyle,
Ojai, 1946–48.
Photograph by Julius Shulman

8.

Back West:
A Regrouping in Patterns,
1944–1948

We headed southwest, St. Louis, Kansas City, and Oklahoma City . . . Only when we entered Arizona on a straight hundred-mile road on the Painted Desert in a violently colored sunset, did I react. It may have been because I was at the wheel, while Harry dozed. I felt a desire to overtake that sunset as if it were a rainbow, before it faded. . . .

Then he took the wheel until we got into Los Angeles at nightfall. The ride through the downtown section with its dark, shapeless office buildings alternating with parking lots, railroad tracks and grimy streets was short; we entered Hollywood which gave me the impression of a frontier town. No buildings seemed to be higher than two stories, the sky was visible everywhere, pierced occasionally by shafts from searchlights as in Paris during the war, to spot enemy planes; here it heralded the presentation of a new film or the opening of a supermarket.

MAN RAY
entering Los Angeles in the 1940s,
from *Self Portrait Man Ray*, 1963

HARRIS AND JEAN took the train back to Los Angeles at the end of November 1944. They stopped over four days at Taliesin in Spring Green, Wisconsin, after receiving a telegram from Frank Lloyd Wright that he was directing Wesley Peters to meet them at the platform in Madison. Harris remembers fondly the music on Saturday evening (a Taliesin tradition) and conversations with Peters and his wife, Svetlana (Wright's stepdaughter), outside on the open roof connection between two parts of the house. He was enthusiastic about the early Wright residences in Oak Park and the Sullivan buildings in Chicago, but more than anything he was enthusiastic about getting home to Los Angeles. He and Jean had enjoyed New York immensely. Because of the war it had seemed small and quiet, cosmopolitan on a modest scale, but it wouldn't stay that way for long—neither, he feared, would Los Angeles.

Back home, at last, he taught design at the University of Southern California and kept up with the Ingersoll Steel house, on which construction had begun soon after he arrived.[1] This house for the frigid climate of Kalamazoo coincided with another house design at the time for a very different climate. He had won a Libbey Owens Ford competition for the design of a solar house. (He tied with Neutra on the first ballot, but the second time around he took the prize away from his former teacher.) The perspective drawing showed gardens and entrance walks on the south side of the house that were protected from the sun by twelve-foot-long sliding louvered panels which could be adjusted according to the angle at which the sun was striking. But the war was still raging and it seemed doomed to go the way of many other designs of the period.

It might be said that Harris's attitude about his home state had never been so warm, so robustly connected. When he received a phone call at this time from Joseph Hudnut, dean of the Graduate School of Design at Harvard University, inviting him to join the faculty, he had to say no. As flattered as he was by the invitation, which he might have accepted had he still been in the East, he knew that California was his element. There he had had clients who understood his work. Moreover, he felt especially qualified to respond to the landscape and culture. Instead of the artists and intellectuals of the early days, he now got an occasional Hollywood star. He designed a warm wooden house for actor Robert Ryan, but, like the ranch house he had designed for movie director John Huston in the San Fernando Valley, it was destined never to be built.[2]

In one of the worst of such disappointments, a plan he had been working on with John Pennington, the first violinist of the London String Quartet, who had come to Hollywood to perform in the filmed musicals that were then popular, collapsed just as the war appeared to be ending. It was a combination house, music studio, and concert hall on a beautiful site looking over the Arroyo Seco in Pasadena. Tall trees screened the house on all sides and framed the view. It was an arrangement well suited to a Harris form. The wide wall of the concert room was all glass and in wide panels that slid horizontally to provide a clear opening to the large garden terrace just outside. The levels of the hall and the terrace differed only by a few inches, an arrangement that allowed the audience or the orchestra to have a choice of inside or outside seating. After deriving the plan, Harris and the Penningtons began waiting for the war to be over. Harris's recent description of what ensued tells how meticulously he worked and how raw his disappointment still is:

John decided that he would like to do a little gardening on the property and he asked me to design a small shed where he could keep tools and maybe make a cup of tea; hence the name "Tool and Tea." He declared his intention of building it with his own hands. Because I didn't put much faith in him as a carpenter, I designed the building in pieces that could be made in the mill and merely bolted together at the site. None of the pieces weighed more than a man could lift; this was true of the floor and roof as well as the walls and the sliding doors. . . . But before even the Tool and Tea could be bolted together, . . . John's wife Doris suddenly died and John immediately gave up all thot of building and returned to England. Quite a bit later, Marcia, sister of Doris and a longtime friend of Jean, visited John in London. Marcia was again single and John asked her to marry him. She refused. Even if she had married him it was too late to build even the Tool and Tea.[3]

Of the nineteen commissions Harris received between 1945 and 1946, eleven were never built. Two of these are most unfortunate because they would have shown Harris working with problems he had not yet faced. The first was a projected plan for the Pottenger Hospital in Monrovia, California, and the second was an automobile sales and service building for Jelton Motor Company in Oakland, a job he shared with William Wurster of San Francisco.[4]

Harris had known Wurster since 1934, when the Lowe house was first published, and the San Francisco architect sent him an admiring note. He would come to know him much better later and to see in him a kindred spirit.[5] Wurster was also influenced by the indigenous wooden architecture of California, so much so that Lewis Mumford, writing in the *New Yorker* in 1947, coined the label "Bay Area Style" to describe the work of both architects. Mumford's larger goal was controversial, namely, to pit the rigorous functionalists, "who placed the mechanical functions of a building above its human functions," against the warmth of his favorite American architects.[6] For the purposes of this argument, he must have reasoned, Harris might as well be in the Bay Area. Yet from his very Southern California vantage point, Harris seems to have found the connection a little strange, in spite of his respect for Wurster and Mumford. It was an awkwardness, however, he could live with. It was Jean Harris who soon found the opportunity to set Mumford straight not just about the geographical limitations of the Bay Area but about the stylistic ones as well.

Since their return to Los Angeles Jean had been busy uncovering all the information she could about Greene and Greene. She looked through telephone books and city directories (old as well as new), but found no help in them or in the AIA directory of its members. They had apparently given up their membership in 1915, believing they could no longer afford the dues. Finally, Jean got the name of Henry Greene's daughter and the couple drove to her house, where he had gone to live. The elderly architect told them that he had left the firm's collection of drawings (410, Harris believes) in the garage of the last house he had lived in. The current owner of the house had no objection to their looking in the garage, and so it was there in a backless and rat-infested cabinet that they found the derelict drawings.[7]

After their find Jean and Harwell reunited the architects for a photograph by Cole Weston, their friend Henry Eggers paid for photographs to be taken of all the Greene and Greene homes, and they organized a traveling exhibition. When Howard Myers, editor of the *Architectural Forum*, came to Los Angeles soon afterward Jean took him to see the early, original California bungalows by the architects. Harris reports: "Myers said, 'Why didn't I know about them?' and Jean answered, 'Why didn't you?' On the spot he commissioned Jean to write an article for the *Forum*. Myers died very shortly afterward but the editor who took over made the article a feature of the Oct. 28, 1948 issue, prefacing it with an excellent introduction."[8]

With a confidence that belied her inexperience as an architecture writer, Jean Bangs Harris chastised Lewis Mumford for misusing the word "style" to describe

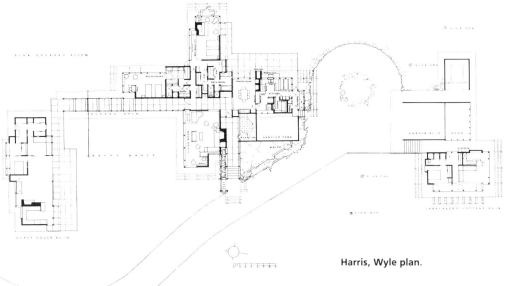

Harris, Wyle plan.

Harris, Wyle house living room.
Photograph by Maynard Parker

Bay Area architecture (which she contended was too diverse for the term) and for failing to notice that that word could have been more aptly used farther south to describe the ubiquitous type of architecture Greene and Greene started. She documented the lives of these forgotten men, put their ideas in the context of trends in American thought, and analyzed their rise and fall with a perspicacity that has left all subsequent chroniclers of Greene and Greene in her debt.[9] As a result of her efforts, the elderly gentlemen were given a special award by the American Institute of Architects.

Harris, who recognized the affinity he had with the Greenes, could hardly have avoided being influenced by the exposure to them his wife's efforts made possible. The Clarence Wyle house, begun in Ojai, California, in 1946 (the year in which the Birtcher house idiom dominated Harris's sensibility), emerged in 1948 and owed much to his contact with the Greenes. The Birtcher house had been distinctive because of Harris's extremely subtle handling of wood. Joints were de-emphasized in favor of the continuous lines of three boards that flowed into and out of the house. Punched-out openings in the boxed-in eaves provided the only interruptions in the overall picture of smoothness. In the Wyle house, by contrast, Harris was far more interested in revealing the structure of his house, and for this reason the gable roof became a favorite new element. "I like not having the boxed-in eaves that I usually had with the hipped roof," Harris has said. From this simple admiration of the roof he quickly arrived at an appreciation for extended open rafters. "You see framing members anyway with a gable roof," he mused, "and it seems nice to see them keep coming.[10] By using rafters that were two inches deeper in the open section he assured himself that they would never appear as if part of the roof had been "blown off in a storm." The two inches would make the extension appear bold and intentional.

The extended open rafters were dramatically exploited in the Wyle house, where Harris was presented with a site in a mountainous region. In his plan, Harris sent four wings away from the house out into the landscape to maximize view

Harris, house for Mr. and Mrs.
Ralph Johnson, Los Angeles,
1947–48.

Photograph by Fred R. Dapprich

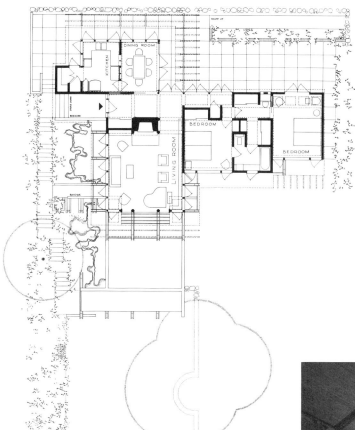

Second, main level

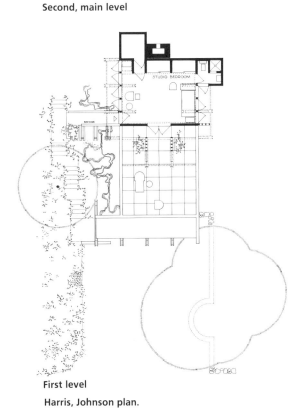

First level

Harris, Johnson plan.

Opposite, Harris, Johnson house: dining room, bedroom, and dressing table.

Photographs by Maynard Parker

Harris, Johnson house living room.

Photograph by Fred R. Dapprich

gazing, an arrangement Esther McCoy has traced to the cruciform plans of his expandable postwar housing ideas.[11] Not only did the wings appear to reach out into the surrounding landscape, but their nature—narrow and long—enabled the architect to provide windows on three sides of the four principal rooms. He celebrated the importance of these rooms by marking their terminations on the outside with extended open rafters. One gabled wing, a porte cochere reaching to the drive, had an exposed roof construction overhead and a rock wall with built-in bench below. It was a clear homage to the Greenes.

For all its exposure to the outdoors, Harris did not fail to give the Wyle house intimate spaces: A brick chimney created an alcove for a desk in the master bedroom, and a built-in sofa and hi-fi table perpendicular to the living room hearth suggested a kind of updated inglenook. Harris might have taken the straightforward Arts and Crafts vocabulary of the Greenes to a simpler, more Modern stage, but the warm woodsy spirit was the same.

If the Wyle house suggested the influence of the Greenes, Harris's next important commission, the Ralph Johnson house of the following year, would make the connection explicit. Anyone who had read Jean's article in the *Architctural Forum* and remembered her descriptions of the Greenes' work would have been struck by the connections between her husband's recent houses and it. "In their work," she wrote, "we are constantly aware of the stick, used as a post, as a beam or composing a lattice, trellis or truss. We see the stick joined together by notch, dowel or strap; the stick making the rhythmic pattern and the joints the decorative detail."[12] In the Johnson house, far more than in the Fellowship Park, Havens, or Birtcher houses (or any preceding work), Harris rejoiced in wood, its ending, its beginning, and its connections.

"If you can think of a rectangular umbrella, then you can understand it," says Harris of his use of wood in the roof of the Johnson house. "I've always been fascinated with an umbrella, the way you have a support and then a support on that and it goes on out. You look up through the whole thing and that's the way you do here."[13] The rafters in the ceiling of the Johnson kitchen protrude through the wall and meet the rafters of the adjacent dining room, which move upward, only to be countered by rafters rising up to join them. Beyond the dining room, outside on the Johnson patio, more rafters rise and fall in contrary slopes.

On the outside of the house Harris made an event out of the splices in the pergola fascias. Believing that what cannot be concealed should be turned into a feature, he multiplied the number of splices and inserted a twelve-by-twelve-by-

Harris, Gerald M. Loeb pavilion,
Redding, Connecticut, 1947–50.
Photograph © Wayne Andrews / Esto

four-inch block in each. Highly visible and regularly spaced as they are, they become a part of the rhythmic pattern of the house. The two-story arrangement, which rises above a garage facing the street, is covered with boards and battens. Entrance comes at the far side of either of two bridges that connect the house to a staircase leading upward alongside a stream. Because "everything," Harris said, "was to take your mind off the long path to the door," he created not a continuous path but rather a "dotted line" leading to the entrance. The lower bridge connects to the room of the Johnsons' son and his private balcony; the upper leads into the

Harris, the Chadwick School,
Rolling Hills, 1951.
Photograph by Quinlin

public area of the house and beyond to the living room and its floor-to-ceiling window. Above the window, the skeletal framework of the roof continues outward in the form of open rafters to frame an image of the Johnson house that evokes the east wing façade of Greene and Greene's Blacker house in Pasadena.

Throughout 1948 and 1949 the pattern continued. The Chadwick School in Rolling Hills was a composition of overlapping gable roofs, imitating and merging with the undulating landscape it occupied.[14] The Mulvihill house in the Sierra Madre was a spectacular example of the type. Looking toward the San Gabriel Mountains, this house dominated its site at the same time it collaborated with it. The living room wing that thrust so boldly into space became the roof of an open-air patio below, in which a closer experience with nature might be had.[15] Perhaps one of the most successful Harris houses of this period was a pavilion for E. F. Hutton president Gerald Loeb that was hidden in the woods of Redding, Connecticut. There was the Greene and Greene influence again, but tempered by the very quiet Japanese forms of the much earlier Fellowship Park Harris.[16] Floors were covered with grass mats, and wall panels of rice paper lined the perimeter of the living room. To this simple beginning drawn from his early practice, Harris added the open rafters and gable roof of his current idiom. With its stronger Craftsman overtones, it was a Modern look that particularly suited his client.

Loeb had contacted Harris as early as 1942 while the Harrises were still in New York.[17] He had been intrigued by photographs of the Havens house he had seen and, as he was a native of San Francisco, he hoped to arrange with Harris to

see the interior of the house on his next trip home. He had hired Frank Lloyd Wright
to design a house for him and he told Harris that he was not placing any limitations on the architect because he had made the mistake of doing that before. As a
young boy, his mother, a widow, had put him in charge of supervising an architect
she had hired to build them a home. He exercised his power more than once, saying no to many of the designer's ideas, with the result that later when he was older
he knew that he had ruined the house. Its architect, he told Harris, was Bernard
Maybeck. When Harris told Loeb about Jean's interviews with Maybeck, the businessman offered to give her a grant to write a book on him. Loeb's plan was to give
the money to the Museum of Modern Art, which would administer the payments
to Jean. She, however, objected strenuously, saying that the sympathies of the museum were completely out of character with Maybeck's work. She urged Loeb instead to give the money to the University of California at Berkeley, which he did.
Although Harris remembers friendly relations with the Museum of Modern Art,
Jean apparently mistrusted it. The museum had introduced the European Modernists and, Jean seems to have believed, enabled them effectively to co-opt the
very idea of Modernism in this country.[18] She wouldn't let it get credit for her re-
discovery of the long-neglected Maybeck.

As with Greene and Greene, Harris became an admirer of Maybeck, though he
knew that there could never be a direct influence on his own work, not even in the
Loeb pavilion, where it might have been most tempting. Harris has said: "His use of
historic forms prevented me from borrowing his forms. This may seem strange

because I did borrow features and details from Greene & Greene; I suppose I could imagine myself originating a Greene & Greene detail but not a detail Maybeck had borrowed."[19]

Although Jean would never complete her book on Maybeck or, for that matter, the one she planned on Greene and Greene, she did write a series of articles for *Architectural Forum, Architectural Record, House and Home,* the *Journal of the American Institute of Architects,* and *House Beautiful.*[20] As a result of this publicity, Maybeck's work enjoyed the scrutiny of a younger generation. He was subsequently awarded the Gold Medal of the American Institute of Architects. Jean kept the photographs and drawings Maybeck had given her for years, actually until her death in 1985, when Harris donated them to the Bancroft Library at Berkeley.

In 1987, when an exhibition of photographs of Maybeck's architecture was mounted by the School of Design at North Carolina State University, Harris made a speech that showed how he had come to terms with the elder architect's historicism. Forgetting perhaps for a moment the contemporary architect's reacquaintance with and acceptance of historical buildings, Harris began:

I hope this will dissolve a prejudice,—a prejudice your first look at these pictures may have aroused. If you are the way I was, you will begin by insisting on today's architect finding his forms in the present. Or, if you are a history-minded architect and believe in using forms from the past, you will probably insist on all forms in the same building being from the same period of the past. Purists hate conglomerations. But Nature is not pure as Maybeck knew so well.[21]

Through the medium of Nature and California Harris had come to see Maybeck as someone he could admire as much as Sullivan and almost as much as Frank Lloyd Wright. Describing the great natural beauty of California at the time Maybeck was designing Wyntoon, a country retreat for Phoebe Apperson Hearst, Harris noted:

From the time he was building Wyntoon onward, Maybeck would return to nature to renew his fertility of invention, to re-create his spirit, to heal his wounds. Nature is complex. Even its plainly visible elements are myriad. Yet in Nature there is no ultimate rejection of a single one of them,—only a re-grouping in patterns where relations are harmonious and each element is engaged in doing what is natural for it to do and, in doing that to enjoy a kind of democratic acceptance. This understanding of nature lay behind the most abstract of Maybeck's creations. It resembles Frank Lloyd Wright's concept of nature.[22]

"Only a regrouping in patterns . . ." There are no better words to describe the changes that Harris's own architecture had begun to reflect.

Bernard Maybeck, the First Church of Christ Science, Berkeley, 1910.
Photograph by Julius Shulman

Charles and Henry Greene, the Blacker house, Pasadena, 1901.
Photograph by Lawrence Speck

9.

The Schism Intensified: Regionalism Becomes an Issue, 1948–1949

I shall not imagine for my future house a romantic owner, nor shall I defend my client's preferences as those foibles and aberrations usually referred to as "human nature." No, he shall be a modern owner, a post-modern owner, if such a thing is conceivable. Free from all sentimentality or fantasy or caprice, his vision, his tastes, his habits of thought shall be those most necessary to a collective-industrial scheme of life; the world shall, if it pleases him, appear as a system of casual sequences transformed each day by the cumulative miracles of science. Even so he will claim for himself some inner experiences, free from outward control, unprofaned by the collective conscience. That opportunity, when the universe is socialized, mechanized, and standardized, will yet be discoverable in the home. Though his house is the most precise product of modern processes there will be entrenched within it this ancient loyalty invulnerable against the siege of our machines. It will be the architect's task, as it is today, to comprehend that loyalty—to comprehend it more firmly than anyone else—and, undefeated by all the armaments of industry, to bring it out in its true and beautiful character.

JOSEPH HUDNUT,
"The Post-Modern House,"
Architecture and the Spirit of Man, 1949;
reprinted in *Roots of Contemporary Architecture,*
1952

HARRIS'S USE of the word "democratic" in his 1987 description of Maybeck harks back to the period surrounding 1948 when Jean's articles on Maybeck and Greene and Greene were appearing. In a reference to the biblical passage from Mark 6:2–8, in which Jesus Christ explains his persecution with the words "a prophet is not without honor, except in his own country," *House Beautiful* entitled Jean's Greene and Greene piece "Prophets without Honor." The battle between those who believed the Europeans had brought Modernism to America and those who believed it had been evolving here all along was still waging. Jean opened her Maybeck story with a 1942 quote from Talbot Hamlin that read, "Where American life has most truly developed along its peculiar and most characteristic lines—let us say roughly along the Pacific Coast—where in general American mores, as distinguished from those of Europe, are most freely accepted, there is evolving a kind of domestic architecture that is perhaps the most advanced domestic architecture in the world today."[1]

It was also in 1948 that Harris wrote his oft-quoted comment describing his houses for an exhibition of California work traveling to Melbourne, Australia: "The soil in which these houses are rooted is the same soil that led to the flowering of California architecture almost 50 years ago. It is a combination of abundance, free minds, love of nature, and an unspoiled countryside. Simple as such a combination seems, it has happened but seldom in the world's history. The eventual reward for its cultivation is a spontaneous architecture in tune with democratic aspirations."[2] He was talking about the work of Greene and Greene and Maybeck, not of the "flowering" of Modern architecture in progress when he first stumbled onto Neutra's and Schindler's Jardinette Apartments in the 1920s. Six years later in a 1954 talk before the Northwest Regional Council of the AIA in Eugene, Oregon, Harris would explain why Modernism as it developed in California was at peace with the architecture that preceded it, happy to be a part of the continuum of American architecture. The answer was regionalism, and Harris's speech was marked by an affectionate and informed description of his home state as well as a discerning commentary on what it had produced. He called the regionalism of California the "Regionalism of Liberation" because the hallmark of the area was "that it was more than ordinarily aware and more than ordinarily free." He continued:

A region may develop ideas. A region may accept ideas. Imagination and intelligence are necessary for both. In California in the late Twenties and Thirties modern European ideas met a still developing regionalism. What was relevant was accepted and became part of a continuing regionalism. In New England, on the other hand, European Modernism met a rigid and restrictive regionalism that at first resisted and then surrendered. New England accepted European Modernism whole because its own regionalism had been reduced to a collection of restrictions.[3]

Harris had become an articulate spokesman for the truth of twentieth-century American architecture as he understood it. The concept of regionalism had allowed him to unite his two great passions—California and Modern architecture—and he had done so in a convincing, even-handed way. It was for others to work out the differences between the two sides.

There was no want of advocates for either the European or the American view. Wayne Andrews, who became a friend of Harris, wrote the following comment in his immensely popular book *Architecture, Ambition and Americans*, published for the first time in 1947:

The battle of the twentieth century, which is fierce enough to amuse anyone who recollects that this is not the first time that artists have disagreed about art, is not over whether we should build in the modern or in the traditional manner, but over what kind of modern is worth building. In spite of the fact that a poll of a hundred architects might give an innocent observer the impression that there are no fewer than a hundred varieties of American architecture, it is safe to say that there are only two brands marketed in our generation by designers positive they are accomplishing a mission.[4]

Andrews labels these two brands Veblenite and Jacobite, after Thorstein Veblen, who, he says, "deplored the expression of untrammeled individualism in any form," and William James, who believed that the distinctions between individuals "went to the heart of the matter." Writing rhapsodically of Harris, Andrews stressed that he, "more than any other Jacobite, was dedicated to the principle that a house must be designed by an individual for an individual."[5]

Besides Andrews, other writers of the time, most notably Lewis Mumford and Bruno Zevi, attempted to clarify the boundaries between the two brands of Modernism. As Peter Blake has pointed out, Mumford pressed for an architecture of humanism and Zevi for one of democracy.[6] However the terms differed, each championed an organic approach. In his *Towards an Organic Architecture* of 1947 Zevi answered Sigfried Giedion's *Space, Time and Architecture*, an International Style manifesto, with a strong argument for the organic approach. And he made clear that "the recognition of space as the protagonist of architecture" was the crucial difference between the International Style and organic architecture.[7] Vincent Scully writing in 1961 would categorize the two aspects of the movement as Modern classicism and Modern romanticism before throwing both terms out in 1965 and declaring that there was no difference between the two, that Harris's Johnson house of 1949, like Gropius's own house of 1938, was predominantly suburban and thus, like it, antiurban.[8]

As Scully's change of thought indicates, one's perspective on American Modernism was likely to change with the passage of time and with increased knowledge. In light of the controversy, no rethinking of the issue was as crucial as that of Lewis Mumford, who in all his early writing on American architecture ignored the contributions of Sullivan and Wright and, at least as egregious in his own estimation later, ignored the connections between them and H. H. Richardson. Later he would become the most prominent advocate of an American evolution toward Modernism predating the European immigration period, but in 1931 it was his first opinion that prevailed. When he wrote then that following the 1893 World's Columbian Exposition in Chicago American architects were led "to wander for forty years in the barren wilderness of classicism and eclecticism" he set into place the mythology of Modernism in this country.[9] All that was needed to complete this mythology was for Swiss polemicist Sigfried Giedion to pick it up and reiterate it: "After the structural forthrightness of the first Chicago School during the eighties, after Louis Sullivan's outstanding purity of architectonic expression and Frank Lloyd Wright's exciting example around 1900, the spirit of American architecture had degenerated into a mercantile classicism." He then made the critical addition, "The impulse to break free from this disastrous development had to be initiated from the outside."[10]

In her book tracing the Modern underpinnings of the American skyscraper, Deborah Pokinski argues that during the 1930s "modernism in America was already underway. Indeed, by 1933 it had come to maturity. It did not have to await an impulse from Europe." She bases her argument on the American Modernism as it was represented in the Century of Progress exhibition of 1933 in Chicago and, ironically, on the architectural values promulgated by the American writers Henry Russell-Hitchcock and Philip Johnson. Her reasoning is as convincing as it is ingenious when she states that the issues on which they organized their book, *The International Style*, "reflected the contemporary American perspective on Modern architecture and implicitly defined a style which addressed primarily American concerns." Very un-European was their interest in historical precedent, in decoration, "indeed," Pokinski writes, "the very conception of a modern style."[11] Hitchcock and Johnson could not help having American points of view.

In the late 1930s and early 1940s such subtle insights into the book were less often the case. One did not think of Hitchcock and Johnson when arguing for the acceptance of an intuitive, native American yearning for a Modern style. Those who had uncovered a continuous thread running through early building (that is, those like Mumford and Andrews and even T. H. Robsjohn-Gibbings) ran the risk of sounding reactionary or a bit too nationalistic in their defense of American Modernism. It was an issue on which everyone took sides or tried desperately to straddle a middle position. James Marston Fitch, for instance, wrote an article for *House Beautiful* in 1944 tracing the evolution of American architecture over the past seventy years, with special emphasis on Modern precedents. In later writing, he spoke of the democratic values of Walter Gropius, whose ardent belief that architectural design should be the outcome of a collective enterprise struck many as socialistic.[12] Joseph Hudnut, dean of the Harvard School of Architecture and the man who brought Gropius to America from England, worried in 1949 that science had replaced values like "good manners, common sense, and love."[13]

Regionalism became a focus of the debate. Harris maintained the strong conviction that "it is a false modernism that sees a contradiction between modernism and regionalism," but it was William Wurster, dean at MIT and UC Berkeley and an outspoken proponent of individualism, who became the symbol of the cause. Calling up the "Bay Area Style" of Wurster, Lewis Mumford argued in support of an American organic architecture.[14] The setting was a symposium at the Museum of Modern Art in 1948 on "What Is Happening to Modern Architecture?" On the opposite side of the issue was Marcel Breuer: "I don't feel too much impulse to set 'human' (in the best sense of the word) against 'formal.' If 'human' is considered identical with redwood all over the place, or if it is considered identical with imperfection and imprecision, I am against it; also, if it is considered identical with camouflaging architecture with planting, with nature, with romantic subsidies."[15]

In his important series of books *American Buildings and Their Architects*,

William Jordy, a proponent of European Modernism, recorded this episode in architectural history with these words:

The regional aspects of modernism, unfortunately led to flag-waving, as the vulgarization of any kind of regional idealism always does. Thus an "American" modern was suddenly proclaimed in the pages of consumer magazines. And its "humanism" and "individuality" were implicitly, and sometimes overtly, contrasted with the "mechanistic" and "communal" (even "communistic") of early European modernism.[16]

Jordy was speaking here, in not so veiled terms, of Elizabeth Gordon's editorial philosophy at *House Beautiful*, whose "stridently American prejudices" offended him. An American Modern movement had become popularized by 1950 and the regional consciousness it displayed, the comfortable humanism it celebrated, represented, he noted, "a genuine threat to the integrity of the Modern Movement."[17] His desire is to set the "uncompromising clarity and abstractness of form" of Breuer's work against the "flabby sentimentality" and tender-minded Modernism of organic architects. The hallmark of the International Style, he reminds his readers, was the "objectivity implicit in the method, aims, and moral implications of an idealized view of the mass production of the period." Through a technological analysis, he observed approvingly, a truly Modern "design lost its overtly personal, its excessively subjective, quality. It thereby approximated the objectivity of a type, standard, or norm. As the typical took precedence over the unique, the architect expected to move from the periphery of modern society to its center, from the studio to the factory, from his elitist role of custom designer for a few to the popular role of designer for mass production."[18] Perhaps the words "typical" and "unique" best denote the differences between the inorganic, technologically minded architects and the organic, personal, and artistic architects.

Harris had been faced with the choice between the typical and unique as far back as the 1920s, when he encountered the buildings of Neutra and Schindler in Los Angeles and found a way of merging both. His buildings had utilized the technological innovations Neutra had taught him, but they became the means by which he created his organic forms and ultimately his very personal houses. The International Style exhibition had been moving to him, but he had not come away from it a convert to the social ends implicit in its emphasis on the typical. On the contrary, he noticed *architectural* features that were to become the individual trademarks of various architects—Mies's lightness of form, Wright's foreshadowing of Falling Water, and what he considered to be a certain lack of originality in Raymond Hood's McGraw-Hill building.[19]

He was looking for the unique, but he was certainly not being shabbily sentimental about it. Sentimentality, he had learned as a child, was what resulted when a style was applied to a building irrespective of its form and when the style made a statement or an allusion to something outside the immediate concerns of the building. A distaste for sentimentality and a resistance to contrived style almost prevented him from looking at Maybeck's very unique forms. Much earlier it had kept him from seeing the Modernity in Irving Gill's Mission Revival houses in Southern California. The aspects of the International Style that appealed to him, the very qualities that made it a style, were to him no more than a means to an end.

Upon his return to California in 1944 Harris was more actively aggressive in the pursuit of his architectural forebears. It was a measure of his confidence that he sometimes used an idea observed in Greene and Greene or Maybeck. Although he knew the type of style they had started, he was once again seeing "the familiar in new light," as Bernard Shaw had taught him to do many years earlier. These California architects were new to him, just as Schindler and Neutra had been new to him in the 1920s, but now, trusting his spontaneity, Harris could give a fresh, unstudied expression to what he admired. The wooden houses of this time might have Greene and Greene details here or there, but the overall result was original. Such had not been the case when a younger Harris was briefly under the spell of the Lovell Health House, learning to copy the look of modern architecture.

Harris's response to the European Modernists he met in New York might have inadvertently encouraged him to seek out his California roots, but once he found them, the expression became completely his own. He was, besides, temperamentally and artistically incapable of designing with a political aim in mind. Neither did he cater to the tastes of the American public. Andrews, Elizabeth Gordon, and others might hold him up as the quintessential American designer of his generation, and indeed his sensual, warm Modernism was popular with the public. But Harris was at all times an artist. When tastes (or, rather, styles) changed, as they inevitably would, the train would have to leave without him.

In this he was once again closer to Schindler than to Neutra. In the late 1940s, when the postwar building boom was beginning, Schindler was almost a forgotten character. He had his own reasons—reasons of pride as well as artistic integrity—for refusing to conform to the dictates of the International Style. He had actually become outspokenly hostile toward the movement and certain, as Wayne Andrews reported in his book, that it threatened everything he believed in. He was convinced that form was unimportant to these architects and he was outraged by their neglect of regional considerations. Esther McCoy told August Sarnitz in 1982 that Schindler thought highly of Harris's work and regional ideas, though, according to Sarnitz, his own "late formal idiom remained far removed from the Bay Regional Style concept." Still, his antipathies were clear: "The classical mode of set forms for columns, architraves, and cornices," he wrote, "is replaced by a stereotyped vocabulary of steel columns, horizontal parapets, and corner windows, to be used . . . both in the jungles and on the glaciers."[20]

And what of Neutra? In the late 1940s he fared rather better than Schindler. His International Style credentials had been impeccable and his passion for its objective (typical) values above suspicion, but he had begun to change, using redwood in his 1939 Davey house and board and batten in the 1942 Nesbitt house in Los Angeles.[21] Even though these developments came several years after Harris's early redwood houses and those of Wurster in San Francisco, Neutra managed to get credit for them from important members of the cognoscenti. Elizabeth Mock of the Museum of Modern Art wrote in her 1945 catalogue for the "Built in the U.S.A." exhibition: "Neutra was at first rather alone in his experiments with new types of wood construction, but before long many architects were exploring the endless possibilities of the material and creating new and appropriate forms."[22] In 1949 Neutra would appear on the cover of the conservative *Time* magazine. The creator of the machine-inspired Lovell Health House was praised as a leader in the movement to "humanize and domesticate" the International Style.[23]

The Museum of Modern Art symposium did not solve the problem of Modern architecture in 1948. As the *Architectural Forum* made clear in the headline and subhead of their coverage of the event, "Coziness is All Right. But architects think functionalism has quite a future ahead." There had been no reconciliation. Mumford might have taken away "a badly bruised Bay Region," as it reported, but such a minor injury wouldn't bring the battle of Modern architecture to a close. In many ways it is raging still. The forces were never to be unified. The late 1940s was nevertheless a good time to pause and reflect. Something *was* happening to Modern architecture, but it was far removed from the concerns of that day—the redwood warmth and natural landscaping of a Wurster or a Harris, the tense compositions and social idealism of a Gropius or a Breuer. In Chicago a high-rise architecture of steel and glass was beginning to catch on. It had the potential to be urban, monumental, and, stripped of its European social ideals, corporate. Tomorrow in America belonged to Mies van der Rohe.

10.   Decline of the West, 1950

Charles Eames, Case Study house #8, 1949.
Photograph by Julius Shulman

Harris, beach cottage for Rex Hardy, Portuguese Bend Club, Los Angeles, 1950.
Photograph by Robert C. Cleveland

A S THE HARRISES SEARCHED for the roots of the regionalist style of California and celebrated their finds in articles and houses, the place they knew and loved was becoming almost unrecognizable to them. The postwar years had brought a population explosion that had overtaken the aspect of the region they loved most—its nature. Thousands of newcomers to California wanted houses, and the ensuing development not only covered the hillsides and the beaches but gobbled up the intervening countryside separating the cities of Southern California. Los Angeles was now the land of urban sprawl and superhighways.

It might have been the ideal time for Harris's career. He was by now a famous architect whose reputation was largely based on his special sympathy with the state of his birth. It was not, however, an ideal time and the reasons it was not are both obvious and subtle. In the first place, Walter Webber's prediction to Jean that "they would get your husband" the way they got Greene and Greene turned out to contain a truth that neither she nor Harris had anticipated. Harris had been copied extensively. People who could not afford an architect could hire a builder who could quickly understand and imitate the kind of straightforward techniques that had become Harris's trademark. In such a context his ongoing original work was lost to any but the most discriminating observers.

Second, among the discriminating, among those who did want to hire an architect, a new taste was emerging that was at odds with the woodsy, natural idiom that had come to be associated with Harris. This new taste was connected to the steel and glass buildings of Neutra, but the more meaningful source was Mies van der Rohe.[1] John Entenza, who had become editor of *California Arts & Architecture* in 1938, played an influential role in the spread of a kind of minimalist, residential style of steel and glass.

The machine aesthetic that interested Entenza had not changed since Harris designed his house in Santa Monica for him, but it had become more spare. He chose to play an active, decisive role in shaping the postwar development in Southern California when in January 1945 he initiated the Case Study program in the pages of *California Arts & Architecture*. Essentially, the magazine became the client. It sponsored an architect and followed the design through construction, public exhibition, and actual use of the house, documenting the entire process for its readers. Harris was one of the first architects invited to participate, but he re-

127

Harris, Hardy beach cottage.
Photograph by Robert C. Cleveland

Pierre Koenig, Case Study house #22, 1959.
Photograph by Julius Shulman

fused because Entenza's takeover of the magazine, he believed, had not been handled well at all.[2] Neutra and Raphael Soriano accepted, but the houses that came to epitomize the program were by Charles Eames, Craig Ellwood, and Pierre Koenig, the thinnest steel structures, glamorously supporting glass walls above the twinkling lights of a Los Angeles stretching endlessly into the distance.[3] This was the image of California Entenza could support—an international image.

Harris admired the Case Study program but was disappointed when Entenza decided to drop "California" from the name of the magazine. Jean and Harris believed the magazine's strength had been its regional bias—the way it showcased the distinctive aspects of California design.[4] To Harris the Case Study houses fit in well with California architecture, but Entenza's aim was to turn the magazine into a national magazine. Distinctive regional qualities that California embodied apparently seemed more provincial to him than distinctive.

Harris construed the idea of California regionalism broadly. Although he loved to work with wood, regionalism connoted not only Greene and Greene but Irving Gill and Myron Hunt, Schindler and Neutra. It referred not simply to wood but to stucco and concrete and steel. It was the International Style interpreted for California just as surely as it was the Craftsman bungalow. To Harris the Eames house, for instance, was an obvious descendant of Neutra's Lovell Health House because it exploited the same technology and it was noteworthy because it had done so in an original way.[5]

He was wise to see that the Eames house stood out from the other Case Study houses. He had come to value the continuity within his "region of liberation" that the house represented, but he may have sensed too why the house had a special allure for a younger generation. Reynar Banham has written that the Eames house was the first building he and other English architects wanted to see when they arrived in Los Angeles in the 1950s.[6] David Gebhard has explained why: "On the surface this was a perfect product of the International Style, a volumetric box which asserted its machine origin; yet underneath it was highly subversive, for it suggested (as Schindler had done earlier) a highly potent anti-European and anti-classical mixture of high art and low art. . . . The English Brutalists of the fifties marginally sensed what the Eames house was about."[7] But the Eames house did not generate a brood of likewise subversive houses, at least not right away (the gauntlet would be picked up later by Frank Gehry); at the moment the trend was toward a machine style ever more admiring of Mies van der Rohe minimalism.

Meanwhile, Harris continued to give himself over to his penchant for wooden, Craftsmanlike exterior forms. In 1949 his enthusiasm for Greene and Greene was still new, after all. For the A. H. Hopmans he designed a house that looked like a wooden pavilion. The Elliot house in North Hollywood of 1950–51 was aptly described by David Gebhard and Robert Winter as "a late Craftsman masterpiece."[8] But it is the tiny beach cottage for Rex Hardy, Jr. (no longer standing), that said strongly, in abbreviated, nutshell fashion, where Harris's interests in wood were taking him in 1950.

Hardy, recently divorced, had purchased a lot on the Palos Verdes Peninsula not far from Lloyd Wright's Wayfarer's Chapel in an area called Portuguese Bend. The country club for the subdivision sold the lots and specified that a house could be no smaller than four hundred square feet. Because that was all the space Hardy believed he needed, Harris was able to realize a scheme he had been dreaming about and toying with for years. The beach house became a perfect square, crowned with Harris's favorite roof for a square, a petal roof. This petal roof was essentially a hipped roof in which the corners were turned ingeniously to create a charming image of shelter. At the last minute Hardy announced that he really needed an additional room for the occasions when his young daughters visited. Harris described the changed plan:

Naturally I couldn't let my dream roof stand between a wonderful father and his two innocent and lovely daughters. So I spoiled my petal roof with a pigtail appendix. If I had thot we could have afforded the additional cost, I would have put the guest room in a separate and still smaller square and connected the two squares with a flat roof low enough to slip under the eaves of both buildings, making the passage beneath it narrow enough and subdued enough to really look like a link.[9]

As the Hardy house demonstrated, Harris gave precedence to the needs of clients. These needs and the specifics of a site had always formed the basis of his organic architecture. This is the underlying reason why the term *regionalism* was not an idea that sounded inhibiting to Harris. He knew too well that others in California, particularly Schindler, had shaped an organic architecture around these same needs with results that were superficially, at least, very different. Although he ultimately became contemptuous of the International Style, many of Schindler's buildings of the 1930s and 1940s share with Neutra's more orthodox structures the particular Modern look it advocated. Harris had attempted such an International Style organic building in his Entenza house of 1937, but had afterward followed his instincts toward a greater use of wood and a return to the spontaneity of his Fellowship Park house. But he seems never to have believed that a so-called machine for living had perforce to place design purity before personal needs. Indeed, the house of his career that was most personal—the home for Harold English, who was in poor health—took shape in an organic way but looked unmistakably European and International Style. One of the finest houses of Harris's career, this house demonstrates how truly free he felt, how loose the stylistic demands of a California regionalism were to him. Neither Elizabeth Gordon nor the Museum of Modern Art could have pinned the English house to a particular Modern ideology.

It is important to realize that Harold English first contacted Harris in 1948, the year in which the Europeans and Americans had seemed most polarized. Harris was finishing up his Wyle and Ralph Johnson houses and describing the California soil in which his ideas had taken shape. English, an American and heir to the United Gypsum fortune, had returned home from France in 1938, following the German invasion of Austria. While in France, where he had been since World War I, English had married a French woman and begun a career as a painter and art collector. Although the couple kept their house in Paris, they had finally decided to purchase a lot in Beverly Hills and to hire Harwell Hamilton Harris. English's interest in European art and ideas may have suggested to Harris the possibility of a more European appearance for the house, but it is doubtful the connection was any stronger. The house was simply so natural and unselfconscious, so much tied to Harris's own intuitions and experiences, that the notion that the inspiration came from without seems highly unlikely.

Harris, skylight over English house stairwell with Matisse stained glass in background.
Photograph by Fred R. Dapprich

Harris, *right*, house for Mr. and
Mrs. Harold English, Beverly
Hills, 1949–50; *below right*,
English house patio with Harris-
designed, movable wind screens.
Photographs by Fred R. Dapprich

Harris, English house living room.
Photograph by Fred R. Dapprich

Few houses in Harris's career demonstrate the evolution of an organic idea better than the English house.[10] Harris's starting point was the precarious health of his client. From this factor came the need for an elevator, which, Harris believed, must be centrally located and near the front door. Around the elevator shaft a staircase took shape, moving upward at a slow, even pace—six steps and a turn, six steps and a turn, six steps and a turn—until the second floor was reached. The stairwell was bathed in sunshine from a ceiling that seemed coffered in light, essentially a wooden grid supporting sandblasted glass and illuminated by means of a skylight above. Straight ahead was Harold English's studio, signaled by glass panels mounted next to the door that Gauguin had painted for his Tahitian studio.

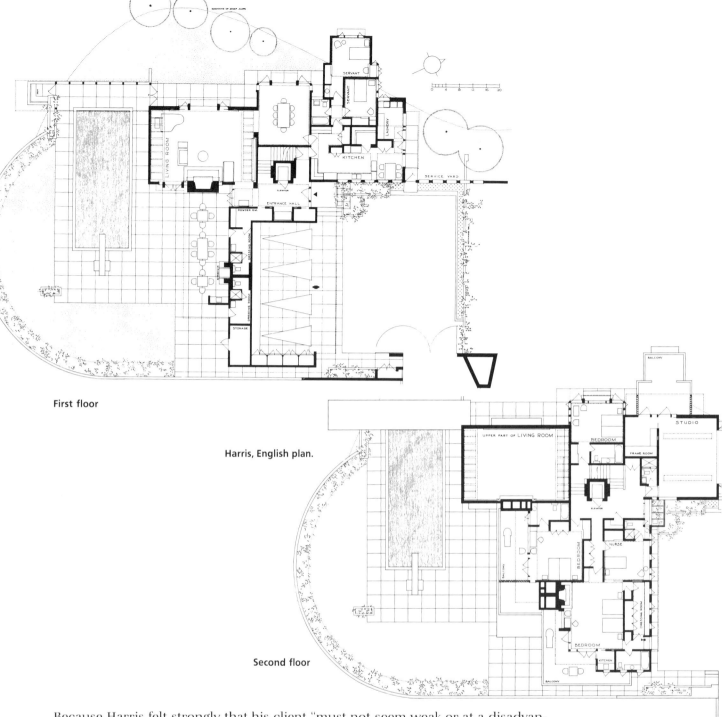

First floor

Harris, English plan.

Second floor

Because Harris felt strongly that his client "must not seem weak or at a disadvantage with others," he was careful to place the master bedroom on the same floor as the studio, and, near the bedroom, in easy eyeshot of English's bed, he arranged for a nurse's room. In the bedroom proper Harris designed a small kitchen—what Harris's one-time client and English's friend Arnold Schönberg called a "tea kitchen." It was convenient to a balcony facing south and a roof terrace facing east, views that were different from English's studio view. Thus could Harris write, "The provision, shaping, and linking of spaces suggest a pattern of private occupations—working, reading, sleeping, eating, day-dreaming, star-gazing, convalescing—all of them possible almost without moving."[11]

Privacy was a key factor in the design of the rest of the house. Two bedrooms for the frequent visits of two nieces and a nephew were discrete from the master

bedroom. One, on the second floor, was entered directly from the stairwell hall-way, and while it actually shared a wall with the master bedroom, its bath was opposite against a far wall; its balcony on the south exposure was enclosed to screen the view of the Englishes' balcony. The second bedroom continued the spi-ral begun by the staircase, taking the house up another six feet to a sequestered area with a western view. Harris had observed that the Beverly Hills lot, high on a ridge, offered views in all directions, views that were dramatic and varied. By giving each room its own view he guaranteed movement through the house. "To enjoy the whole view one will have to visit every room in the house," he predicted.

English offered Harris the largest budget of his career. Able at last to build in a larger scale, Harris abandoned his usual three-foot module in favor of the more standard four feet. It was not, however, a change meant to facilitate the use of prefabricated wall boards. The English house was covered, inside and out, with a soft cream-colored plaster, uninterrupted by joint lines. Rhythm was created not simply in the movement up the staircase but with four-foot windows and doors that ran in continuous lines above and below the flat protruding eaves surrounding the house. The window of the studio is clearly by the hand of the Lowe house architect, but instead of breaking sliding wall panels into very small panes to create a Japanese effect, Harris has left two central window panels free of panes and broken the side windows into three panes each. Here, and in the dining room's western exposure of glazed doors, Harris pushed the glass wall out from the room with a line of half-module windows, creating a niche or bay window effect. Combined with the very tall ceilings, plaster walls, and wooden mullions painted in a soft gray green, these rooms and all the others partook of an unmistakable grandeur. They also bore a strong resemblance to Frank Lloyd Wright's compositions.

Harris was comfortable with the antique furniture the Englishes moved into the house because, like the paintings in their collections, the pieces were originals, not reproductions. Because they were a natural aspect of the lives his clients led, they seemed also void of the pretenses such furnishings usually suggested to him. He believed that the plain white walls, which had no period connotation, set the paintings off.[12] Of course, the plain walls were destined to connote the Modern Movement in architecture. The white at the Lovell house had done so intentionally. Harris wasn't thinking about styles. He was not trying to be didactic or monumental. Fred Dapprich's camera moved over the surfaces of the English house with the same caressing light that had warmed Harris's wooden houses. In place of Neutra's formalism at the Lovell Health House was the kind of velvet tactility that had defined Fellowship Park for the public.

Harris's English house received little national press coverage. Those who had pigeon-holed the architect as the exponent of an updated Greene and Greene aesthetic were no wiser after its completion in 1951. To the young Los Angeles designers so strongly influenced by the high-tech minimalism of Mies, the English house would have been an enigma. It could have seemed like an anachronism, a throwback to the themes—both International Style and Wrightian—of the 1920s and 1930s. There was in this house, as original and vitally appropriate to its owners as it was, still a sense of longing for an earlier California. For this reason it seems to give closure to the Los Angeles that had been "a place and a time" to Harris.

There were numerous reminders that the times he knew were gone, but the most interesting, though in its own way bittersweet, was his involvement with the

Harris, National Orange Show,
San Bernardino, 1948–55.
Photograph by Maynard Parker

National Orange Show, orange
displays in the suffused light
beneath a white canvas tent,
ca. 1918.
*Photograph by a very young Harwell
Hamilton Harris*

National Orange Show exhibit buildings in his old hometown, San Bernardino. The National Orange Show was an annual event in the "citrus belt" of California. It was usually held in February, and Harris could remember going to it as a child. It was then in the center of town, beneath a canvas tent which gave a dreamy, suffused light to the orange displays below. He remembered the alligator pears (avocadoes), but mostly he remembered the oranges, an endless array of oranges, shaped into castles and all manner of gimmicks to get one's attention.[13]

He had been contacted in 1948 by Everett Swing, an acquaintance from his youth, who had been elected to the chairmanship of the Orange Show commission. They were interested now in building permanent exhibition spaces for the orange show and related displays. A previous building had burned and a newer steel building had been left unfinished. Harris was asked to come in as a consulting architect for it and the remaining buildings. Because he had always admired the Lamella domes he had seen used for markets in the 1920s and because he liked the way the curve of the arch was produced using straight wooden studs, he suggested that the Orange Show exhibition building be a Lamella dome.[14] To create a Lamella dome Harris adapted the concept of a Lamella arch, which, simply put, was an arched roof made of relatively short pieces of lumber bolted together to form a mutually braced and stiffened network. Before such a structure was covered with the final roof cover, its patterning was like an immense and lovely spider web. Harris dreaded the day that his steel Lamella dome for the National Orange Show exhibition building was to be roofed.

From ground to ground the frame took shape, spanning a distance of 225 feet. Remembering the white canvas circus tents of his youth, Harris suggested that they cover the roof with a translucent material to create the same lighting effect. Different exhibitors objected, however, because they wanted to use their own lights in their booths. The roofing material Harris chose was Robertson Steel decking with a square corrugation and a galvanized finish. It was the same steel decking Neutra had used in his Von Sternberg house.

The Orange Show had become big business. To his disappointment oranges played a very minor role in the exhibitions. The trend was toward showcasing automobiles. The involvement with the Orange Show brought home to Harris how irrevocable the change to Southern California really was. Hundreds of acres of orange groves had been leveled by the people who moved to California after the war. And it wasn't only the Orange Show that had given way to the automobile, it was the fresh, smog-free environment.

In 1950 Harris was commissioned to design a house in Fallbrook, California, for Mr. and Mrs. Alvin Ray. He gave their wide-open hillside site a design that traced its origins back to the Wyle house of several years earlier. Wings stretched out into the landscape and large glazed areas furnished the interior with abundant views. A library at the core of the house, removed a bit from the light-filled wings, nevertheless received a softened, indirect sunshine through a skylight Harris created by lifting a small section of roof above clerestories. A patio made a feature of a dramatic natural granite outcropping on the property. Harris had reacted to the spirit of the landscape as he always had, but the experience with the Ray house

Harris, Ray house living room wing.
Photograph by Fred R. Dapprich

Harris, house for Mr. and Mrs. Alvin Ray, Fallbrook, California, 1950.
Photograph by Fred R. Dapprich

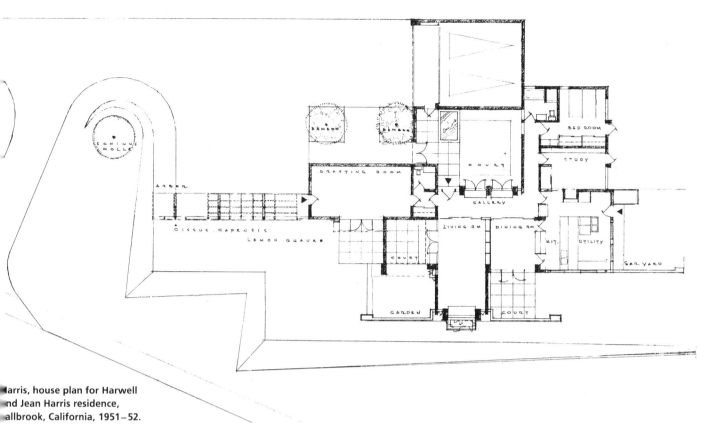

Harris, house plan for Harwell and Jean Harris residence, Fallbrook, California, 1951–52.

evoked a more personal response than he expected. It made him miss the California of his youth. As they drove through the avocado groves of Fallbrook he and Jean decided that they would build a new house for themselves in this area. Thus they might recapture their lost California.

For his own house Harris turned his back on the very wooden Craftsman idiom that had guided him through the Ray house. He chose instead concrete block construction, plastered and painted white. As he wove patio and courtyard spaces into the house, so too did he wind pieces of wooden trellis painted a burnt orange. One first saw it as a pergola above the entrance walk and later as a simple

Harris, Fallbrook house exterior.
Photograph by David B. Barrow, Jr.

trim over specific window and doorway areas. It even appeared at the opening to the courtyard, on its side, ladderlike against the plaster. Strong light and shadow made the wooden detailing as mutable as it was decorative. In this it was quite unlike the cast stone ornament of the Hollyhock House, but there can be little doubt that Wright was behind Harris's articulation of it in the composition of his Fallbrook home. A backward glance at the words he used to describe what he liked about the Hollyhock sculpture suggests the comparison. He remembered:

The ornament would follow around a wing and then it would come back again on another wing. And then I suddenly saw the ornament on each side of the large opening in the wall of what turned out to be the living room. It opened the living room out to a rectangular pool. I could see this same pattern but now incised . . . and then I discovered it in the full round coming up out of the center of the building mass, from places you couldn't see from where I was, couldn't see what the ornament was a part of.[15]

A small rectangular pool at the entrance and a living room with a window treatment that overlooked an exterior plant box were details that underscored that Harris was still studying and rethinking the Hollyhock House.[16] At Fallbrook, however, he was less nostalgic—perhaps less romantic—than he had been in Beverly Hills with the English house. However much the details might call Wright to mind, however much the wood and stucco and relaxed southwestern spirit might even conjure up Schindler, one feels something expectant about the Fallbrook house. To focus on it is to sense one of those ineffable and invisible moments of evolutionary change in an artist. Like the hands of a clock that dare you to catch them moving, such moments may also prove elusive. To see where they are leading one must follow their movement forward. Development is critical. Without it, there is only the empty certainty that time has passed.

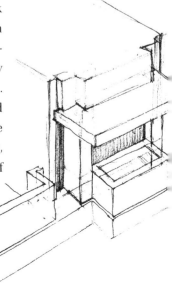

Harris, Harris house sketch on butter paper of front planter showing Wrightian influence.

Unfortunately, Harris left behind the themes of the unfinished Fallbrook house before he and Jean had completely settled into it. With an apprehension that too many ripe moments of his career were passing him by, he made the extremely radical decision to leave California. He did not have the foresight to know that it would be the final break with the state that had so completely shaped him. He only knew that the Korean War had begun, that work in his office was slow, and that the University of Texas at Austin held out an interesting opportunity. Could he be the first director of the newly formed School of Architecture? It was a challenge, an adventure, and, not least, a secure income. It was also, they thought, only a brief interlude away from home.

11. "We're Not Canning Tomatoes": The University of Texas at Austin, 1951–1955

remember once, and I don't know whether it was in Austin or not, Donald Barthelme (Houston architect and father of the writer by the same name) had come to a conference on school design. And he got up, drew some pictures and he spoke in a very positive way, rather slow, and he had a refrain he kept repeating. It was, "We're not canning tomatoes." I'll never forget that. "We're not canning tomatoes," he said. "We're not canning tomatoes."

HARWELL HAMILTON HARRIS
to author, January 1988

THE ALTERED LANDSCAPE of postwar California had prepared the Harrises to welcome a change, but the move to Texas was destined to play a more pivotal role in their lives than either could have expected. What they believed they needed was a temporary change of scenery. They got that—Jean was particularly thrilled as they drove across the openness of West Texas—but they got a great deal more besides.[1] Harris, who loved nothing better than to design from morning until night, had accepted the position of director of the newly formed School of Architecture at the University of Texas. He had taught at a number of schools—Yale and Columbia as well as the University of Southern California and the University of California at Los Angeles—but he had never held (nor had he wanted to hold) a permanent position on the faculty of an architecture school.[2] Now, rather suddenly, he was not just an architect, he was the director of a whole school.

From every indication Harris's administrative skills were rusty. Since 1934, when Jean quit her job as a social worker for the County of Los Angeles, she had assumed the responsibility of keeping the office records, of typing the correspondence, of public relations—in short, taking care of everything that interrupted the work of her husband. One young architect has recalled that she even insisted that work in the office stop when she served tea to Harris's draftsmen twice daily, late morning and late afternoon, believing firmly that it would renew their energy.[3] In Texas it would be her impulse to help Harris in any way she could. Although it was a natural enough impulse (and was actually beneficial to the school, particularly in regard to alumni relations), she and Harris had not appreciated fully how nervous the faculty of the new school was or how threatened it felt about his arrival. They were heralded as a most glamorous couple, Harris as one of the bright lights of the Modern Movement and Jean as the incisive scholar of Greene and Greene and Maybeck, but they were to be carefully scrutinized.[4]

Harris was in an untenable position. Prior to his arrival, architecture at the University of Texas had been offered under the auspices of the College of Engineering. When the school succeeded in breaking away and becoming autonomous, Harris was a good choice for director because he was widely known as a designer. With his selection the faculty would seem to have sent a message that the UT School of Architecture was not interested merely in the technical aspects of build-

Harris, *left*, at a University of
Texas party with faculty member
Roland Roessner, *center*, and
Nolan E. Barrick at the right.
Photograph by Laughead

ing but in the artistic aspects as well. Nevertheless, the faculty was greatly divided
over the hiring of Harris. The hostility they had previously felt toward the College
of Engineering they now directed at each other and at Harris.

Harris has said that the problems were more personal and political than
philosophical. It seems that Goldwin Goldsmith, for whom the current architecture building is named, had written a protest letter to *California Arts & Architecture* following the publication of its special Modern issue edited by Pauline
Schindler in 1935. Harris's Lowe house had figured prominently in that issue, but
by 1951 Goldsmith, quite old, was friendly toward the new director and Harris
liked and respected him.[5] Philosophy, nevertheless, did enter into the situation
Harris faced at the University of Texas. Because the school's independence had not
brought with it any increase in budget for the hiring of new faculty members and
because, moreover, Harris was not free to fire those of his detractors who already
had tenure, it seemed he was fated to perpetuate a rather dead curriculum. Ironically, out of this stalemate Harris was able to put together a young faculty over the
next four years that would do credit to his image as an educator and would put
Texas on the map as the home of a progressive school of architecture.

Two replacements had been made before Harris's arrival in the fall of 1951,
and one of these, Bernhard Hoesli, turned out to be an amazing bit of luck. Hoesli
was young and, Harris has said, "comparatively inexperienced," but he was a dedicated and inspired teacher.[6] He was from Zurich, having been educated at the
Eidgenössische Technische Hochschule, to which he would later return as pro-

fessor, dean, and, finally, director. He had also worked two years in the office of Le Corbusier. He and Harris shared a knowledge of the European designers as well as a respect for Frank Lloyd Wright, and the two became close friends. With his intense intellectual curiosity about aspects of the Modern Movement (particularly the spatial concepts of Wright, Mies, and Le Corbusier), his commitment to original thinking, and his generosity with students he was an inspiration to many and, in a quiet way, a rallying point for other young faculty members yet to arrive. Another close friend on the faculty was Hugo Leipziger-Pearce, who had worked in the office of Bruno Taut and on miner housing for Upper Silesia, an area of Germany that became part of Poland following World War II. Leipziger, a planner, was also an admirer of Frank Lloyd Wright, whose organically evolved Broadacre City had deeply impressed him. Although Harris told Leipziger that planning was not a special interest of his, the two men formed a strong, mutual respect. Harris could count on Leipziger's loyalty in conflicts with the other members of the faculty.

As with his architecture, Harris did not have a tight, rigid ideological platform on which to base his design curriculum. Equally opposed to the Beaux Arts method of copying historic detail in an eclectic manner and the Bauhaus method of working collectively on Modern architecture, Harris chose to replicate as far as possible in an academic setting his own experience. His own emotional vulnerability in the face of Modern architecture and his predisposition to seek out discoveries were the attitudes without which he knew he would never have become an architect. Thus he hoped his students would be open to the artistic values latent in architecture while he and the faculty encouraged an atmosphere of discovery. He was well aware that this approach was open-ended, but since his goal was to foster originality, he did not care. *He* did not want to can tomatoes.

My ideas in teaching grew out of my experiences in learning, first in sculpture, next in architectural projects I worked on with Neutra. I learned to distrust abstractions that were not my own abstractions. I believed in starting with the real. I considered design to be discovery. In design I looked for the natural and the simple. This is what the artist looks for. I hoped to find this approach in the teachers I hired, but I could hire so few, and they with little warning.[7]

Nevertheless, through various means—firing nontenured faculty, creating a community class to supplement a faculty salary, and so on—Harris succeeded in adding a handful of new teachers to the architecture faculty. Of these, at least three were artists.

When he was presented with his first job opening to fill, Harris contacted Joseph Albers, whom he had met while visiting at Yale in 1952, and asked him to recommend one of his art students for the job. Albers had taught at the Bauhaus following the departure of color theorist Johannes Itten and was at that moment developing and teaching his own principles of color at Yale. But Harris, unimpressed by Bauhaus attitudes generally and at peace with his own instincts for color, shaped largely by Stanton Macdonald-Wright, was not motivated by ideological concerns. He simply wanted to hire an artist and he liked Albers personally and felt he could trust him. His faith was well placed. Indeed, Harris was so pleased with Albers's choice of Lee Hirsche for the job that he ended up hiring two more art students from Yale, with the result that by the fall of 1954 Robert Slutsky and Irwin Rubin were in Austin.[8]

Harris had already angered the faculty over the hiring of Colin Rowe, a British architect, graduate of the Warburg Institute and author of the "Mathematics of the Ideal Villa," the first of his many important writings on architecture. He had met Rowe and another British architect traveling with him after the two arrived at his Austin office in the spring of 1952. They had just come from Mexico, where they had happened to make the acquaintance of Harris's former client and friend John Adams Comstock. Comstock told them that Harris was now in Texas, and they decided to pay him a visit.[9] Later, in the summer when the Harrises were in Berkeley, staying in Weston Havens's house while he was out of the country, they got a call from Rowe. Harris recalls the conversation: "'Can I get a job?' he asked. Well, I knew that something was going to be open. I don't know what it was. It wasn't free hand drawing. I don't know what it was, but I just said yes. I didn't realize that protocol called for all the tenured faculty to select appointments. I just said, 'Yes, come on.'"[10]

When Rowe joined the faculty in 1953 the dynamics of Harris's situation would begin to change. Rowe and Hoesli shared the same intellectual interests and immediately struck up a friendship that would last until Hoesli's death in 1985. Both men were single at the time and spent many evenings with the Harrises. Jean was fond of them, and in the case of Rowe, particularly, she had found someone to match her own acerbic wit.[11]

Harris now had his supporters, though they would never be tenure-bound, and he was becoming increasingly more determined in his efforts to have an influence on the curriculum. When, at the suggestion of Bernard Hoesli, he hired John Hejduk, who had acquired his education at the University of Cincinnati, Cooper Union, and Harvard University and had spent one year studying in Italy, he made another move toward strengthening his position.[12] The arrival of Hirsche, Rubin, Slutsky, and Marcus Whiffen, another British architect who wrote Harris from Yale seeking a job and was willing to accept one of the low salaries Harris had to offer, in the fall of 1954 would round out his new circle of influence. Though they had no vote on issues of policy, Harris would see to it that their presence was felt by the students.

In his important study of the Harris years at the University of Texas, "Towards a Unified Vision of Modern Architecture: The Texas Experiment, 1951–56," David Thurman has observed:

Harris emphasized four elements in the new program. First, he initiated a course dealing with architectural theory for all students above the freshmen year, which would examine both historical and contemporary architectural works. The course was designed to closely examine buildings, considering the cultural and historical conditions at the time, and principles related to structure and planning. Second, a new course was proposed to allow an expressive, freehand approach to drawing, not so much as a means of presenting reality as a method of abstracting it. Third, the scope of the critic was enlarged to include lecturing on architectural theory in the studio, and to participate in occasional collaborative projects with students. Fourth, and finally, Harris created two versions of the "Manual for the Conduct of Courses in Design," with one version for students and one for faculty. Of special interest in the Manual were the creation of . . . "design coordinators," as well as a heavy emphasis on the design process in the sophomore and junior year studios. Also of special note during the junior year was an emphasis on "spatial logic" as opposed to "functional expediency."[13]

In the implementation of these goals Harris's young faculty would play important roles. Thurman has noted that three of Harris's five "design coordinators" were Harris appointees: Rowe, Hoesli, and Hirsche, a situation destined to antagonize tenured faculty members, many of whom were merely assistants to the coordinators. Because Rowe was interested in a critical approach to the history of architecture, Hoesli fascinated by the study of spatial concepts among Modern architects, and Hirsche by the expressive qualities of art, each of their particular areas were integral to Harris's plan. The same would be true of intellectual Hejduk, artists Rubin and Slutsky, and historian Whiffen.

With the exception of Whiffen, whose stay at Texas was not long, and the addition of Werner Seligmann, Lee Hodgden, and John Shaw, who came after Harris's resignation in 1955, these are the men who would come to be known as the "Texas Rangers," a term reflecting not only their Texas experience but the continued educational interests that experience would have on their later careers. Harris is to be credited with the hiring of such promising teachers. His qualifications were seemingly modest—he wanted good teachers who could get along well with the others he hired. In exchange for this, he was eager to let each teach "in whatever manner he found most productive." The result was a group of individuals capable of igniting sparks of creative energy not only in students but in each other. By no means, however, can Harris be seen as the instigator or provocateur of the intellectual concerns that would hold the group loosely together for years. As he wrote Thurman, "My interest was in having teachers who really liked to teach and in letting each teach the way he found most productive. I would have opposed a [Texas] Ranger ideology as much as any other ideology."[14]

For his own part, Harris directed time and energy to the collaborative element of design, broadly hinted at in the manual. In his insistence that students have the opportunity to work on real problems as well as theoretical ones, he was remembering the importance of Richard Neutra to his own early thinking. UT students who had the good fortune to be in the architecture program during Harris's brief tenure there were exposed to Modern architecture, not just by means of working with the director on one of his commissions but by visiting important landmarks of the movement and meeting some of its illustrious players. (When, for instance, he heard Buckminster Fuller would be in Houston, he called "Bucky" at home and easily persuaded him to come to Austin as well, though he could not offer him an honorarium.) His desire to expose the students to everything he could within his means was obviously true from the beginning:

A month or two after my arrival, 4 or 5 students came to my office to ask where they would be going on their field trip. Until then I was unaware of a catalogue requirement of a field trip in the student's fourth year, and for which he should be prepared to spend as much as thirty dollars. I asked them to where past trips had been and was told it had usually been to a mill in East Austin but one had been to a cement plant in San Antonio. I then asked where they would like to go. They said "Puerto Rico." "Why Puerto Rico?" I asked and was told that one of UT's former instructors was now an important planner in Puerto Rico and they believed he could show them interesting work there. Just that morning I had received notice of the coming VIII Pan American Congress of Architects in Mexico City. Trying to go them one better, I asked, "How would you like to go to the VIII Pan American Congress of Architects in Mexico City?" Instantly, that was where they wanted to go, and immediately started talking about how they would get there, and how to pay living costs there for a week.[15]

After complicated negotiations in which students solicited the help of relatives and friends in Mexico, the total cost per individual had been reduced to $82, still too much. Harris's next step illustrates that he was beginning to understand some of the political aspects of his deparment.

I discovered the School had been given some money by the Central Texas Chapter AIA. It was the accumulation of members' payments for meals they had not consumed. It was earmarked for scholarships, but the faculty had decided only the interest could be spent. I knew I would get nowhere by asking in a faculty meeting for any of this money so instead I went to each of the older members separately with the proposal of a "collective travelling scholarship,"—and got it.

Finally, with the money raised and all efforts to get a visa for an Asian student exhausted, Harris and his students arrived in Mexico City.

Meetings of the Congress were in the unfinished buildings of the University of Mexico on the new campus in the Pedregal. We were the only students at the Congress. On the morning of the first day I was sitting in the hotel lobby when Frank Lloyd Wright entered. I told him I had 21 students from the University of Texas there with me and I hoped he would find time during his stay to talk to them. He agreed readily. At lunch I ran into Walter Gropius and made the same request of him; he refused to answer and I didn't see him again. . . . I had letters, telegrams and telephone conversations with our embassy in Mexico trying to arrange [the visa for the Asian student]. Consequently, the U.S. Embassy knew we were coming and we received an invitation to a party at the Embassy. It was not a large party but Frank Lloyd Wright was there and posed for pictures with the boys. Our ambassador was O'Dwyer, a former mayor of New York. He was at the door to greet each boy when he entered and to shake his hand when he left. Out on the university campus I found Diego Rivera up on the sloping walls of the giant Coliseum, directing with a long bamboo pole about 40 workmen who were carrying and placing (as they were shown) stones of various

Harris at the Wainwright tomb by Louis Sullivan, one of the many architectural sites visited when Harris took U.T. students on an architectural tour of Chicago and Saint Louis in 1954.
Photograph by Buford Pickens, courtesy of Harwell Hamilton Harris

colors to form an enormous mural decoration. I had had dinner with Rivera at a friend's house in 1939 when he was painting in public a mural at the San Francisco Fair. I called up to him and he invited us up on the scaffolding with him. Before leaving [for] Austin I told the students that because fully half our trip's expenses was being paid with money given by the Central Texas Chapter, we would have to report to the Chapter at the first meeting following our return and that each boy would have to say something. [One boy nicknamed Toline from Moline] was chosen master of ceremonies; at the meeting I was amazed to see him overcome with emotion, something his happy-go-lucky manner had led us never to expect. About a week after our return to Austin my wife came by the School to bring me something. One of the boys who had been on the trip saw her and rushed up to tell her what a wonderful trip they had had. "And do you know," he said, "for the first time in my life I felt like *a professional man!*" [16]

This is precisely the reaction Harris hoped most to provoke. He wasn't trying to impress the students by placing them in the rarefied situations to which his career had entitled him. Rather, he seems to have wanted to show them that the people they had read about were just people who had grappled with the artistic problems of real life.

On the next field trip, to Chicago and St. Louis, the focus was on buildings. In Chicago they had a special guided tour of the buildings in the Loop, and an associate of Mies van der Rohe took them on a tour of his own penthouse apartment on the roof of 860 North Lakeshore Towers. They saw the Frank Lloyd Wright houses in Oak Park and the other surrounding suburbs before heading to St. Louis, where Buford Pickens, the dean of architecture at Washington University, showed them the Wainwright building and mausoleum, Harris's favorite Louis Sullivan designs. [17]

Finally, Harris hoped to involve students in his own work to give them a feeling for the ways in which "real problems are much more stimulating than the artificial problems" necessary for academic instruction. [18] The perfect opportunity for such an intense involvement with students did not present itself immediately, though at least one student, David Barrow, was obviously privy to the designs Harris made in connection with a house for his parents. (Barrow, a serious student who, with Bernhard Hoesli, made an ambitious camping trip through the Midwest and West to see all the Frank Lloyd Wright and Harris buildings, would later become an associate in Harris's Dallas office.) [19]

Harris's first years at the university were so filled with administrative responsibilities that he hardly had any time to design. In 1952 he managed to finish the Fallbrook house he had begun for himself and Jean while they were still in California and, with the assistance of a young Harvard graduate, Eugene George, he com-

Harris, exterior and entrance
gallery of the Tom Cranfill house,
Austin, 1952.
Photographs by Hans Beacham

pleted work on the National Orange Show buildings. George assisted him in two other houses, one for Mr. and Mrs. Sylvan Lang in San Antonio and another for a UT English professor and art collector, Thomas Cranfill.

The Cranfill house brought Harris's early wooden style to Texas. Perceptive students might have seen in it traces of the Lowe house and the Granstedt house. Like the Lowe, it was board and batten with a shingled, hipped roof and a front garage that shaped a garden court, prefacing the front entrance. Like the Granstedt, it occupied a hillside and thus opened its back to a view, while the more closed front was illuminated by means of Harris's favorite clerestory windows, folded into the ridge of the roof. As in the Granstedt house, Harris separated the entrance hall from the living room by means of a wall that forced movement along it through a space that became a gallery. Without an entrance on axis with the front door, the living room became more private. Harris made one major sacrifice to the budget: he had to give up his idea of covering the house in one-inch-thick slabs of native Texas shellstone measuring three feet by six feet, eight inches. The next concession, cypress rather than redwood for the house exterior, was an accommodation to Texas. He did manage to use the shellstone material for the panels in Cranfill's entrance art gallery. In time and with increased familiarity with the climate of the state, he would make other adjustments to his California idiom.

Finally, in 1954 Harris was given his golden opportunity to involve his students in a real building. Harris described the unusual circumstances of the commission and the collaboration as follows:

The commission for the *House Beautiful* Pace Setter House had been given to me, but I decided if I really wanted students to have a chance to work on a real project, from selection of site to completion, ready for occupancy, this was my chance. *House Beautiful* was selecting the architect, acting as client, lending its name, providing the furnishings, photographing it and devoting two full issues of the magazine to publicising it. It was the idea of the Dallas Power and Light Company to build the house at the Dallas State Fair and it was putting money into it to publicise all-electric living. *House Beautiful's* demands so increased the cost that building was postponed for a year while Dallas Power and Light looked for more money. It got from General Electric the gift of all the electric equipment plus $10,000 in cash. It got from the State Fair $30,000 in cash in addition to our choice of a large, tree-and-grass-covered site, well situated on the fair grounds. At an *Architectural Forum* Round Table Conference in Chicago, to which I was invited I mentioned in my talk the *House Beautiful* Pace Setter we were planning. The moment I sat down Phil Farnsworth, president of the California Redwood Association, jumped up and announced his Association would give all the redwood we would need. The amount of selected, all-heart redwood we received was enormous; we were using it inside as well as out. On my way back to Austin I was delayed two hours in Dallas by plane failure. Having lunch in the airport with another delayed passenger, I happened to mention the Pace Setter project and the Redwood Association incident. My luncheon partner asked me if I would mind his mentioning this to Latane Temple of the Temple Industries. "If I do," he said, "I'll bet you'll have a call from him before noon tomorrow." Temple called and offered all the long leaf yellow pine we could use. As in the case of the redwood, the amount of yellow pine used was enormous; the house was large with a roof area well beyond that of the floor area. To provide the very best, Temple cut one of its last stands of long leaf, milled it, kiln dried it and got it to us well in advance of our need. Let me add that the eaves minimum projection was 4 feet and much of it was 8 feet; the ends and the undersides of the eaves rafters were exposed and, of the hundreds of exposed rafters only 7 had to be replaced on account of warping or twisting. The Dallas Home Builders Association offered to provide labor and supervision of construction and appointed Joe Maberry as supervisor. . . .

For collaborators I chose six students: David Barrow, Don Legge, Bill Hoff, Neil Lacey, Pat Chumney and Haldor Nielsen. Some were 4th year, some 5th and one was a graduate. We divided the design into six parts and each student took one part. We met every afternoon, and for the first hour each student showed what he had been doing and thinking and received the criticism and suggestions of the others. Each always knew what the others were doing and so was a participant in overall design decisions. To my mind, this is the fastest way to learn. To complete the detail drawings, David Barrow and Don Legge spent the Summer in Dallas with me and worked in a room of a building overlooking the Pace Setter now under construction. They watched their details being built and joined together. They made additional details as needed. During the Fair over 80,000 people visited the house. On the opening day I took Governor Allan Shivers thru the house. Even before the opening, newspapers throughout the State carried stories about the UT School of Architecture's house at the Fair. This is the way I wish architectural design could be taught.[20]

The State Fair house, unlike the Cranfill, continued the very strong, Craftsman-like features of Harris's late California work. It seemed to pick right up from where the Johnson and Wyle houses left off. Rafters from the gabled wings of the house extended outward for shade and lighting was subtle, built into troughlike brackets supporting the roof's wide overhang. The strong, visual image of the second-floor façade of the Ralph Johnson house, with windows reaching to the roof, now rested on the ground, a part of a larger composition of forms. Construction was board and batten and the roof was white gravel.

Because of special arrangements Harris built into the house that could make it easy to dismantle and relocate, the State Fair house was purchased and moved off the fair grounds.[21] Harris had gotten all the exposure and good publicity an

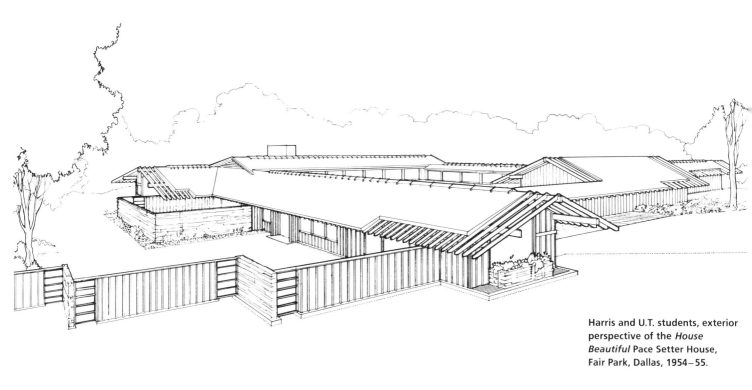

Harris and U.T. students, exterior perspective of the *House Beautiful* Pace Setter House, Fair Park, Dallas, 1954–55.

architect recently arrived in a state could want. At least three future commissions—the homes for the Townsends in Paris, Texas, the Woodalls in Big Spring, and Ruth Carter Stevenson in Fort Worth—can be traced to its influence. The Stevenson commission, for the daughter of Fort Worth oil and newspaper magnate Amon Carter, was quite large and challenging. It would have the effect of keeping Harris in Texas following his 1955 resignation from the University of Texas post.

The conflicts within the School of Architecture had intensified. Because Harris had not given in to his initial sense of powerlessness, because, on the contrary, he had pushed ahead by being as creative as he could to get what he wanted, he had fueled the resentment of several tenured faculty members. His falling out with one of these men, Robert Buffler (the former acting director), had happened soon after his arrival. For unexplained reasons, Buffler continued to keep his desk in the director's office after Harris began work. Further, he encouraged Harris to let him handle duties that, in truth, Harris did not yet fully understand: "In the beginning, I was glad to have Buffler's constant help but soon realized I was becoming more and more dependent upon him for everything,—that he probably wanted to keep me that way,—and that to the faculty I probably looked like Buffler's puppet. So I removed Buffler's desk from my office and incurred his lasting enmity."[22]

By March 1954, Harris, buried under the load of his administrative duties and worn out by the bickering of the faculty, appealed to Logan Wilson, president of the University of Texas, for a staff person to lighten his load. Thurman has sug-

Harris and U.T. students, Pace Setter House dining room.
Photograph by G. A. McAfee

Harris and U.T. students, Pace Setter House kitchen.
Photograph by G. A. McAfee

gested Harris was also motivated by his desire to spend more time developing his academic program, but it is doubtless also true that Harris, supervising the Pace Setter House, hoped to free some time for designing. In any case, Wilson declined to help, leaving Harris to fend for himself.

Did Jean Harris begin to have undue influence on the running of the School of Architecture, as some of Harris's critics charged? Was she able to resist the well-established routine of helping her husband with administrative chores? It is true that Jean was too devoted to Harris and too contemptuous of those who would hurt him not to use what few means were available to alleviate the pressure of his situation. Moreover, she saw him not just as her husband but as her partner and, as she told the women's club in San Angelo in 1956, this brought with it certain rights:

As a house wife you are a partner in an important business, not merely [a] drudge. As a part owner of a business, you operate on the policy level. More than this you are in charge of operations. You manage the plant, you do the purchasing, handle the public relations and the personnel problems as well. It is an exciting and an exacting business—but you begin at the top. The reward is an integrated personality, an outlook based on real values and the promise of continuing growth and development, which means an ever-expanding life.[23]

Elsewhere in her speech Jean urged the West Texas matrons to have confidence in themselves, and she reminds them that "the shrewdness, the sagacity, the forbearance of the mature man or woman, can be more interesting than the uncertainties . . . of youth."[24] Later in the same speech she prophesied the day when women would say to themselves, "I don't want to look young. I want to look as if I owned a national industry." It is here that she began to betray the characteristics of her personality that made her the focus of some of Harris's UT troubles.

Jean was an early feminist. Even before she went to New York to gain experience in labor unions she had worked her way through college, describing one of the more colorful jobs—on Cannery Row—for the Berkeley student newspaper. In addition to her studies of American architects in the 1940s, she had begun to probe the relatively uncharted waters of the history of food, hoping to mine out the aspects that made it a telling reflection of the society that produced it. By the time the couple arrived in Austin, she had become the food editor of *House Beautiful*, heading up a whole new section of the magazine devoted to "The Daily Art of Good Living." She was remarkably self-possessed. Nevertheless, and in spite of her sermon to the San Angelo group, it is difficult to judge how much confidence she really had. (Her failures to finish the three important books of her life—on Greene and Greene, Maybeck, and the history of food, begun in 1950—suggest that on some level she didn't really believe in herself.) She was, however, not easily intimidated. As she told her San Angelo audience:

In middle age you are in the group which rules. You don't have to do what your parents or your teachers decide. You decide. More than this—your contemporaries are the senators, the judges, the regents, the trustees, the policy makers of society. Just being the same age as these men, has certain advantages. You can never be entirely overwhelmed by a man when you can reconstruct for yourself what he was doing in high school.

Jean's candor could charm or sting, and many who sensed the strength of her character shrank from her quick intelligence. It was the 1950s in Texas, after all, and very few men and even fewer women were up to the kind of challenge Jean posed. There is no doubt that her independent, nondeferential attitude caused some to think she was a controlling person. Those who were predisposed to be ungenerous may have contrasted her outspoken manner with Harris's extremely gentle and polite manner and come to the wrong conclusions about who was running the school.

It was, most emphatically, Harris. Harwell Harris was a man with very strong convictions who since earliest childhood had desired to submerge his passion and channel it beneath an image of serene politesse. Contact with Jean and a desire to express his architectural ideas to his clients had opened him up, but his soft-spoken, courtly manner still masked his innermost thoughts. Jean, who knew him well, picked up on the cues of his interests and beliefs, always taking them further and making more of them than he would have, but usually broadening his original opinions. Because she was more demonstrative, one's perception of who was influencing whom in their marriage could be deceptive. For instance, Harris exposed her to the ideas about wood and construction that made it possible for her to understand Greene and Greene and Maybeck. Harris exposed her to the tensions of the American and European Modernists, and she had enough restless intelligence to pursue it. Harris needed to entertain clients, visiting architects, editors, and students, and Jean became not only a gourmet cook but an authority on the history of food. When Harris needed a collaborative project on which to involve students, *House Beautiful*, for whom she worked as a writer and idea source, came through with the Pace Setter House. However independent Jean was, however brusque or strident she might become, the final impression with which one is left is how much she believed in her husband's abilities, how really selfless she was in helping him pursue them, how creative and humorous she could be about the events they shared. Because she did not have a conventional attitude regarding the duties of a proper, supporting wife, because, moreover, she had once had quite high ambitions for herself (secretary of labor), her contributions to Harris's career are all the more impressive.

Jean's influence on Harris is important to establish not only because of the UT events but because of her ongoing work for Elizabeth Gordon at *House Beautiful*. When Harris insists that "Mrs. Harris had no roles [at the University of Texas] other than those of encouragement and support" and when he says that "because Jean was clearly with me in any controversy, she naturally shared any faculty enmity toward me," he is not defending his wife as much as he is relaying the truth.[25] In all things architectural Harris made the decisions. Harris clearly listened to Jean, but in very many ways he was still that young boy in Redlands, a little detached, keeping his own counsel, making up his own mind. They seemed to have agreed on many of the basic issues of their lives; the differences were of degree and style. But, as the UT interlude demonstrated, these were important differences.

In the early 1950s Elizabeth Gordon's editorials were becoming xenophobic to the point of hysteria. This was the period when Mies van der Rohe's popularity had begun to make itself felt all over America. Gordon's response was to assign her executive editor, Joseph Barry, to interview Dr. Edith Farnsworth, whose Mies-designed glass house of 1949 he called "an emptied aquarium on a steel stand."[26] The article was titled, "Report on the American Battle between Good and Bad

Modern Houses," and it focused on the owner as victim of European International Style dogma. In a later issue she published another attack on Mies under her own byline. This piece, with its second-coming tone and title, "The Threat to the Next America," reads as a kind of parody of reactionary rhetoric and provoked outrage within the architectural community.[27]

Jean Harris and Gordon must have shared their attitude toward European art, even their boosterism for American design. The two were close during the 1950s and, as Harris reports, Gordon depended on Jean:

I had forgotten Jean was still working for *House Beautiful*. Part of the time she was listed as Food Editor, at other times as the author of a particular article. But most of the time she was thinking up ideas of various sorts for Elizabeth Gordon to use. Elizabeth would often push an idea so close to the bounds of provability that Jean would be afraid the idea was about to go over the cliff and she and Elizabeth with it.

Jean's titles for the pieces sound innocent enough: How to Cook by Ear; Herbs; The American Tradition [in Architecture]; What is Truly an American House?; When is Garden American Style?; Beginning of the Modern House; Nature Colors; Social Elements Behind Style; Social Implications of Architecture, etc, etc. . . .

Reading this old material makes me realize how very much there is to admire and respect in Jean.[28]

While Harris might have had few complaints with the magazine's insistence on American themes, he probably did not know that Gordon had "gone over the cliff" more than once. The Mies obsession alone would have found him unsympathetic. Jean was worried for good reason. By simplifying the intellectual debate of Modernism into good versus bad, by moralizing as she did, Gordon did push ideas too far. Jean's own writings on American subjects were far more interesting and persuasive. She used America's insecure reliance on European ideas to put in relief the originality she had found in Greene and Greene and Maybeck, an originality that had too often been forsaken. In one particularly noteworthy passage she described the eclipse of the Greene brothers in the aftermath of interest in Beaux Arts eclecticism:

Thus is was inevitable that when the force of the propaganda for the imported style had spent itself, public attention would again be focused on the Greene work. It was part of a cultural movement which found expression in every aspect of American life. It was an early and fruitful chapter in what we are at last finding the assurance to recognize as our own architectural traditions.[29]

Harris and Jean Murray Bangs Harris at a social event in Texas, ca. 1955.

Harris had good reason to respect his wife's lively, curious mind. "Everything she did," he has written, "was well-researched and she expressed it clearly and from an imaginative viewpoint—usually her own."[30] The *House Beautiful* excesses may have had some connection with Jean, but only in the broadest sense (it was a good vehicle for seeing new American homes) did the magazine reflect Harris's ideas.

While caution should be used when equating Jean's articles with Harris's opinions, there were many occasions when he was quite thrilled by her erudition, her tact, and especially, her point of view. This was certainly true of the Greene and Greene and Maybeck articles, and it was also true of a lengthy book review she wrote for *Progressive Architecture* in 1953.

Lewis Mumford had just published his *Roots of Contemporary Architecture*, a compilation of writings by and about American architecture and ideas.[31] Harris, who greatly admired Mumford, was proud of her favorable review, a review concluded with these restrained but passionate words:

The accumulation of knowledge of this sort about the last 100 years of architectural design will make it possible to have an informed body of opinion competent to check on statements of theory and fact. This should go a long way towards eliminating the cultism, the teleocism, the myth-making which play such an important part in the architectural world today. A critical re-evaluation of ideas, reputations, and history is bound to result.

All of this points toward the millennium, or a reasonable facsimile thereof.[32]

The following year Jean's friend and Harris's employee Colin Rowe wrote a review of the same book for the *Architectural Review*, expressing his profound disappointment that the people around whom the cults and myth making had occurred were not included. What had been the supreme virtue of the book for Jean was the fatal defect for Rowe. He wrote:

One looks around for the big operators, the neo-academicians, the lunatic fringe. One perceives dimly the outlines of the empire of Mr. Wright, one looks around in vain for indications of that rival Chicago empire of Mies van der Rohe; but Mies and (more surprisingly) Gropius have been neatly kept off the stage.

No exposition of contemporary American architecture can claim to be complete where there are such omissions.[33]

It was the same old argument again, but this time conducted not in the inflamed language of a popular magazine editor or the personal or didactic tone of architects at a symposium, but rather on the intellectual high ground between friends who had had a simple, reasonable difference of opinion. It is for this kind of interaction that Jean must be remembered. She could rise to meet and challenge anyone—she seems to have taken on Sigfried Giedeon in New York for errors of judgment made regarding the future kitchen in his book *Mechanization Takes Command.*[34] She could be witty, candid, and, if provoked, rather ferocious. But she was always willing to get embroiled. Harris benefited in many ways from her feistiness and he, quite rightly, admired her courage.

Colin Rowe left the University of Texas in 1956. Neither his contract nor those of Slutsky and Hejduk were renewed. Hoesli and some of the other new faculty stayed on until 1957 or 1958, but before long they were all gone. Nevertheless, committed to ideas and projects begun at the university, they (Hoesli and Rowe, particularly) would keep up with each other. They were scholars of architecture as much as they were architects, and the particular mix of individuals at UT had had the magical effect of stimulating their intellectual sensibilities. Harris, seduced by the Ruth Carter Stevenson commission, moved to Fort Worth in 1955. Close friends commented on the unmistakable joy he exuded upon being back at the drafting table again.

12.

The Ten-Fingered Grasp of Reality in the Split Cultures of Fort Worth and Dallas, 1955–1962

Around 1900 Louis Sullivan, in his Kindergarten Chats, sought to arrive at "the true meaning of the words 'Organic Architecture'" through contrast, by exploring "what the word 'organic' does not mean". Organic, he said, means living, means development, and not, as in the reigning American Architecture of 1900, "pitiful in its folly, . . . functions without forms, forms without functions; details unrelated to the masses, and masses unrelated to anything but folly . . ." "Organic" means for him the "searching for realities—a word I love because I love the sense of life it stands for, the ten-fingered grasp of things it implies". Organic in the sense of Sullivan and Wright is a protest against the split personality, against a split culture. It is identical with "the ten-fingered grasp of reality" or with that development in which thinking and feeling approach coincidence.

Bruno Zevi, from
Towards an Organic Architecture, 1949

THE FORT WORTH of 1955 was not, as it is today, a cultural center remarkable for its lack of pretense, the result of a felicitous mingling of cattle, oil, art, and architecture. Where Philip Johnson's Amon Carter Museum of 1961 and the Kimbell Museum of 1972 by Louis Kahn now face each other across a broad stretch of land, a kind of museum-size portion of prairie, there was in 1955 only the nearby tower of the Will Rogers Coliseum. On the edge of town could be seen the architecture that started the city: stockyards, where the state's cattle could be corralled and auctioned. But if Fort Worth was "cow town" it was also, and somewhat more discreetly, a place where oil business was conducted, where fine works of art were being collected and viewed privately in grand homes that tended to look like French chateaux or English country estates. Harris's client was that rare exception. The daughter of one of the city's most prominent citizens, Ruth Carter wanted a Modern and unpretentious home where she could live with her husband and four (later five) children, a place where her art collection seemed natural and personal, not monumental and aloof. The program, the scale, and the client were made to order for Harris following his ordeal at the University of Texas. Who could guess what the long-term repercussions of moving to Fort Worth instead of back to California would be; the short term was a bird in the hand.

Harris's conception of the Carter Stevenson house was ambitious. Through an entrance alongside the brick wall of the garage and a small garden, one arrived at the front door. Just beyond it on the inside of the house was the juncture of two corridors that bordered an interior atrium with walls of glass. The opposite walls, splashed with soft light from the atrium, became the art gallery. The first corridor led straight ahead, past a door to the master bedroom, beyond to a wing of four children's bedrooms. The corridor to the right led past a dining room and kitchen to a large playroom, filled with light from clerestory windows and glass doors opening onto an arc-shaped balcony overlooking a wooded ravine below. A sharp left from the entrance hall would have placed a visitor in the living room, which in its turn gave way first to a small library and then to the master bedroom and bath.

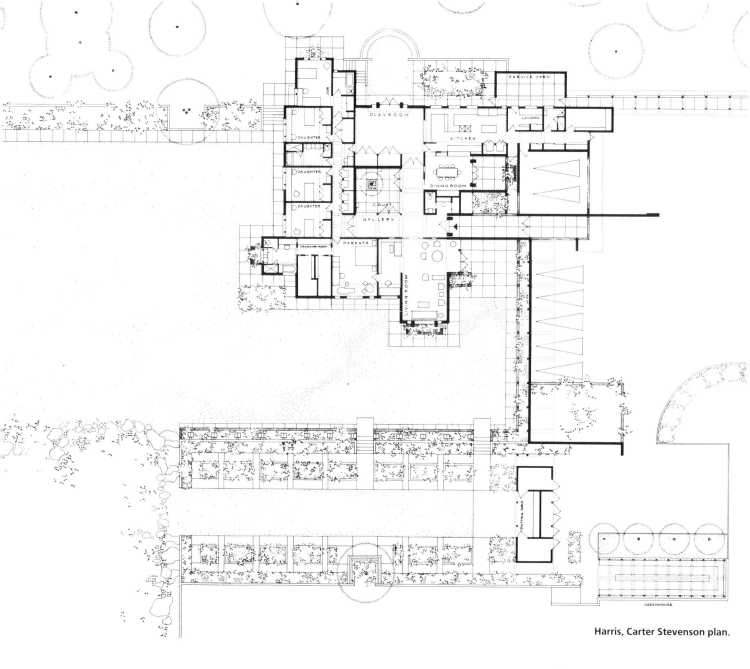

Harris, Carter Stevenson plan.

Harris, the Ruth Carter Stevenson
house, Fort Worth, 1955–56.
Photograph © Wayne Andrews / Esto

The plan of the Carter Stevenson house was larger than most Harris had designed, but it expressed again many of his fundamental attitudes toward living. The door was, more or less, at the center of the house; nature came inside by means of a small garden at the end of the dining room and the central atrium. The two public corridors of the atrium became a gallery, while the two enclosed sides allowed children and parents to pass through the house and around and into the playroom or kitchen in privacy. The module was four feet and the ceilings were a little higher, but Harris provided a lower, human scale in lighting troughs in the corridors and elsewhere, particularly over doorways leading into rooms with light soffits the width of one module.

The exterior of the house was quite unlike anything Harris had ever done before. While working on the State Fair of Texas house he had decided that wood might not be the best material for Texas; and he had resolved to try brick. The Carter Stevenson house was thus sheathed in a warm coral brick (from a company in which the family had stock) that nevertheless cut a bold shape against the open field of grass and the sunny Texas sky. Harris did not group windows in a ribbon fashion as was his custom. Instead, windows were separate from each other but connected by a white stucco fascia that came down from the flat roof to the window line and cantilevered out at 90 degrees to form eaves. Where there were no windows the pink brick rose without interruption to the roof. The window treatment and the massing of the house generally were heavier, more sculptural than one might expect from Harris.

In Texas, Harris realized, nature was not always as gentle as it was in California. The atrium, the entrance courtyard, and the dining room garden brought the

opposite, Harris, Carter
Stevenson house: planter detail
and patio, later enclosed.
Photograph at left © Wayne Andrews/
Esto; at right by Walter de Lima Meyers

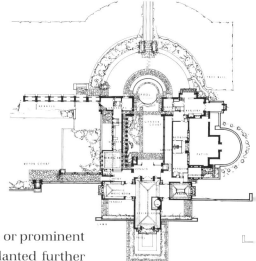

Frank Lloyd Wright, Hollyhock House plan for Aline Barnsdall, 1917–22.
Frank Lloyd Wright Archives

effects of a softer nature into the house. Large groupings of windows or prominent windows were given brick planters on the outside which when planted further enhanced the exchange between inside and outside. Otherwise, vistas to the outdoor gardens were not emphasized. This too must have been a function of Harris's new respect for the heat. Where nature was not shady and inviting, as it was from the playroom out into the sylvan ravine, Harris either modified and ameliorated the view or turned one's attention inward.

The garden, however, was a focus point, as much to Harris as it was to Thomas Church, the landscape architect, and Ruth Carter Stevenson, an avid gardener. He orchestrated the placement of a greenhouse, a potting shed, a pergola, and a series of walkways within this large, open space. The wall that protects the garden from the driveway was wooden with a trellis to create a contrast to the brick and stucco of the house. It meets the house, Harris says, "associates with it, but doesn't pretend to be it."[1] For another walkway, stretching across the garden and demarcating the first of a series of terraces leading up a hill, Harris added the finishing touch to an outdoor lantern he had originally designed for the Lek house in La Jolla. In place of the Venetian glass globe of the earlier lamp, he used an inexpensive plastic globe of the sort generally used for outdoor parties. It didn't hurt that in spirit this plastic globe, sold in a long string of identical globes, was just one step away from the very fragile, temporary Japanese lanterns. As had happened often in his early California days, the idea had taken shape around an inexpensive material he admired. Harris cut them apart and "to give them a setting so they weren't just a ball out there, I put this roof over them."[2] Harris had always liked gardens that could be walked through or along; the lanterns made such strolling a possibility at night when the sun had gone down. Because they became a favorite motif for entrances and driveways, they gradually emerged in later work as a kind of Harris signature.

And yet something more important than a pleasant coordination of garden and house seems to be going on at the Carter Stevenson residence. It had taken Harris thirty years, but in the Ruth Carter Stevenson house he was finally in a position to pay homage to Wright's Hollyhock House. On the most superficial level, both programs called for the integration of small subsidiary buildings in a garden landscape dominated by a house. A comparison of the plans suggests what Harris has admitted was an unconscious influence of Wright's house—the arc-shaped balcony extending from the playroom and overlooking the ravine. Of the semicircular shape of a pool emerging from the Hollyhock House, Harris says, "I am sure it had something to do with this." "One doesn't always know until after he's seen it [the house finished], then he can begin to see where certain things influenced him."[3]

Robert Winter and David Gebhard have suggested the English house is Harris's tribute to the Hollyhock House, a picture of how that house would have looked without the hollyhocks, but that observation more accurately describes its connection with the Carter Stevenson house.[4] In these two houses the eaves are of the same material and color as the fascia and can thus be read as roof. In the English house the painted wooden fascia is a darker shade of gray-green than the off-white stucco wall from which it emerges, suggesting another, separate plane moving laterally through the structure of the house. The point is best understood in the bay that protrudes into the Carter Stevenson garden. Here the Hollyhock House is evoked not only in the fascia and eaves but in the window treatment below, where a wide, double unit of glass is interrupted by two masonry supports.

Finally, and most important, the Carter Stevenson house—with its more massive materials—had the kind of sculptural presence that had overwhelmed the young Otis art student in 1926 and "decided [him] to be an architect." That the house still felt light and immaterial, more like a Harris house than a Wright house, was dramatically brought home soon after its completion when a young man named Mitchell Wilder was hired to be the first director of the new Amon Carter Museum. While he was being entertained at the Carter Stevenson house, he announced to his hostess that her house must have been designed by Harwell Hamilton Harris. He was certain because he had once lived briefly in the Fellowship Park pavilion in Los Angeles.[5]

Almost concurrent with the building of the Carter Stevenson house was the design and construction of a house in the northeast Texas town of Paris. Dr. and Mrs. Courtney Townsend had seen the State Fair house and it had gotten them started thinking about a new house. The Townsends with their three young boys owned a lot where an old family home was shaded by an enormous oak. When they saw the Pace Setter House they decided to demolish the old house and ask Harris to design them a Modern house. The resulting brick house had a hipped roof, a deep entranceway alongside a court, a dining room facing a private garden, and, in a homage to the Hollyhock House, a living room looking onto a lily pond shaded by the oak tree. The children's room, where all three boys lived dormitory-style, had its own second entrance from a side yard. In the end, the Townsend house received almost as much exposure as the Pace Setter House because it was chosen to be published in the September 1958 issue of *Life Magazine*. Several months

Harris, house for Dr. and Mrs. Courtney Townsend, Paris, Texas, 1956.
Photograph by Paul Lamb

later *House and Home* reprinted the *Life* article under a headline that spoke clearly of the concerns of the day—"A House to Show the Fun of Family Life."[6]

The 1950s, the decade when all postwar baby boomers were still children, was indeed a time to design for the fun of family life. Although neither Jean nor Harris had ever wanted to have children of their own, Harris was interested in the desires of young people and had always been particularly adept at respecting their privacy and their need for creativity.[7] His playrooms for the De Steiguer and Bauer houses were fine early examples. The Eisenbergs, for whom Harris would design a house in 1957, warmly recall that the architect insisted on planning a space where their infant son could later put together model airplanes.[8] And yet, for all his youthful sympathy with the passions of children, the late 1950s was not a boom period for Harris. In Texas it couldn't have been because of the fashion for steel and glass, International Style houses that had begun to populate the California landscape. Although there were isolated examples of the type, the fashion had never caught on in the state. The most plausible explanation was that Harris did not have quite the same name recognition, a reality that must have had a particular sting since houses imitating his wooden details and hipped roofs were everywhere. It was perhaps the old Greene and Greene curse again.

Of the six residential commissions that came to Harris in 1956 and 1957, four came from clients outside the state. A case in point was the house commission for Mr. and Mrs. C. R. Antrim. While they were in college in California they had both fallen in love with the Fellowship Park house. Years later, after they had purchased two and a half acres of a fig orchard in Fresno, California, they remembered Harris and contacted him in his Fort Worth office. They knew that the distance would make the job difficult, so Cal Antrim made a model of their house so that they could monitor the way light would fall across the house during the day. As it turned out, the Antrim house did take Harris back beyond his late Arts and Crafts houses to the period of Fellowship Park. Of the many glazed doors that opened the house to nature, there were some that were translucent and recalled, for those who were observant, the still earlier Lowe house.[9] For this reason and because the Antrims appreciated the simple, quiet forms that had always shaped Harris's most elegant work, this house, the last of his California designs, was an unconscious touchstone in his ongoing yet transplanted career.

On the opposite side of the country in Fairfield, Connecticut, another wall of glazed doors opened up a view of the Connecticut River. This house for Mr. and Mrs. Andrew Kirkpatrick, who had previously lived in a house by McKim, Mead

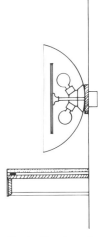

Harris, Eisenberg house, drawing of Jean Eisenberg's dressing table mirror constructed from a kettle drum.

Harris, Dr. and Mrs. Seymour
Eisenberg house, Dallas,
1957–58.
Photograph by Harwell Hamilton Harris

and White, slipped into the wooded lot unnoticed because of its shingled exterior. Although the lot had a steep drop-off, Harris supported the house at the entrance ground level with steel piers. He used the grander four-foot module, scoring the concrete entrance walk into two-foot squares. The Louis B. Fredrick residence for Barrington, Illinois, also fit into a wooded region. The roof plan with clerestory windows overlapping more clerestory windows was a virtuoso example of the kind of ingenious roof arrangements that had become standard practice for Harris.

Designing for Texas again in 1957, Harris combined wood and brick in the flat-roofed Eisenberg house, one of his most successful Texas houses and still beautifully maintained. A wooden fascia didn't appear to weigh down and restrict the windows as had been true in the more sun-bathed Carter Stevenson house. Moreover, glass in continuous lines of windows and doors provided views of the shady lot. Other wooden details, like the board and batten entrance gate and the trellis over the courtyard, became the intermediary or transitional phase between the permanence of the brick and the more delicate, temporal aspects of human life it was meant to contain.

The Eisenbergs had a wooded lot that sloped gradually down to a small stream. Drawing again from his very early Granstedt plan, Harris situated the house on the lot in such a way that the house itself and even its porte cochere were barely visible from the street. By focusing attention not on the house but on how the experience of it could reveal the beauty of the natural site, Harris seemed to make the exterior brick walls disappear. He worked out careful plans for the entrance garden, which, through floor-to-ceiling windows in the entrance gallery, brought nature into the house. He dropped another enclosed garden into an out-door spot at the end of the dining room. And he made sure that the two wings of bedrooms were given abundant exposure to the outdoors, creating what he called a "Juliet Balcony" for the Eisenberg's daughter. As in the Granstedt house, however, Harris saved his greatest outdoor views for the living room and study, which opened to the wooded backyard via a redwood deck. He did not repeat the same clerestory windows he had devised to bring light into the central core of the Granstedt house. Instead, he made a slight break in the level of the flat roof, inserted a band of ver-tical glass in the break, removed a strip of ceiling board below it to let light enter, and left the rafters unchanged but visible as deep dividers in the illuminating strip that then bordered the room's rear wall. Morning sunlight entering between the regularly spaced rafters would then cast a rhythmical succession of identical sun-spots on the brick wall. Emphasis on wood and craftsmanship was picked up and elaborated on in the Eisenberg deck and in a Harris-designed bridge crossing the stream that was never built.

Harris also designed a built-in bar and hi-fi, two freestanding tables, and a desk. The desk for the Eisenberg study was identical to the desk he had designed many years earlier for Weston Havens. In the simplicity of its crisp wooden edges and interlocking forms, it sums up much of what Harris valued in good design throughout his career. The same held true for the more whimsical, ad hoc nature of Jean Eisenberg's mirror above her dressing table, where the looking glass inside a kettle drum (supported from behind by two light sockets) seems to float in a circle of light.

Finally, color in the Eisenberg house aided Harris's creation of architectural form. However much the walls of the house were hidden in nature, the wide front door, in a luminous terra cotta orange, came forward and announced the exis-tence of the house beyond. Inside, the opposite was true: soft yellow-green walls dissolved in light and seemed only a bit more substantial than the ubiquitous glass windows and doors.

Aside from these residences, what began to emerge in the late 1950s was a greater involvement with commercial architecture. It was at this time that Harris, collaborating with Perkins and Will, designed the Motel-on-the-Mountain for Mount Hillburn, New York. The Japanese spirit of the motel was much touted, and Harris surely contributed to it. He, however, was not at his best with big collaborations and, as *Architectural Forum* reported, architect Junzo Yoshimura "was responsible for overall development and design of the restaurant and new units in conjunction with Architects Steinhardt & Thompson." Nevertheless, Harris's sensibility is unmistakably present in the series of walkways, covered as they had been at the Wyle house with gabled roofs.[10]

In Fort Worth he remodeled the office for the Bond Radiological Group, taking it from a banal, asbestos-siding before picture to a Modern after image of vertical lapped cypress siding and long, slit windows. The modernization of America that had begun in California thirty years earlier with intellectuals and artists now was broadly accepted. Although ideally Harris preferred to shape his organic architecture around the lives of his clients, he was not averse to reshaping the look of their surroundings with new materials. As early as 1932 he had reorganized a house for his cousin Fred Hasennauer, giving his conventional bungalow with double-hung windows an addition with casement windows and a hipped roof. Although he has been taking on this kind of house remodeling challenge ever since, the most important such opportunity came to him while he was in Fort Worth. It involved a commercial building with an uncommon significance to Harris.

Late in 1956 Harris received a call from Cliff Sommer, the president of the Security Bank and Trust Company in Owatonna, Minnesota. He knew the bank, one of Louis Sullivan's fine monumental buildings for a midwestern small town, and he listened with interest as Sommer described the problems he had faced trying to update the building. He had had plans drawn up that were rejected by the Minnesota State Art Society, the Twin Cities Chapter of the AIA, the Minnesota Society of Architects, and the University of Minnesota's School of Architecture for sacrificing too much of Sullivan's original design. A five-man committee proposed that a consulting architect "with exceptional talent and understanding of Sullivan's work" be hired. Harris's name headed their list.[11]

Harris accepted with enthusiasm, but he faced a daunting task. The bank had been a monument to Sullivan's credo "form follows function," and now Harris had to leave intact the form of the building while changing the function.[12] The form of the building, on the corner of a city block, was a cube. Built of brick with an orna-

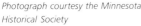
Photograph courtesy the Minnesota
Historical Society

**Harris, renovation to Sullivan's
National Farmers Bank, 1956–57.**
Photograph by Clark Dean

mental cornice at the top edges and ornamental molding outlining the perimeters of the two exposed exterior walls, the building was blocky and heavy. Sullivan offset the heaviness, however, by means of two semicircular arches of glass. On the inside the two remaining walls echoed the other arches, but where soft light came through the windows of the others illuminating the green terra-cotta decoration, these arches enclosed murals of cows and corn and cloudy blue skies. They were tributes to the farmers who banked there. Opposite the entrance a brick wall shielded the view of the bank vault embedded in another brick wall that was surmounted by an elaborately ornamented clock.

When Harris took over the remodeling this was not, however, the building he faced. A 1931 renovation had knocked out the first wall (opposite the entrance), exposing the second and, along with it, the vault itself. The new plans called for removing the second as well and thus destroying not only the massing in the room but the support for the clock. The bank needed more room, and these drastic measures seemed as warranted in 1958 as they had in 1931. Using the space of another Sullivan-designed building behind the bank, Harris chose to move the vault back into it, redoing the rest of it for the bank's new departments. He then partially altered the brick wall, keeping the top where it had the strongest visual effect because of the clock but cutting away below where the vault had been. This cantilevered brick area now became an observation deck, a point from which one might study the mural or ornamentation at a closer range. Below the brick he added much-needed tellers' booths. More tellers' booths lined the right of the bank, and Harris developed a loan officers' platform on the left. The acoustics and lighting of these open office spaces were provided through a trellis or pergolalike construction that rose no higher than the bottom line of ornamentation of the arches.

The trellises were all Harris. He did not attempt to reconstruct Sullivan's office designs nor did he try to put his mind in the mind of the late architect and try to guess what he might have done. Although it was different it was respectful. It was so light and skeletal it tended to disappear under the refurbished ornament and repainted murals. Only in a single incident is it possible to see the younger organic architect grappling with a reconstruction of a detail by his ancestor, and this occurred in the redesign of the check-writing tables.

Louis Sullivan, National Farmers Bank, Owatonna, Minnesota, 1908.
Photograph courtesy the Minnesota Historical Society

Sullivan's original tables were supported by pedestals with a strong Arts and Crafts style of interlocking forms that provided balance and visual interest underneath. The sides rose above the tabletop to give the bank customer, who could use either end for writing, a sense of privacy. The tables had been replaced in 1931 with plain, no-nonsense, four-legged tables that could accommodate more people because they were without the raised sides. Drawing upon the originals, Harris recreated the idea of the pedestal, but he thinned the mass out of the interlocking forms and made them more articulate and clean. The effect was related to what he had done with the gabled rafters he had observed in the work of Greene and Greene; namely, he expressed the modernity latent in the spirit of American Arts and Crafts designs. One feels here the presence of Harris the sculpture student intrigued by the idea of finding *a priori* forms inside the clay, fascinated by Michelangelo's *Prisoners* escaping from the weight of their marble confines. And because he shared Sullivan's respect for privacy, he called for two small tables, near the entrance, to be given raised sides.

In his address at the dedication of the newly renovated bank, historian James Marston Fitch commented specifically on the aspect of the bank that was least Modern—its elaborate ornamentation. It became a vehicle for him to address more contemporary architectural concerns:

The professional architects in this audience tonight may well have some personal reservations about the decorative ornament which Louis employed on this building. That would not be surprising. We have all become so acutely self-conscious in these matters, so unsure of our taste, so unwilling publicly to commit ourselves to one or another of the various schools of art available to us today, that we take the easy way out: we simply use no art or ornament at all.[13]

Fitch never alluded to the great debate between European and American Modernists, though on this issue of ornament he might have. From Richardson and Sullivan and Wright on down through Edward Durrell Stone, many American Moderns had not been able to isolate Modern form from ornament. They did not see that they were mutually exclusive.[14] For Europeans, on the other hand, there seems to have been a consensus that Adolph Loos's book *Ornament Is Crime* expressed a central truth for twentieth-century design. On Sullivan's ornament, Fitch made a suggestive comment: "He never made the vulgar error of thinking that mere mechanical or structural function were the only values to be expressed in architecture. Above and beyond them stood social and cultural functions: these too had to be given expression in symbolic form. The architect, no less than the poet, had to extract and celebrate these functions." Finally, he added: "I am sure that Mr. Harris has different, perhaps even better, concepts of architectural ornament than those of Sullivan. But he also has, I know, a strong sense of historical continuity, of the significance and value of this building as a part of our cultural heritage."[15]

In fact, Harris did not have stronger "concepts of architectural ornament than those of Sullivan." While he had never believed ornament to be criminal, his own talents and inclinations had been at cross-purposes with it. How could he lighten the mass and simplify the forms while encumbering the structure with decoration? On this point his own work had diverged not only from the eclecticism of his father, the decoration of Greene and Greene, Maybeck, and Sullivan, but Frank Lloyd Wright and even Schindler. Furthermore, he did not care for symbols that were not born out of one's own unique experience in the world. He had never valued the monumental in architecture, because its permanence seemed to outweigh and kill the individual's ability to discover a more immediate and vital organic life inside the building. Yet, for all this, Harris cherished a piece of Sullivan's green terra-cotta coping that had been removed from the bank. He took it home and placed it in a prominent position in his otherwise spare, efficient office. Next to it, over the years, he would pose for a number of photographs.

Harris in 1962 with green terra-cotta coping from Sullivan's National Farmers Bank.
Unknown photographer, courtesy of Harwell Hamilton Harris

What did this mean for a man of Harris's bent who was, on top of everything else, also unsentimental? Fitch hinted at it in his speech: It was related to the continuity of American architecture. Like a family heirloom that to a child seems irrelevant and perhaps even unattractive, the green coping, discovered at a mature point in Harris's career, was not only beautiful but a potent and private symbol of his aesthetic and philosophical roots. As the taste for Modern buildings on a monumental scale began to grow in the America of the 1950s, it was also a re-

Harris, the Greenwood
Mausoleum, Fort Worth, 1956.
Photograph by Harwell Hamilton Harris

Harris, Greenwood Mausoleum.
Photograph by Paul Lamb

minder of the link he had with American monumentality. While others looked at Le Corbusier and Mies van der Rohe for guidance, Harris continued to explore Sullivan and Wright, mining out and rethinking the elements that he could claim, it would almost seem, by birthright.

At the same time Harris was working on the bank he received a commission for a mausoleum, a monumental building where some of his unconscious preoccupation with Sullivan's forms would play itself out. His client for the Greenwood Mausoleum in Fort Worth was John Bailey, and it was Bailey who suggested that they take a sightseeing tour to California to acquaint themselves with mausoleums. What Harris found was that most mausoleums consist of monotonous repetition of very long corridors without natural light.[16] He also found out that it was a rule of thumb among morticians that overbuilding was a mistake. Having a small backlog of unsold crypts encouraged buying early rather than later. The mausoleum would have to be built in installments.

Before he was finished Harris would know all the tedious details about such moribund topics as crypt ventilation, Westminster crypts, and companion crypts, but his concept of the building took shape immediately. He imagined a cluster of buildings so that Bailey could expand discreetly; this avoided the problem of one building perpetually in the ruinous state of construction. The separate buildings in the cluster were what Harris called "square doughnuts" as they were shaped around courtyards equipped with horizontally rolling roofs of clear glass, motorized to open in good weather and close in rainy weather.[17] The doughnut shape also alleviated the long hallways Harris had hated. Floors were of a dark green marble having a "quiet pattern." The marble walls of the corridors were an off-white warmed with fine veins of green and ochre. Deep-colored marble framed large openings and appeared in the larger areas called "family rooms."

The building became one of Harris's favorite buildings. Here was a monumental building of great permanence (what could be more permanent than a mausoleum?) with heavy massing (the entranceway was six feet deep), motifs strongly connected to earlier architecture (the arched entranceways recalled the Security Bank and Trust arches, though Harris's were more earthbound), and, not least, decorative detail (the cast concrete ornament of the entrance arches in a manner not unrelated to Frank Lloyd Wright's geometric shapes, but the repetitive quatrefoils breaking up the space on the interior recall Maybeck's medievalizing motifs). It is impossible to imagine the young Harris taking up a commission so ostensibly at odds with his sensibility, but in 1958 it was an opportunity to enter into a completely different kind of problem and solve it following its own peculiar dictates and without compromising his own.

As early as the State Fair of Texas house Harris had observed that Texans did not use their garden courts the way Californians did. The heat would not allow it. He had decided that one day he would design an air-conditioned courtyard in the center of a house. Contained within his Greenwood Mausoleum solution were ideas—heavy masonry, Toplites which controlled the light and the angle of desirable light and deflected the rest—that would one day make his air-conditioned courtyard possible. Nevertheless, in his next buildings, for the very harsh climate of Big Spring, Texas, Harris reverted to his wooden, California idiom.

His Saint Mary's Episcopal Church combined concrete block (in the distinct pink tone indigenous to the soil there) and soaring open rafters. Because he built the church complex in stages (the first sanctuary becoming the later fellowship hall), there are a few awkward places where the dominant buildings, comprising the two sides of a quadrangle, seem to compete with each other. One wishes the open rafters and wooden joinery of the fellowship hall had been stripped off or stripped down when the sanctuary took over as the preeminent building. This building, the current sanctuary, is in some ways the apotheosis of the strain of Greene and Greene running through Harris's sensibility. Though Harris never acknowledged the gothicism hidden deep within the gabled roofs and exquisite joinery of Arts and Crafts forms, he nevertheless intuited the uplifting, emotional effects such stylistic choices could create. In Saint Mary's the open rafters at the altar end of the church actually rise up and fly away a bit from the roof so as to create a break that becomes a skylight capable of pouring natural light on the litur-

Harris, Saint Mary's Episcopal
Church, Big Spring, Texas, 1960.
Photograph by Paul Lamb

gical center of the interior below. The exterior walls were marked by square eight-inch glass inserts, equally spaced both vertically and horizontally, that provided a sprinkling of daylight and an impression, whether intended or not, of dozens of flickering candles.

His involvement with Saint Mary's prompted a handful of residential commissions in this rather isolated West Texas city. And for the first of his commissions, homes for the Garretts and Bristows, he returned to aspects of the Greenwood Mausoleum that he hoped would work for an inwardly turning house. Neither of these houses were built, and the two that were, one in wood for Dr. and Mrs. Milton Talbot and another in brick for Dr. and Mrs. J. M. Woodall, were hipped-roof houses closely connected to the landscape. Dr. Talbot, who played a major role in hiring Harris for the Saint Mary's commission, knew the architect's work from his own prior study in the field; the Woodalls knew it from the Pace Setter House they had seen at the State Fair of Texas. It is possible that both clients urged Harris in the direction of the kind of wooden detailing they had admired, but the experience of these houses, their locations above wild, undeveloped canyons, suggests another source for their appearances. Big Spring, with its hills and canyons, its dry climate and desertlike vegetation, may have seemed strangely resonant of Southern California. Harris's California houses would fit particularly well there.

Because both houses have their primary exposures to the west and north where their canyon views are the most dramatic, the deep eaves of Harris's hipped roofs provided needed protection from the sun. In the Woodall house, particularly, Harris's disposition and interior articulation of a living room on the northwest corner of the lot, almost hovering above a canyon, created the effect of shady

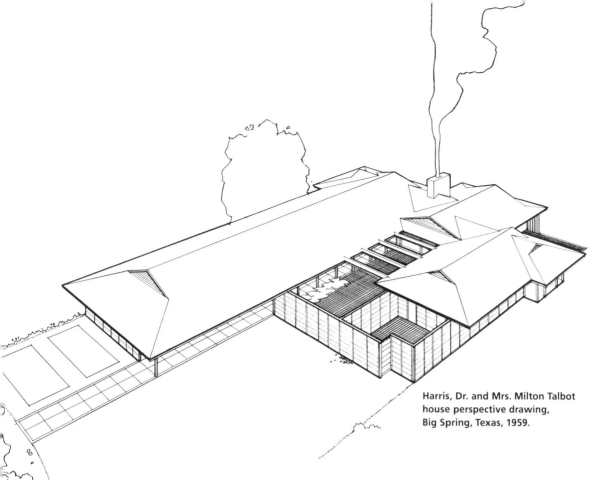

Harris, Dr. and Mrs. Milton Talbot house perspective drawing, Big Spring, Texas, 1959.

coolness. In one of the few ceilings of his career that was neither white painted gypsum board nor Celotex panel, the Woodall living room ceiling, a square of thirty feet by thirty feet, was stained Philippine mahogany. Divided into the three-foot squares of Harris's standard module, the ceiling followed the lines of a perfectly square hip, rising up and through the crossbeams holding it together. Because it also extended over a gallery on the eastern entrance and courtyard side of the room, the effect of shelter was doubly emphasized. After the extreme glare of the late western sun had faded, one might watch the spectacular West Texas sunset from a most serene vantage point.

The roofs and their interior expressions in both houses were of primary interest to Harris. He often used a ceiling to connect rooms that were functionally separate but somehow spiritually related. For instance, the Woodall living room was separate from the entrance gallery, with its glassed-in view of a courtyard pool, but as the defining wall continued no higher than the line of lightweight, Japanese-inspired sliding doors, the strong ceiling form above connected the areas. It was the same with the Talbot house entrance and living room. The master bedroom was bound together with a small library by the upper embrace of a hipped ceiling. On the interior Harris joined together the various hipped ceilings of master bedrooms, dining rooms, and living rooms (most of the lesser rooms had flat ceilings) with light shelves composed of three-foot-square sections of translucent glass.

Because the wild canyons were meant to be viewed from the houses but not brought inside, Harris dropped protected gardens in front of the windows of the Woodall dining room and the Talbot bedroom wing, to a lesser extent. The en-

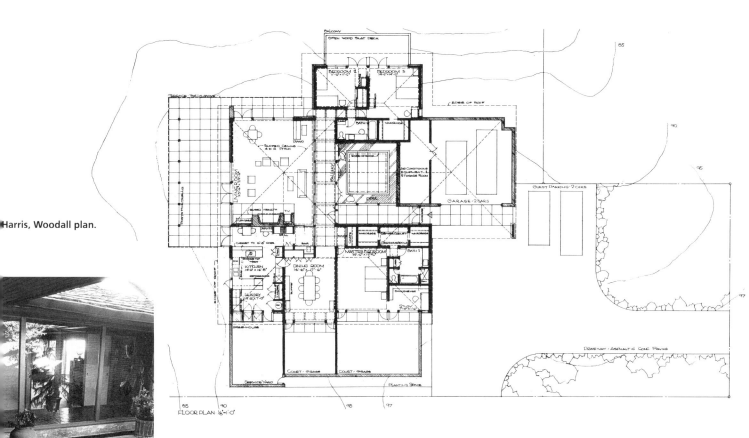

Harris, Woodall plan.

Harris, entrance patio of house for Dr. and Mrs. J. M. Woodall, Big Spring, Texas, 1958–59.
Photograph by Paul Lamb

Harris, Woodall living room.
Photograph by Paul Lamb

trance courtyards were particularly refreshing, and the Woodalls', a pool of water, greeted the visitor with the sights and sounds of the element that to West Texans is the most precious. It was this reshaping or channeling of nature through architectural prowess that made the Woodall and Talbot houses almost stronger statements of Harris's skill than the early houses for the very temperate California or the State Fair house (which, after all, was designed only for a temporary site). What was strong and seductive about the land Harris framed and dramatized; what was harsh and ugly he manipulated and subverted.

Harris finally had his opportunity to build his air-conditioned courtyard when his former clients, the John Treanors (for whom he had designed a house in Visalia, California, and a sales shop), moved to Abilene, Texas, to open a dealership for Caterpillar farm equipment.[18] Harris's approach toward Texas home building had evolved even more since he had struck upon his garden court idea. In the Southwest, he had concluded, glass was for view and shade for comfort; where there was no view, glass was still used for light and heat. The Treanor house, for instance, was shaped in relation to a line of trees bordering the bank of a long and narrow lake. All eastern rooms, including the master bedroom and a library, were given floor to ceiling exposure to the shaded view. Southern and western rooms like the kitchen, dining rooms, and laundry room were given enclosed gardens where wooden trellises could support plants and the rooms could enjoy light and openness. The center of the house, around which all other rooms were shaped, was Harris's courtyard, now an indoor garden room, the focus of the house.

The gold-tan brick used on the exterior of the house was brought inward for the square garden room. The four doors into the room were covered with matting,

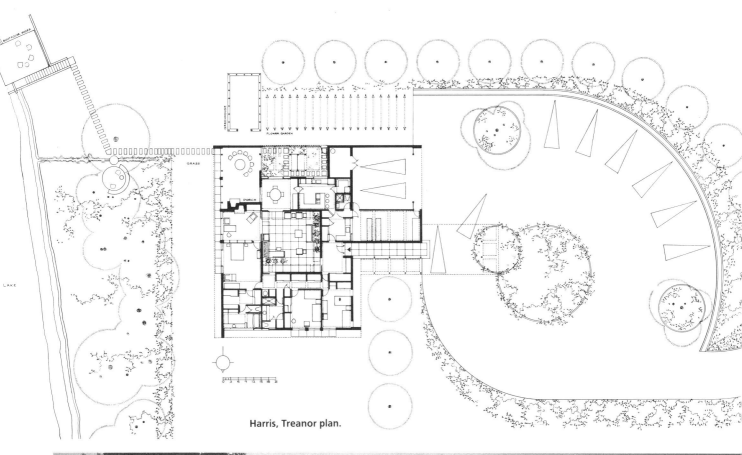

Harris, Treanor plan.

Harris, Mr. and Mrs. John Treanor
house, Abilene, Texas, 1958–59.
Photograph by Walter de Lima Meyers

Harris, eastern, lakeside elevation
of Treanor house looking into the
back courtyard.
Photograph by Walter de Lima Meyers

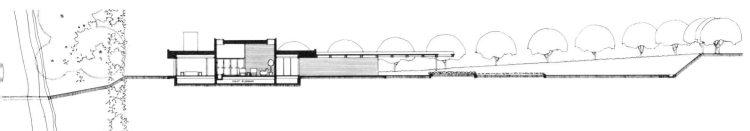

Harris, Treanor house cross section.

and wall sections above the doors were painted sheetrock. The floor, heated from below, was white marble with ochre and green striations which Harris said "made it a very easy thing to look at."[19] Furniture was designed by Carl Anderson—two low chairs of the sort used in the New York World's Fair "America at Home" exhibition—and tables and a sofa designed by Harris. One sofa had an open end because Harris imagined an idle person languorously trailing his fingers into the small fountain built into the marble floor below.

The ceiling of the garden room rose another three feet, ten inches above those in other rooms, a feature that was dramatized on the outside in the form of a central cubic core. On the inside, light filtered down around the perimeter of the room through a roof with Toplites fitted into three-foot-square metal frames. Double beams protruding from the wall in three-foot intervals held in place what counted as a diminutive ceiling. The central sheetrocked area was like a canvas tent pulled taut by the beams. Below, where light poured in around the edges, the Treanors placed large trees in pots to underline the connection with a garden.

The façade of the Treanor house looked solid and closed. A porte cochere reached out over a circular drive and alongside an entrance garden, but otherwise this western face had only a couple of narrow but long windows. There was a precedence in Harris's experience for such a massive-looking exterior followed by a light-filled, natural, and open interior. Schindler's Kings Road house in Hollywood of tilt-up concrete walls and slit windows gave way to rooms open to a patio by sliding doors. The patio was open-air and far more casual than Harris's garden room, but the former was intended after all for California bohemian life in the 1930s, the latter for a businessman new to the market and the heat of Texas in the late 1950s. It was not a strong connection—the organic forms were conceived differently according to their different uses—but it may indicate, once again, that Harris never really forgot the buildings that had most moved him. They were like recessive genes: they belonged to him but were silent, hidden, almost forgotten until the right mixture of circumstances brought them to the surface of a completely different organism. In a similar way, the double height, rectangular box quality of the Charles Eames house in Los Angeles with its open-mezzanine second floor may have worked subtly on Harris as he designed three apartments in Austin for Tom Cranfill at about this time.[20] Hidden behind a conventional house on a remote street, the concrete block apartments held out Harris's favorite surprise: a rich and private exposure to nature. Quiet and elegantly functional, they are among his best work.

Harris, Tom Cranfill apartments, Austin, 1958.
Photographs by Paul Lamb

By the time he finished the Treanor house Jean and Harris had lived in Dallas for a year. It was a city that struck them as much more sophisiticated than either Austin or Fort Worth. They moved into a high-rise apartment (designed by Dallas Modernist Howard Meyer) overlooking a section of Turtle Creek just on the edge of the very posh and privileged Highland Park neighborhood. They could see Frank Lloyd Wright's newly completed Dallas Theater Center from the apartment, and Harris became a passionate fan of the building.[21]

The Harrises became friendly with Mr. and Mrs. Edmund Kahn, who also lived in the building, and Harris remodeled their apartment with such signature details as lights built into opaque-glass soffits that, combined with his internal spatial organization, could make entering their apartment a little like entering one of Harris's houses. Louise Kahn, an interior designer, had worked with Harris in selecting and acquiring fabrics and other interior furnishings for the Treanor house.

The Kahn job was not a major commission, but it was destined to be one of the few Harris received during his four years in Dallas that tapped his special design skills. Another for Mr. and Mrs. Wesley Francis Wright, Jr. (Mrs. Wright was Tom Cranfill's sister), was an elegant home also near Turtle Creek. The Wrights had four children, and one of the most striking aspects of their house was the children's wing, where the hall passages had built-in bookshelves and cabinets and each of the four rooms had access to a special garden. Harris handled his bedroom wings quite differently from Frank Lloyd Wright, who made an event out of the hallway. Harris might make use of an open plan, connecting living and dining areas, but his private wings seemed more private, even remote. They benefited

Harris, apartment interior for
Edmund and Louise Kahn, Dallas,
1958.
Photograph by Doris Jacoby

from his respect for the individual, secret soul. This was especially true of the Francis Wright house, where the foyer encouraged movement beyond into a living room instead of to the right (toward the children's hall) or the left (toward the master bedroom). Three of Harris's other house commissions from this period, including one for photographer Edward Weston's son Cole, were never built.[22] The Weston plan showed Harris responding to a stunning California site with octagonal forms that were unusual in his repertoire of shapes.

It was a time for large, commercial buildings. Mies and Le Corbusier dominated the stylistic trends, but Louis Kahn's and Alvar Aalto's very personal renditions of Modernism were beginning to be understood and appreciated. Aalto's regionalism and Kahn's spiritualism were both able to make the transition to large scale. Kahn's aesthetic particularly cried out for monumentality. Harris's regional modernism would not fare so well. His region had encouraged a gentle, collaborative approach to nature, and the resultant lightness and temporality were not qualities that commercial developers sought. In addition, developing an organic form around a speculative business was not easy. Harris was more and more out of his element.

One of the largest, most prestigious, and most problematic commissions Harris received during the late 1950s was for the design of the U.S. Embassy in Helsinki, Finland, which was destined never to be built. It was the kind of big job that affords an architect a great deal of exposure, that encourages him or her to rise to the occasion and create something memorable. Harris's embassy was one of his least inspired buildings, however. Part of the problem was in the very bureaucratic pro-

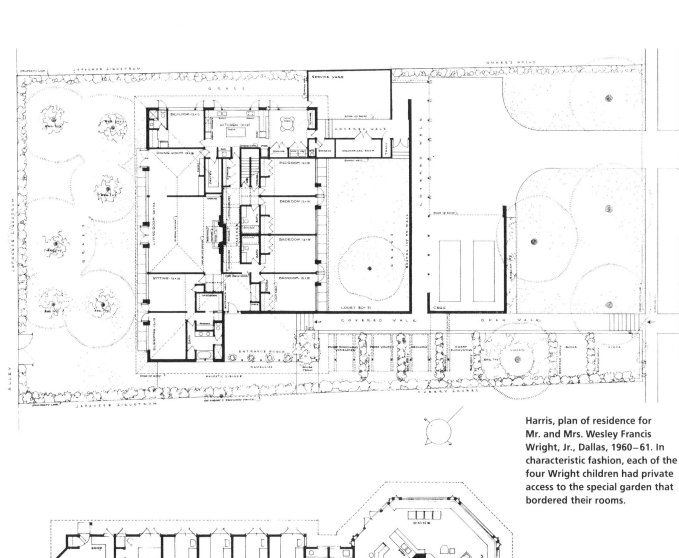

Harris, plan of residence for Mr. and Mrs. Wesley Francis Wright, Jr., Dallas, 1960–61. In characteristic fashion, each of the four Wright children had private access to the special garden that bordered their rooms.

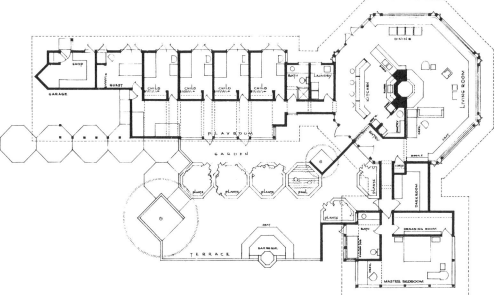

Harris, Cole Weston plan, 1959. Although this house was never built, Harris's use of the octagonal living room/kitchen was his response to Weston's scenic property above the Pacific Ocean in the Big Sur, Carmel, California.

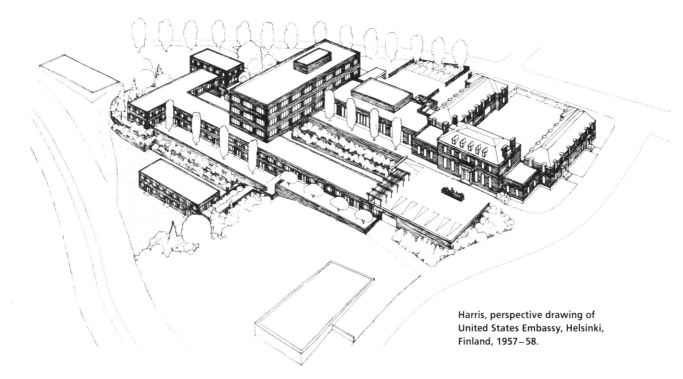

Harris, perspective drawing of
United States Embassy, Helsinki,
Finland, 1957–58.

gram with which he had to work. The other part may have been his desire to build
the kind of regionalized Modern building he had seen in Finland by Alvar Aalto.

Harris knew Aalto from the 1930s when he and William Wurster took the
Aaltos on an architectural tour from San Francisco to Harris's house for Marion
Clark in Carmel. Aalto had introduced the American architect to his Finnish colleagues by saying that Harris was "the second best architect in America" (after
Wright).[23] Certainly Harris had regionalized Modernism in much the same way as
the Finn Aalto had done. And when Harris began the embassy design, a brick building with Thermopane windows and a flat roof, he may have sought unconsciously
to reflect his increased knowledge of Aalto. The Helsinki climate was new to Harris,
however, and between the restraints it placed on him and the bureaucratic demands of the government, there was none of the robust quirkiness and finesse so
characteristic of the Finnish architect. David Barrow, an associate in Harris's office
during this time, has recalled that Harris wondered out loud why, of all the embas-
sies in the world, he had managed to get one in Finland.[24] In Southeast Asia he
might have found new ways to use his hipped roofs, his wooden details, and his
forms where delicacy of mass was the rule.

Herein lay the critical question for the architect: Supposing that he was in a
familiar, temperate climate, could Harris's idiom make the transition from the
scale of a house to the scale of an embassy or an office building? Barrow has further recalled that Harris always did his best work when something—the client, the
site, or the problem—sparked a special chord in him. This had been true of the
English house, the Havens house, even, in a curious way, the unlikely Greenwood
Mausoleum, where he knew he had ingeniously solved the difficulties inherent in
the genre and satisfied the client's demands. Mies van der Rohe had demonstrated
that the lightness, the fragility of his Barcelona Pavilion or Farnsworth house could

be writ large in multistory buildings like 860 Lakeshore Drive Apartments in Chicago. Harris respected them but finally decided they were too diagrammatic. To Harris a building lived only if was free to follow the patterns of life in an organic fashion. He was eager for the client who would give him a chance to see his fine details, his elegant proportions, writ large. When it happened, he would count on the spark to lead him to the organic solution.

To the extent that this organic approach to design was based on an American outlook, a belief that each individual life shapes different and unique patterns in the world and that architects in a democratic society must be absolutely free to follow those patterns, there is an element of pathos, if not irony, about the dilemma in which Harris found himself in the late 1950s and early 1960s. The American businessman, to whom the paradigm of the rugged individual would seem to be sacrosanct, did not necessarily see architecture as the means to communicate that point. It was a point that Harris seems not to have grasped fully until he was well into his working relationship with Dallas developer Trammell Crow, who had retained his services in 1958.

Crow and Harris had a propitious beginning in the immense court Harris designed for the developer's Trade Mart in Dallas. Essentially, the Trade Mart was the place where buyers for retail stores and interior designers could visit hundreds of showrooms and buy (at wholesale prices) what they would stock the next season or what they would show their clients. Because there were designated "market" days when the buildings were filled with people, Crow wanted Harris to design an area for relaxation and refreshment.

The Trade Mart Court was the connector for two market buildings. Because showrooms turned inward toward the corridors on every floor, buyers and sellers were without any contact with natural light. It was a situation that appealed very strongly to Harris's faith in nature to restore and refresh people. It followed, then, that Harris would make the court an atrium. His solution, however, departed from the kind of arrangements he had made for the Greenwood Mausoleum and the Treanor house, though it did rely on the same principle that made them effective. The Toplites, or glass prism blocks, he had used in them were designed so that they allowed only desirable light to enter an interior; harsh light was reflected. Harris made the Trade Mart Court roof sawtoothed to accomplish the same goal. The nearly vertical surface of each tooth faced north and was glass to admit the soft light; the less vertical surface faced south and was opaque to exclude the harsh sun.

Harris, the Trade Mart Court, Dallas, 1959, showing in foreground Harris's gazebo with what he called "an X-ray" version of his petal roof.
Photograph by Martha Dillon

When he was thus sure of a gentle light, Harris designed a large dome fountain for the end of the atrium where meals were served. The opposite end, where newly arrived visitors entered, was given a pool where water lilies and water hyacinths floated in the shadow of a Harris gazebo, essentially the same square building with the petal roof he had wanted to give Rex Hardy. Trellises and benches of natural, unstained redwood surrounded the pool. Because the rectangular atrium space was banked on all four sides by the railings of the floors that opened onto it, Harris simply framed the gazebo roof, making it what he called "x-ray"—to invite the gaze of shoppers on upper levels. And because he was fascinated by the task of providing additional ways for people to cross the space on upper levels, he designed metal suspension bridges supported by cables. The criss-cross shape of the wires suggested a trapeze to him, and he chose to paint them in gold and vermillion because these were the colors of circus wagons he had seen as a boy in Redlands. These were colors, he also believed, that suited metal.[25]

Harris had never been doctrinaire about his choice of materials. His balloons for Grandview Gardens, his chain-link fence for the railing of Weston Havens' balcony, his plastic lanterns for the Ruth Carter Stevenson garden all had a mixture of invention and whimsy in the right proportion for the context. The colorful bridges of the Trade Mart Court were of this essential character, but this atrium also satisfied his insistence on organic form. Looking over the railing at the elegant Dallasites on opening night, Harris has recently recalled, "You could see the pattern people made on the floor!"[26] It would be the last time a project for Crow would elicit such excitement from the architect.

Harris, perspective drawing of Stemmons Towers apartments, Dallas.

The next four years would witness a succession of unbuilt projects that apparently neither the architect nor the patron liked. Sometimes Crow would involve Harris in the design of a building with the idea of frightening off another developer. Sometimes Harris's office would work up sketches and plans for buildings—like the 1960 Stemmons Towers—that were built under the supervision of another architect and without Harris's detailing or proportions. Additions to the Trade Mart were worked out by Harris but then handed over to other people. Several high-rise apartment buildings, office towers, and a shopping mall were all left unbuilt.

Why? Was Crow disappointed in Harris's work? It is a difficult question made more difficult by the developer's continued patronage of Harris. It is further complicated by the drawings that survive from this period in Harris's career, drawings that prove that organic form had been the critical lifeblood of all his previous work. Without it, without the spark from an interested client, the stimulation of a beautiful site (almost all of Crow's buildings were on Stemmons Freeway in Dallas), or a complicated, challenging program, Harris's creativity was stymied. Maybe he could have translated his idiom into the much larger, more monumental scale Crow required, but not without the necessary catalyst. Harris was an artist, and the act of designing buildings that to him, at least, had no soul was destined to demoralize him. The tragedy of the Dallas experience was that it broke Harris's spirit. If his compromised designs had been built, the situation for his reputation would have only been worse.

In many ways it was the classic confrontation between the businessman and the artist. In one of the few glimpses Harris has offered into this period, he tells about designing the Valley View shopping center.

I had been impressed with Southbend Mall in Minnesota. I couldn't talk Crow into building an interior shopping mall. The idea of a string of buildings bothered me. I turned it into an arc so you could get views of windows ahead as you walked. But he didn't do it.

If I had been an architecture student and these things weren't built, then I would expect it, but I expected at least half of these things to be built.[27]

The businessman in Crow may have distrusted Harris's ideas (even ones as visionary as an indoor shopping mall for Texas) because Harris's office, inasmuch as it was a business, was clearly operating on a small scale. Barrow has said that he imagined they, Harris and just two draftsmen, may not have looked very impressive to Crow, who came bustling in with new deals to discuss from time to time.[28] Harris disliked any form of self-promotion and he was not apologetic that his

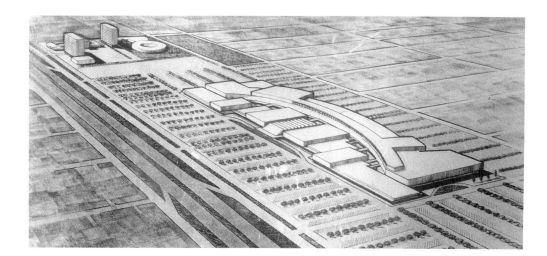

office was small. In 1960 he gave a speech entitled "The Changing Practice of Architecture" before the California Council of Architects at a meeting in Yosemite Valley in which he talked about the advantages of the small office.

How does my office differ from a large office? It differs, to begin with, in having fewer collaborators, consultants, engineers, interior designers, landscapers, business managers, public relations advisors, job-getters, promoters; we are therefore more free from design by office committee. We are also more free from the restrictions of pecuniary self-interest; there is no office accountant calling us to task for spending more time on a job than the fee justifies.[29]

As the speech continued Harris underlined the central point of his talk; namely, that large and small offices attract different kinds of clients. The large office, with a staff of specialists, attracts "the mind of a man whose judgments are based largely on opinions of experts,—on reputations, polls, and *under*-estimations of what the public likes." The small office, by contrast, attracts "more independent men than those usually found heading great corporations and handling large sums of money." The large office is thus handicapped by its "characterless client," while the small office is freer to be "ruled by convictions," freer "to express something deeper and more significant than mere fashion."[30]

What can it mean that Harris, on retainer to Crow and thus not free, in spite of his small office, chose what seems to be a somewhat disingenuous line of argument? It is as if writing the speech had been a means of venting frustration and, in doing so, he unconsciously reminded himself of the kind of architecture he had most admired, architecture produced by small offices for great clients—the kind of architecture he was not likely to do while on Crow's payroll because, as he said, "Having convictions is not a mere luxury,—it is a necessity for a great building. Convictions are needed in both *architect and client*."[31]

At a time when his career was on dead center, when the kind of architecture he valued and of which he was a master was out of fashion, it may have been comforting to hear himself say: "[A small office] does offer you, who are thoughtful and

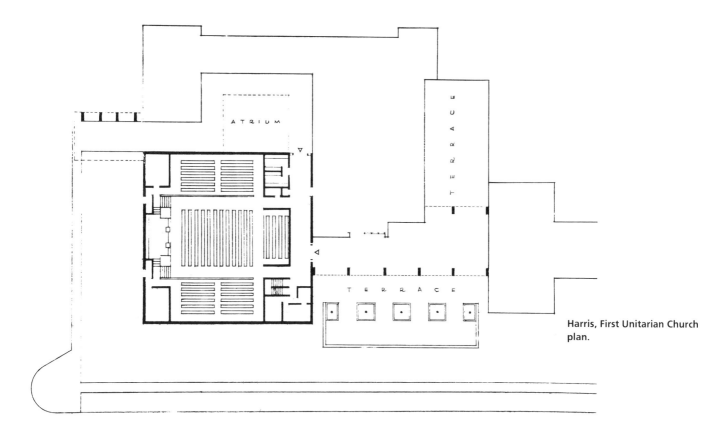

ATRIUM

TERRACE

TERRACE

Harris, First Unitarian Church
plan.

sensitive, an opportunity to look for the constituent facts of the time—not the incidental ones only—, to try to design in terms of reality rather than fashion, to be
un-fashionable or un-modern."

These were words Harris would live by for the rest of his active career. In
1960, however, when he uttered them he was still bound to Crow, whom he clearly
needed in spite of his disavowal of pecuniary interest. The rest of the year was
spent in thinking about parking spaces and access to freeways for apartments and
office buildings that would never be built.

In 1961 all that would change when he received the commission for the First
Unitarian Church. He had always felt an affinity with Unitarians. He had even revealed his admiration for them when, in his 1960 Yosemite talk, he had referred to
Frank Lloyd Wright's clients for his Unity Temple. He had characterized the Unitarians in Oak Park, Illinois, as "a small congregation of people whom, I suspect,
were men of high principles."[32] He had every reason to believe that the Dallas Unitarians were no different (indeed, the new minister's wife, who must have helped
assure his selection, was the sister of one of Harris's former draftsmen in California). This commission was an opportunity at last.

There were two factors governing the Unitarian Church that immediately began to shape its exterior: it was located at a busy, noisy intersection from which it
had to be protected and it was in Texas under a sun whose ferocity Harris had
come to respect. To keep out the sound a structural steel framework supported
windowless walls of concrete block. To keep out the harsh sun, while allowing in a

Harris, First Unitarian Church,
Dallas, 1961–63.
Photographs by Maynard Parker

generous supply of natural light, the ceiling became a variation on the Treanors' top-lit garden room.

It was in 1961 while he was in New York serving as an adjunct professor of architecture at Columbia that Harris came up with his conception for the church. He visualized an ornament that, in the forms of bands on the smooth stucco face of the cubic building, would "glorify the cube." At the same time it would, he reasoned, prevent the spectator from noticing the absence of windows. The ornament's module was three feet so the interruption of the three-foot fire door would not butcher it. The module of the auditorium was twelve feet. The plaster ceiling went across the center of the sanctuary space and turned up around its perimeter, forming a recess where Toplites were concealed. With a ceiling floating in light the room was given a mood of weightlessness, a suffusion of light in keeping with its spiritual function. During the day, all four walls were washed with light; at night, lens lights, concealed in the inner walls of the channel, provided an equally subtle kind of illumination.

Down below this great open space and in contrast to it, Harris designed pews and lecterns in his simple, modern, Craftsman idiom and faced the walls with wood to further suggest warmth and intimacy. As in the Trade Mart Court, where he defined a crafted, natural, small-scale setting far beneath his sawtoothed roof, Harris seemed to be consciously setting apart the monumental and ponderous and the small, transitory, and very human realms. Thus a metaphor for the sanctuary became a clearing into which one stumbles after a walk along a dark and narrow path.[33]

Harris also relished the contrasts on the outside where the cast ornament was set against the smooth stuccoed surface of the concrete block walls. He liked the way the additional classroom building that abuts the sanctuary assumed a secondary role because its monumental columns were flush with the edges they

supported and because ornament was left off. Ornament on each of the faces of the sanctuary building outlined a square parallel to the building's perimeter instead of winding over the corners and connecting the surfaces. Harris believed it created a stronger image and, as it happened, this is the way Louis Sullivan articulated the ornament on the very closed, solid walls of the Wainwright Tomb in St. Louis. It was also closely connected to the interior ornamentation of Wright's Unity Temple in Oak Park. "Don't think for a minute that I didn't have it in mind," Harris has admitted.[34]

In fact, it is easy to see the connections to Wright's church. Like it, Harris's church had sitting areas divided evenly by aisles that served as reminders that the building was an immense cube, not the more traditional rectangle. It followed too that the furnishings, like the Carter Stevenson fascias, were essentially Wrightian forms without the ornament. But to focus on such comparisons, however much Harris may encourage them, would risk overlooking the ways in which the First Unitarian Church in Dallas was a church of its time, maybe the only Harris building of the later period that was.

The more fitting comparison should be with Louis Kahn's Unitarian Church for Rochester, New York, of exactly the same period—1961 to 1963. Harris had no knowledge of the building at the time of his own church design.[35] Nevertheless, a photograph of it would have shown him a central cubic volume with sections of ceiling raised at the perimeter to allow light to flow over concrete block walls below. To use Vincent Scully's words, "In Kahn's Unitarian Church for Rochester, all the hard and solemn shapes were now derived from an analysis of function and, most of all, from the reception of light." The shapes of the interior, shapes not unlike Harris's, Scully called "Brutalist."[36]

There could be no more inappropriate label for Harris's architecture than brutal. And yet, his First Unitarian Church shows that he too, following the dictates of his program and with a small homage to Wright, could be led to produce the kind of mannered urban Modernism that characterized the monumental buildings not only of Kahn but of Aalto, Mies, and Le Corbusier. Harris's church was a good building and an inspired one, but he was not an urban architect. Having to shut out the outdoors for noise or heat reasons was not a job that came naturally to Harris. He might have dealt with what Scully called "the facts of modern life at a level not only functional but physically active and symbolic," but he was not destined to pioneer, along with Kahn and the others, a new moment in architecture. That he had already done.

Harris once said that Jean gave him the courage to be himself.[37] In the early 1960s, he faced the realization that, working for Crow, he had almost lost himself. After the First Unitarian Church got under way, he decided to break out of the gloomy rut that had become his Dallas experience. With Jean's support, he accepted an offer to teach at North Carolina State University in Raleigh. The dean of the school, Henry Kamphoefner, had made the offer many times, but when he mentioned it again at breakfast with Jean and Harris while on a visit to Dallas, he was surprised that they finally answered "yes," with one condition. Could they come immediately? They were ready to leave Texas. Harris was eager to do again the kind of architecture that opened itself to nature and shaped itself around the lives of individuals who, as did he, wanted their houses to be "every inch alive."[38]

Harris and Louis Kahn at North Carolina State University, Raleigh, 1964.
Unknown photographer, courtesy of Harwell Hamilton Harris

Harris with Herschel Luker and student Roddy Cook at Arlington State College, North Carolina.
Photographer unknown

13.
The River Flows On:
North Carolina, 1962–1975

*How should men know what is coming to pass
within them, when there are no words to grasp it?
How could the drops of water know themselves
to be a river? Yet the river flows on.*

ANTOINE DE SAINT-EXUPÉRY

Harris WAS CLOSE TO SIXTY and Jean almost seventy when they moved to Raleigh, North Carolina, for a fresh start. It was a place that offered a landscape particularly sympathetic to Harris's architecture, but in their experience it was a place quite apart. By any standards, California and Texas were America's frontiers; North Carolina was stamped with the gentility of its much older roots as a state in the pre–Civil War South and as a colony under British rule. Raleigh, the capital and the home of North Carolina State University, reflected both cultures. It boasted an abundance of antebellum homes and a Greek Revival capitol designed by the prestigious New York firm of Ithiel Town and Alexander Jackson Davis. Named for Sir Walter Raleigh, the small city was surrounded by the tobacco plantations, which constituted one of the state's major industries. North Carolina State University was the agricultural and technical branch of the University of North Carolina at nearby Chapel Hill.

The School of Design at NCSU had become one of the most important and progressive in the country due to the efforts of its remarkable director, Henry Kamphoefner. In the years preceding Harris's arrival, Kamphoefner had developed a lively curriculum centered on the most current ideas in architectural thinking. He had brought Frank Lloyd Wright, Buckminster Fuller, Matthew Nowicki, and Mies van der Rohe to the school, to name only a few. Lewis Mumford's important *Roots of Contemporary Architecture* had grown out of a seminar he taught at North Carolina State University. Harris later recalled that Kamphoefner did not hire people because they fit a slot in the curriculum but "because they were capable of something for which no slot existed." In his relentless pursuit of Harris, Kamphoefner was following up not only on his personal admiration of the architect's work but what might be labeled his sixth sense for the qualities that lay behind good teaching.[1]

Harris was a natural teacher. He had always been popular at the universities where he had guest taught, and he had exerted a very deep influence on students at the University of Texas. Not until his arrival at North Carolina State University, however, did he have the time necessary to devote to teaching. Here he would write intriguing, enticing course descriptions and put into practice his belief that learning must be a journey of discovery. In later years he would receive prestigious awards for his contributions to architectural education, but from the beginning his presence at NCSU was appreciated. As early as 1965 the students devoted an entire

Henry Kamphoefner, dean of the North Carolina State University School of Design, 1948–73.
Date and photographer unknown, courtesy of North Carolina State University

issue of their student publication to his work and ideas. The two student editors admiringly summed up the design philosophy of their subject with these words:

An architectural experience must be developed from a complex stew of the client's wishes, the functional requirements, the building technique, and the existing environment. The natural design process begins by allowing each fact its way, no matter how demanding. From this melee, full of contradictions, the unique problems are discovered and the unifying direction is established in response to them. Thus a clear continuity flows out of the process charged by the excitement of discovery.[2]

Harris was committed to the task of conveying excitement to his students, but one feels it may have cost him some effort. The practice of architecture was his one true love and, for reasons that are not entirely clear, he felt estranged from it. He has said that he as much as retired when he went to North Carolina, and in some ways he did act like a retiree.[3] He ceased photographing new buildings he built, assuming, it almost seems, that no one would be interested. He was far removed in time and locale from the architectural world that had shaped him, and one imagines the bewilderment he must have felt as he watched a younger generation begin the attack on Modernism that was to dominate the remainder of the sixties and seventies. Robert Venturi's *Complexity and Contradiction* had cast the first stone to shatter the tyranny of Modernist thinking, but how strange it must have seemed to Harris to feel lumped together with those of his contemporaries with whom he had had so little in common. He had not insisted that "less is more." Rather, as the students at NCSU had noted, he had always been dedicated to an architecture in which contradictions were taken deadly seriously.

As always, however, all problems of theory, all tendencies toward bitterness or malaise, were dissolved in the creative act of designing. He may have felt that he had retired, but very few others had that impression. Indeed, he kept up a continuous and distinguished practice throughout the period, beginning each building with the very real excitement that discovery had always held out to him. It almost seems that he purposely shut his eyes to what architects elsewhere were doing. He had never cared for fashion, even when *he* was in fashion. As he had told the architects at the 1960 Yosemite conference, one had "to try to design in terms of reality rather than fashion, to be unfashionable or un-modern . . . to start each new work at the beginning and not where some previous work left off."[4] It was a measure of his own feelings about the state of Modernism that to start each work "at the beginning" (the attitude that had thrilled him so when he had first encountered it in the 1920s at the Otis Art Institute) was now "un-modern" to him.

Clients came to him not only from Raleigh but from the neighboring cities of Durham, home of Duke University, and Chapel Hill. This area, which has now been dubbed the "Research Triangle," was characterized by the kind of flux one might expect from the prevalence of so many universities. Because it was also expanding, a number of Harris's clients would be affiliated with one or another of the academic institutions. Most of them came with few preconceptions about Harris's work and with a willingness to turn the design over to him. It was a combination that had always resulted in his best, his most unselfconscious and deceptively simple houses. "What the architect can accomplish is limited by what his clients can understand," Harris wrote in a 1968 issue of *North Carolina Architect*. "The clients for whom he surpasses himself are the clients who make the most intelligent demands on him."[5] If the clients of California were united by their low budgets and their openness to the very new, the clients of North Carolina were united by a somewhat more mature intelligence. What would become immediately apparent to anyone who had followed Harris's work was that both groups were united by their interest in nature and the expression it was given in their homes.

North Carolina had harsher winters than either Texas or California, but not so harsh that Harris had to abstain from the use of his deep eaves or his affection for trellises and gardens. He had never liked formal gardens, where plants had to stay dutifully behind borders, and he was becoming rather fond of the way pine needles covered the ground and surfaces of architecture, uniting them in a strong, very natural connection. One of his earliest houses for Dr. and Mrs. Roy Lindahl in Chapel Hill seemed almost lost in the woods with its shingled roof and redwood siding. It and an earlier home of redwood for Mr. and Mrs. J. Francis Paschal of Durham proved to Harris that his California regionalism would be just as fitting in North Carolina. Just as the missions were not a point of reference in his former homes, neither were the plantations in the new. "Nature is the context for much of the North Carolina architect's work," Harris, with traces of bitterness, wrote in 1968. "Nature may also be the example the North Carolina architect needs most,—needs even more than he needs the examples of his contemporaries' work."[6]

The Lindahl house had the kind of horizontal redwood framing inside and out that Harris had first used in the Birtcher house—basically, narrow boards battened at the module line. The module, thirty-two inches rather than the more standard thirty-six, was the smallest he had ever used. Harris believed it worked fine for the doors and wall rhythms but worried that it was a little narrow for the hallway that lined one side of a courtyard held within the U-shaped plan. Skillfully

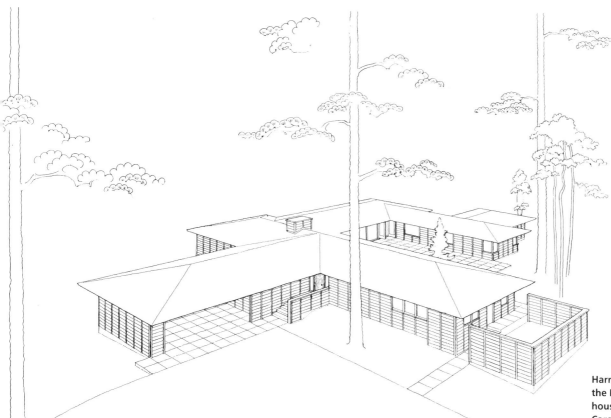

Harris, perspective drawing of the Dr. and Mrs. Roy Lindahl house, Chapel Hill, North Carolina, 1964.

Harris, Lindahl house.
Photograph by David B. Barrow, Jr.

manipulating a wall of cabinets on one side of the hall and by making windows on the other floor to ceiling, Harris created the illusion of a wider space. Lighting in the hallway had the same dual quality he had always valued; that is, light troughs beneath a higher ceiling. This effect was always more dramatic when an area of low ceiling preceded a much grander space, as was the case in the entrance area that gave way to the Lindahl living room and dining room. In these areas Harris carried the ceiling on up to the roof, allowing framing members to show through.

Wings radiated out from this central area of the house and, where possible (as with the master bedroom and two rooms for the Lindahls' sons), Harris gave bedrooms the kind of exposure that could be had only at the ends of wings. It was what the Wyle house had reveled in. The Lindahl house, in fact, fused together the smoothness of the Birtcher house exterior and the rougher, more Craftsman-like spirit of houses like the Wyle. Exposed rafters dramatized the underside of his hipped roofs, and a makeshift gutter became a feature when Harris extended every other rafter beyond the house to give it support.

The Van Alstyne house in Durham for Duke University law professor William Van Alstyne and his wife and children was one of the most successful plans of Harris's career. For a wooded, hillside slope he called for a split-level house of redwood in board and batten. A Maybeck-inspired roof in which two gable roofs splinter off at different points from a large, overarching gable created a unified exterior but an interior marked by the reality of three gable forms.[7] The entrance was on the second level up a flight of stairs. Here a dining room and living room, separated only by a lower six-foot-wide light shelf, provided a large space for entertaining. The space could be enlarged further by a deck opening directly off the living

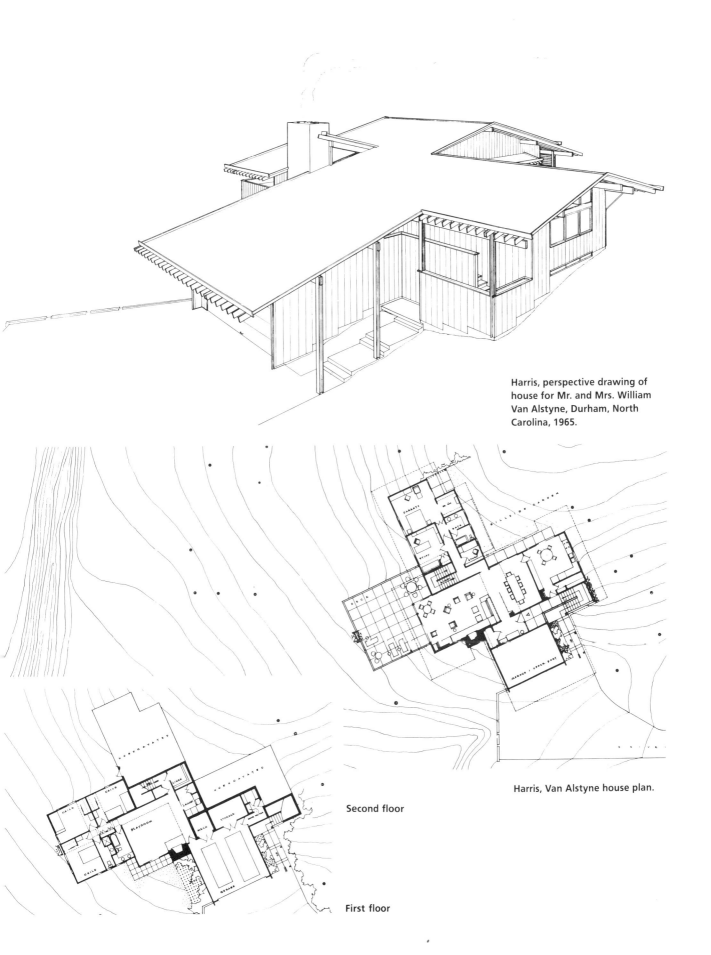

Harris, perspective drawing of house for Mr. and Mrs. William Van Alstyne, Durham, North Carolina, 1965.

Harris, Van Alstyne house plan.

Second floor

First floor

room. Supporting beams of a gable roof were exposed on the inside and could be seen running on out over the rafters of the deck in one direction and, in the other, through the glass windows of the kitchen (on the opposite side of the dining room). Boards and battens had come just as easily inside. On this level also a bedroom suite contained not only the usual dressing, bed, and bath areas but two private offices for the busy couple who occupied it. Down a wide, light-filled staircase, one could reach a playroom and three children's bedrooms. Access to the house through the garage was also here, but Harris, always concerned about function and ease of use, outfitted it with a dumbwaiter which could lift groceries and other parcels directly into the kitchen pantry above.

Sometimes in North Carolina, the pine needles on the ground, the tall trees, and the low dark roofs of his crafted houses made Harris think about the Japanese prints he had admired since his very early youth. Since the days when his Lowe house in Altadena had delighted the architectural world, Harris had always attracted clients who liked and understood the delicacy, the sublime simplicity of his own Japanese sensibility. Those qualities had not been particularly at home in Texas, but now in a harmonious setting they could enjoy a kind of renaissance. Two of Harris's clients would even find in them a valued link to that faraway, Oriental culture.

Dr. Kenneth Sugioka, head of the Department of Anesthesiology at the University of North Carolina School of Medicine, had finally purchased the lot outside of Chapel Hill that he had spotted almost thirty-five years earlier. A steep hillside above Morgan Creek, it was the site of the largest natural grove of rhododendrons east of Winston-Salem. At the home of Mr. and Mrs. Frank Klingberg, for whom Harris had designed a house in 1964, Sugioka and his wife, Mary, a pediatrician, learned the name of Harwell Harris and saw a bound reprint of the special story the *Architectural Forum* had devoted to his early houses in 1940. Klingberg told Sugioka that he didn't think Harris designed private homes anymore but encouraged him to call and find out. Sugioka phoned Harris, and the architect asked if he might see the site. "I remember it was a very ugly and gray day," Sugioka reminded Harris recently, "and you had a hat on—I think it was raining. It was not a very nice day, but you stood on top by the road and looked out and you said, 'Yes, I've always wanted to build a house in surroundings like this.'"[8]

Plans began in earnest soon afterward. The Sugiokas had asked for four bedrooms, a sunny kitchen, and a home that was contemporary but not starkly modern. The house was on a sloping hillside, not unlike the Weston Havens lot, but the

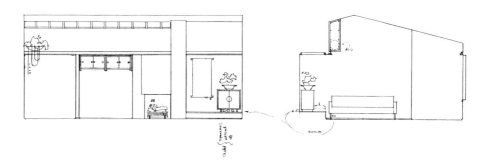

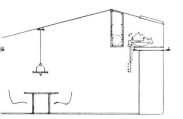

Harris, Sugioka house interior
details.

Harris, Dr. Kenneth and Mary
Sugioka house, Chapel Hill, North
Carolina, 1967.
Photograph by David B. Barrow, Jr.

critical difference was that the view from the Havens house had to be out and up; the Sugioka view had to be out and down toward the creek and the rhododendrons. Three bedrooms and a playroom rested on the hillside and supported the living and dining room above. A broad gable roof covered them. Emerging at either end, with their own smaller gable crowns, were the kitchen and master bedroom, which enjoyed exposure on three sides because Harris let them pull away from the central core of the house. They were supported above the ground by piers and were extended over the site with decks. The house was sheathed with horizontal boards of cypress battened on the module line every three feet.

The interior was exposed to nature through broad expanses of glass. The central two levels of the house were given uninterrupted ribbons of windows, and the upper-level living room had a skylight which brought light in from the more closed, street side of the house. Harris took the ceiling of the kitchen all the way up to the gabled roof, exposing a crossbeam and the rafters that ran laterally through the house. He continued their movement to the outside and made them visible by means of a large plate-glass window that also owed its shape to the gable overhead, not unlike the front window of the Ralph Johnson house. As he had done in the Van Alstyne house, Harris furnished the master bedroom with a private study. "I'm giving you a study with a balcony," Harris had told Sugioka, "so you can sit out there and think great thoughts."[9] This was the kind of encouragement Harris had always liked to give his clients through his organic architecture.

Soon after the Sugioka house was completed Harris received a commission to design a house for another medical doctor, a professor of anatomy at Chapel Hill, who had spent his youth in Japan with his parents, who were missionaries there. Dr. Stanley Bennett and his wife, Alice, had purchased and combined two small, abandoned farms on the outskirts of Chapel Hill where they planned to start an arboretum. Indeed, after they moved into their house, the first plantings of trees had a strong connection with Japan. In the entrance courtyard, around which Harris had shaped the house, they planted a plum, a bamboo, and a pine tree. According to Japanese tradition, the plum tree, because it blossomed early, symbolized the hope of spring, the bamboo represented resilience because it would come back after being killed by winter freezes. The pine stood simply for strength in the face of adversity.

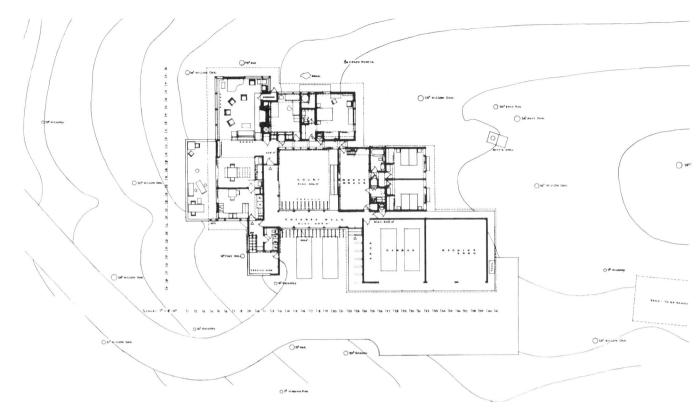

Harris, plan for residence of Dr. and Mrs. Stanley Bennett, Chapel Hill, North Carolina, 1970.

The house was beautifully sited in a clearing that allowed for views in every direction. A visitor could pull his car up to the courtyard where a walkway, up a couple of steps off the ground and covered with a narrow roof, led around two of its sides to the front door. From this approach one could see inside the floor-length windows of a hallway to doors of a bedroom and library in a deep shade of eggplant purple. Walls were of the neutralized green Harris used in many houses; the front door (and all other exterior doors) was a succulent shade of orange-pink terra cotta. The other glassed-in side of the courtyard was a large workroom behind which were two bedrooms for the visits of the Bennetts' grown children.

To the left and directly ahead as one entered the house was a Japanese tokonoma. It formed the termination point of what seemed like a hallway; that is, the kind of open division between spaces that Harris shaped only by means of his dropped light shelves. (In the case of the Bennett house he further defined the space by means of a low cabinet.) Out from underneath the lighting arrangement was the dining room to the left and the living room to the right. Windows and doors looked onto a redwood deck with a built-in bench and beyond to the woods in the distance. Above his horizontal siding of clear-grained Douglas fir battened down at three-foot intervals, Harris called for a standing seam aluminum roof. The Bennetts had told Harris that it was "more important to have a suitable house than to have a house quickly." It was an attitude that he could understand, for it was not until 1968 that he had begun to design a house for himself and Jean.

When Jean was writing regularly for *House Beautiful* in the early 1950s, it was easy to see the connections between some of her stories and Harris's houses. She wrote a small story on "nature's colors" which made mention of the very colors Harris had always preferred. She wrote about the one-woman kitchen at the center of the house, combining her very personal and resolute position that she be left alone in the kitchen with Harris's predilection for making this room the core of his organic form. One story during these years, however, had no real connection with their lives at the time; it anticipated their Raleigh home by sixteen years.

In the July 1952 issue Jean had published a story entitled "What Is a Retirement House?" It was an unusually thoughtful piece for a magazine like *House Beautiful* to publish and it was not only well illustrated with photographs of contemporary buildings, it was also well written. Jean's voice is clear and strong here as she describes a new kind of small house that is

built to serve one set of needs when new—but meets later requirements of an older couple—to help them float through their last years without financial strain and with a minimum of work.

The retirement house is born of a new set of social conditions: high income taxes which make it virtually impossible to save enough money to live on the income thereof, our increasing longevity, and the medical science of geriatrics. As a result, people are building small subsidiary houses in their peak earning years for eventual use during retirement. Because of the diversity of individual requirement, the retirement house takes a number of forms.

Jean Murray Bangs Harris.
Photograph by the Raleigh News and Observer

Two of the forms she described have direct bearing on the house that Harris designed for them in Raleigh. The first was a small guesthouse built on the same property as the main house where, she advocated, the owners might move in later years when they rented the bigger house. The second was an income-producing structure which contained a small apartment or penthouse where owners could live without rent while their property paid the taxes plus a little extra for income.

The property that the Harrises purchased in Raleigh was on the edge of the NCSU campus and was comprised of two lots. One lot already had a home that they might use as rental property for students or faculty; the other was the destination for their new home, a building that would include not only an office that could be rented after Harris retired, but another, smaller apartment that would also bring in rental income. The multiple uses were so smoothly worked out that it was impossible to feel that one was living in an office or working in a home.

The plan bears some similarity to the apartments Harris designed for Tom Cranfill in the 1950s, but where these apartments were entered on the ground floor, the Harris Raleigh house was entered on the mezzanine level, that is if one

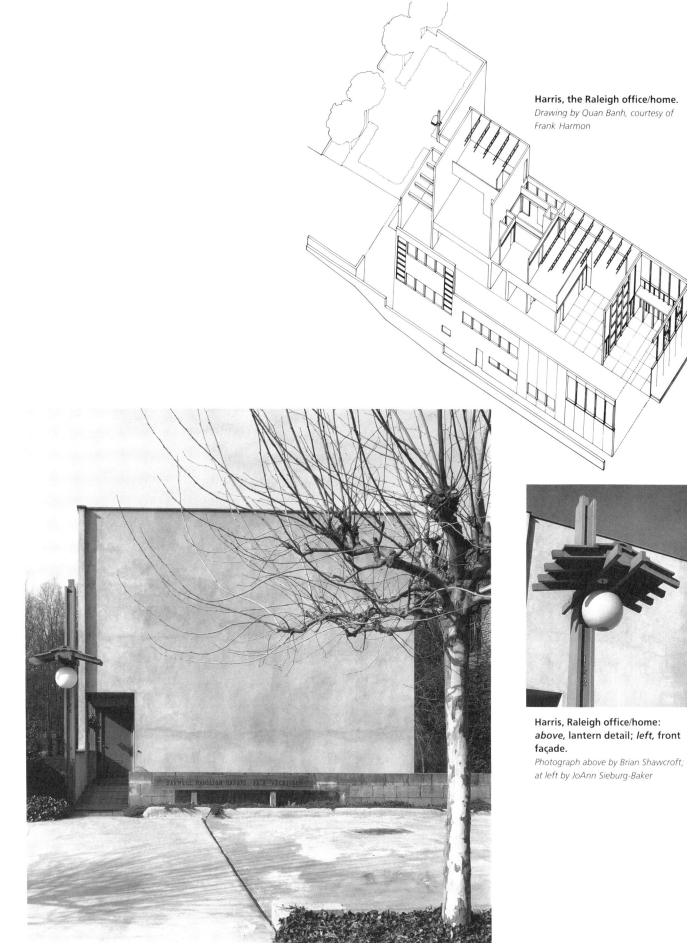

Harris, the Raleigh office/home.
Drawing by Quan Banh, courtesy of Frank Harmon

Harris, Raleigh office/home: *above,* lantern detail; *left,* front façade.
Photograph above by Brian Shawcroft; at left by JoAnn Sieburg-Baker

were to approach it from the front door. A court for parking and a blind stucco façade faced the street. On the right in front of a low wall of concrete blocks a wooden sign spelled out "Harwell Hamilton Harris FAIA Architect." On the left, a lantern of the sort Harris used in the Carter Stevenson garden marked the beginning of an entrance walk to the recessed front door. Inside the door to the right was a reception area and beyond it a large, light-filled drafting room. Straight ahead on axis with the front door was another door that gave way to the Harrises's house. Through it and across a landing was the mezzanine that contained Harris's more private office and library. At the foot and to the right of a single-run staircase was the more domestic area of the house—a combination living and dining area looking into a garden room with high walls for privacy from the steady traffic of students walking to school. Behind the dining room one door led to the Harris bedroom and another to the "one-woman" kitchen. Behind these areas, across the width of the house, Harris had another small, fireproof office where he kept his drawings and where Jean worked long hours on her history of food book. (The door to this area, which Jean had named "El Dumpo," was through their bedroom closet.) Behind this and directly below the architect's office above was another small apartment and enclosed garden. To better meet the Harrises's needs the front door of the house was at the foot of the stairs, easily accessible from the driveway. In her later, declining years it is doubtful that Jean ever had any reason to climb the stairs to the mezzanine. By planning ahead for old age and by clever use of space, the Harrises had succeeded in creating a perfect retirement house.

Of all his late North Carolina work, Harris's essential design characteristics coalesced most beautifully in the Saint Giles Presbyterian Church. If a proposed guest house had been added to the Wyle House in Ojai, it would be tempting to compare it with the Saint Giles scheme. Both perspective renderings show a collection of wooden buildings with gable roofs connected by covered walkways. Unfortunately, too, for Saint Giles, the covered walkways have not yet been built. (The church has been built in installments, so they may go up yet.) Even without them, however, the pathways from building to building take the visitor on a journey of discovery in search of the sanctuary. Not surprisingly, it comes at the climax of the journey, although, in typical Harris fashion, it presents itself with no great ceremony. In character it looks like the other buildings in the complex, except for a balcony that protrudes into the woods from the church narthex.

Inside the room churchgoers find themselves looking across a shallow but wide horizontal space to the chancel and not toward either of the gable ends,

Harris, Saint Giles Presbyterian
Church, Raleigh, North Carolina,
1967–83.

Photograph by Brian Shawcroft

which contain circular windows, each inscribing a Greek cross. If these two crosses on the sides of the sanctuary diffuse the drama of the room somewhat, it may be because Harris never viewed it as the heart of the church. The church's real center, the place which for Harris was always a sanctuary, is the nature outside, accessible from the balcony. It is a fragment of hillside wilderness, tree-inhabited, fern-carpeted, and almost surrounded by the building and covered walks. It is rather elusive and mysterious—perhaps, in its way, more spiritual than the man-made sanctuary that sets it off. To quote Harris, "It's a form and if you have any liking for form, you're apt to approve of it." [10]

Harris, drawing of the Cullowhee
Presbyterian Church, Cullowhee,
North Carolina, 1976.

Harris would design three more churches in the next several years, the Church of Reconciliation for Chapel Hill, the Cullowhee Presbyterian Church, and the North Raleigh United Methodist Church, but of these only the Cullowhee Church would ever be built. About the same time, in 1972, a favorite, inspired plan for a resort on the island of Kinabalu just off the coast of North Borneo was also canceled. Working feverishly on his scheme for the island (which included an eight-story hotel, a Malay theater, a Chinese restaurant, a casino, a floating restaurant, and an assortment of other attractions, including gardens) Harris completed the drawings in only three months without the help of assistants. He learned that the scale of a project didn't matter once he had the idea, but it was a small return for the hopes that were dashed when the job was canceled owing to the death of the client. There is an enormous chasm that separates an idea, however inspired, from a fully realized piece of architecture. Harris, who had always found the disputation of ideas a weak substitute for building, felt the difference most keenly.

In 1975, after remodeling a house for John Caldwell, the chancellor of NCSU, who had just retired, Harris decided it was time to retire as well.

14.   Retirement

Together, spaces make a pattern. It is the pattern of a person's interests, feelings, activities. It is as though those interests, feelings, activities had expressed themselves on some now forgotten occasion, leaving tracks,—and this building has grown up around those tracks. With its form the building satisfies the user's wants—conscious and unconscious. It anticipates, it invites, it implements those wants. So, whatever the indweller now does he does effortlessly, harmoniously, pleasurably. Accomplishing this calls for great art, —doing what great art does in music, in literature, in mathematics, in painting, in sculpture: creating a great unity. Doing this is what makes architecture worthwhile.

HARWELL HAMILTON HARRIS, 1977

Harris talking about his architecture.
Photograph by Brian Shawcroft

HARRIS HAD RESIGNED from teaching, but he wasn't ready to leave his practice behind. He stayed busy with new commissions that, for one reason or another, didn't go. A vacation residence for Ruth Carter Stevenson in Roaring Gap, North Carolina, fell through, as did a new home for William Van Alstyne, who had meanwhile become divorced from his wife. It was a trying time, made more trying by Jean's failing health. She now had the painful heart ailment known as angina.

Her wits still razor sharp, Jean continued to work on her history of food book late into the night in the office near their bedroom. She seemed to have a sad feeling about her husband's experience at the University of Texas and a bitterness that more of his recent work had not been built. Harris, not bitter, was nevertheless in low spirits.

He had always been sought out by students and remembered by former clients and his own contemporaries. This period was no exception. In 1981 he was given a one-man show of his work at NCSU and the next year the Fayetteville, North Carolina, Museum of Art followed with another retrospective. A student at the University of Texas traveled to interview him with his professor in order to write an article for *Texas Architect*. The architecture student, Paul Lamb, had become interested in Harris while living in his Cliff Street Apartments for Tom Cranfill, and the article he wrote with Lawrence Speck, entitled "Rediscovering Harwell Hamilton Harris," began to interest a new generation of Texas students. In 1984 Esther McCoy's important book *The Second Generation* was published, and about the same time David Barrow, a former student and associate from the Dallas years, encouraged Harris to sell his lifetime's output of plans to him so that he could donate them to the Architectural Drawings Collection of the University of Texas Library. Harris agreed, and soon afterward, at the instigation of Speck, an exhibition and small monograph were planned under the auspices of the Center for the Study of American Architecture, part of the University of Texas School of Architecture.

Both of the Harrises were thrilled about the prospect of the show. Jean particularly seemed happy that it was to be held at the University of Texas, the place where she believed Harris had been mistreated. As time for the opening neared, news came that the university had raised enough money to endow a professorship in his name. Meanwhile, Jean's heart had caused her to be hospitalized. She insisted that she still planned to go to the opening of the exhibition in Austin and went so far as to ask what kind of evening attire she should wear. As her health continued to worsen, she tried to convince her doctor to go with her. Finally, she chose to stay behind after exacting a promise from Harris that he would tell her every detail of the festive event. When their good friend architect Frank Harmon decided to go to the opening and made a video of it, Harris left Raleigh. On the following day, as he flew to Austin from Dallas, she died. It was as if the thought of Harris's honorary welcome back to Austin had kept her alive; only after she knew it was going to happen and had actually seen him leave was she able to let go of her life. As she had requested, Harris stayed in Austin for the opening, where a large crowd of friends and former clients had gathered.

Left, Harris with author and Harold Box, dean of the School of Architecture in front of a half-scale rendition of the Ralph Johnson house façade, University of Texas at Austin, opening night of exhibition devoted to drawings and photographs from Harris's long career, February 22, 1985.
Photograph by Debbe Sharpe

Harris, *left,* and Dr. Samuel D. Proctor, *right,* receiving honorary doctorates from North Carolina State University Chancellor Bruce R. Poulton, *center,* May 11, 1985.
Photograph by Herman Lankford, courtesy of North Carolina State University

Since that time Harris has received an honorary doctorate from North Carolina State University, an award he very much cherishes. He has stayed busy trying to find a publisher for Jean's history of food book, jurying architectural work of students at various universities, and traveling to the cities—Arlington, Chicago, and New York—where the small exhibition of his drawings has traveled and where he has discovered a new generation interested in what he has to say about the buildings that seem so unlike what they have come to think of as Modern. He has continued to design additions for Saint Giles and facilities for a park in Cary, North Carolina. In 1985 he received a request to help design a setting in Fort Worth for four sculptures. In his words, the commission was "unbelievable," which is to say that it engaged him completely. He wrote:

After two trips to Venice [Italy], my Greenwood [Mausoleum] client, John Bailey, has succeeded in getting exact replicas of the 4 horses over the entrance to St. Mark's—for $27,000 each. He wants me to design an entrance to Greenwood Memorial Park, using the horses. He has sent me pictures of the original horses, together and separate, in place and now inside for protection from the corroding atmosphere; pictures in great detail of their replacements; pictures of the plaster models from which the models for the castings have now been made; and close-ups of the bronze parts being worked on in the foundry.

The idea is so crazy it's fantastic. I have agreed to try. No courtyard, no surrounding buildings encrusted with elaborate art, the loot of centuries. Instead, a rolling Texas prairie. I have the horses galloping up to the crest of a rise and then galloping right over the heads of the entering visitors. My drawings are far enough along to convince me I like it.[1]

Harris placed the horses on a bridge between two concrete arches that rose out of the ground on either side of the entrance road. To foster the effect of the low "rise" he wanted, the arches were deep and as low and thus earthbound as he could make them. An additional arch on each side of greater width reinforced the idea of a natural ground swell, as did plant boxes out of which one leg of each of the arches appeared to emerge.

After Bailey's lawyer protested that young children would be encouraged to climb up the vaults to the horses' backs and therefore that the design encouraged lawsuits, the plan was dropped. In another letter, Harris recorded his feelings: "A visionary means to break the necks of little boys and to break the cemetery's fortune with liability suits. Bailey asked for time to look for alternate designs other than the one I proposed. I doubt Bailey comes back to my alternate, and I'll be glad if he doesn't. I fell in love with those magnificent horses."[2]

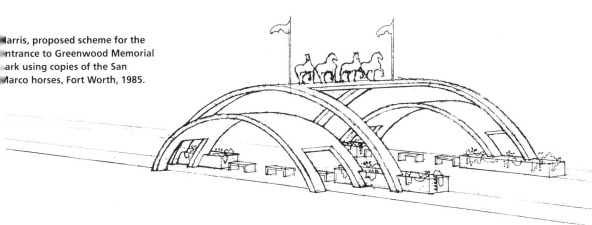

Harris, proposed scheme for the entrance to Greenwood Memorial Park using copies of the San Marco horses, Fort Worth, 1985.

As it happened, Bailey did not come back to Harris. The horses were placed on separate pedestals high above the heads not only of would-be juvenile equestrians but of the more somber visitors passing by them on their way to the cemetery.

And yet, Harris's solution remains a compelling one. It deserves to be remembered alongside his best houses, perhaps even above them as a kind of introductory epigraph containing the essential metaphor of his life's work. Had he not labored for sixty years to take art off the pedestal on which it had been placed? Had he not sought to reveal its natural underpinnings, making the enjoyment of it more personal and immediate, free from pretense and artificiality? As he had always tracked the life patterns of his clients so as to place them in harmonious settings in which they felt at ease and inspired, he looked carefully at what the horses of San Marco had to say for themselves. He refused to be put off by their famous San Marco setting, for he had never been averse to looking at past art and distilling out of it what was essential and alive. He knew that the horses had been given their exquisitely crafted, very naturalistic forms perhaps hundreds of years before they rose to the top of the Venetian church. He could not reconstruct their original destinations in Byzantium, nor did he want to. Characteristically, Harris sought to liberate the horses, to let them come down off their dusty, dead observation points and exercise their powerful legs in a full gallop across a Texas prairie. This was the fresh, natural, very gentle iconoclasm of the good-natured Harris at work. This was the Modern spirit as it was expressed by one of its most passionate disciples.

Right, Stanton Macdonald-Wright, *Synchromy in Purple Minor,* 1918.
Courtesy of the James and Mari Michener Collection, Archer M. Huntington Art Gallery, The University of Texas at Austin
Below, Harris, still life in pastel crayon, 1932.

Above left and below, R. M. Schindler, Schindler Kings Road house, 1922, "With a fire indoor beckoning to another in the garden, indoors and outdoors became even more one," Harris observed.

Photographs by Grant Mudford

Above right, Harris, Lewis Gaffney house and studio, 1932.

MULTI-FAMILY DWELLING FOR ARTHUR JENSEN ON OCCIDENTAL BLVD
HARWELL HARRIS / ARCH. GROUP FOR INDUSTRY AND COMMERCE

HARWELL H HARRIS · JANUARY 1934
RESIDENCE FOR MISS PAULINE LOWE / PANAMINT DRIVE / ALTADENA / CAL

Above, multifamily dwelling for
Arthur Jensen, 1931, signed
"Harwell Harris—Arch. Group for
Industry and Commerce." *Above
right,* Harris, drawing of the
Pauline Lowe house, 1933, before
the flat roof had been replaced
by the later hipped roof. *Below,*
Harris, drawing, street side of the
De Steiguer gift shop, 1939.

A GIFT SHOP FOR MR & MRS EDWARD DESTEIGUER / PASADENA, CALIFORNIA 1939 / HARWELL HAMILTON HARRIS

Harris, Fellowship Park, 1935, with Carl Anderson—designed chair in foreground.

A rare color photograph by Fred R. Dapprich

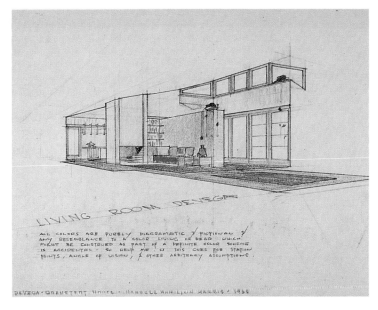

LIVING ROOM DESIGN

ALL COLORS ARE PURELY DIAGRAMATIC / FICTIONAL /
ANY RESEMBLANCE TO A COLOR LIVING OR DEAD / WHICH
MIGHT BE CONSTRUED AS PART OF A DEFINITE COLOR SCHEME
IS ACCIDENTAL — SO HELP ME / IF THIS GOES FOR STATION
POINTS, ANGLE OF VISION, / OTHER ARBITRARY ASSUMPTIONS.

Above, Harris drawing of the Greta Granstedt house, Hollywood, 1937–38. *Center,* drawing of interior of the Granstedt house by Harry Harrison, one of Harris's draftsmen. His comments, intended to amuse his boss, seem to reflect how strongly Harris felt about developing his own interior color schemes (and, indeed, everything else related to the design), without the interference of his assistants. Harrison wrote: "All colors are purely diagrammatic and fictional and any resemblance to a color living or dead which might be construed as part of a definite color scheme is accidental—so help me. This goes for station points, angles of vision, and other arbitrary assumptions." *Below,* Harris drawing of Grandview Gardens Restaurant, Chinatown, Los Angeles, 1940.

GRANDVIEW GARDENS NEW CHINATOWN

HARWELL HAMILTON HARRIS · LOS ANGELES
1940

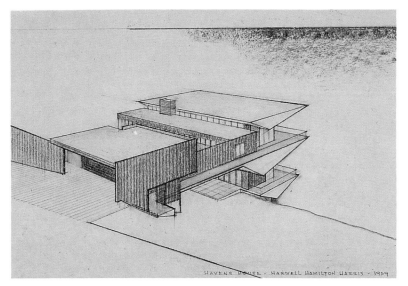

Left, Harris, perspective drawing of the Weston Havens house, Berkeley, 1940–41, showing the eastern and northern elevations.

Below, Havens house living room and balcony.

© 1985 Henry Bowles

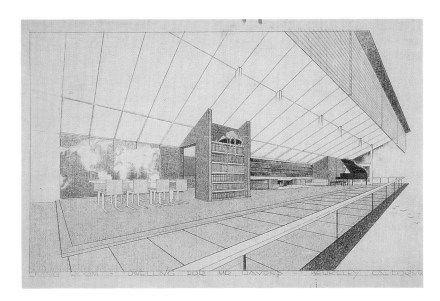

Right, Harris, bird's-eye perspective of the Havens house upper balcony.

Below, Havens house balcony.
© 1985 Henry Bowles

Top left, Havens house pass-through buffet between kitchen and dining room.
© *1985 Henry Bowles*

Bottom left, Havens house dining room with one of the muralled doors open to expose kitchen.
© *1985 Henry Bowles*

Above right, Havens house master bedroom with doors opening onto the outdoor badminton court.
© *1985 Henry Bowles*

Opposite, trough-shaped bridge connecting the hillside with the house and protecting the privacy of the badminton court below.
© *1985 Henry Bowles*

Left, Juliet Man Ray seated on the built-in couch of the Cecil Birtcher house, 1941.
Photograph by Harwell Hamilton Harris, courtesy of David B. Barrow, Jr.
Below, Harris's design (using Carl Anderson furniture), for the "America at Home" exhibition showroom, New York World's Fair, 1939.

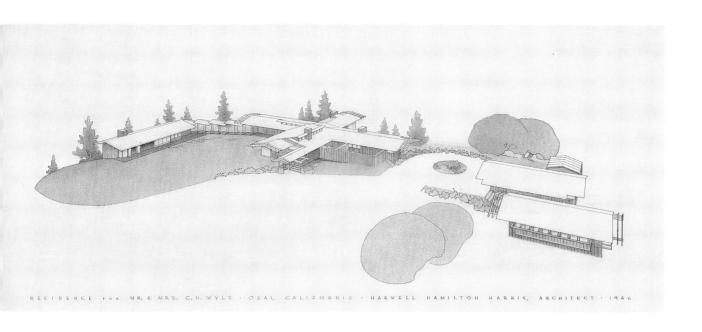

RESIDENCE for MR. & MRS. C. H. WYLE · OJAI, CALIFORNIA · HARWELL HAMILTON HARRIS, ARCHITECT · 1946

Above, Harris, perspective rendering of the Clarence Wyle house, 1946–48, Ojai, California, showing covered walkway and guest house, which were never built. *Right,* Harris, interior perspective of the Dr. Lodewijk .ek house, La Jolla, California, 1941.

Above left, Ralph Johnson house,
Los Angeles, 1947–48.
Photograph by David B. Barrow, Jr.
Left, J. J. Mulvihill house, Sierra
Madre, California, 1948.
Photograph by David B. Barrow, Jr.
Opposite above, Harris's
"springboard into space" detail
from the Harold English house,
1949–50.
Photograph by David B. Barrow, Jr.
Opposite below, far right,
poolside, exterior elevation of
the Harold English house.
Photograph by David B. Barrow, Jr.
Opposite below, immediate right,
Wrightian window detail, Harold
English house.
Photograph by David B. Barrow, Jr.

Left, Harris and U.T. students David Barrow, Don Legge, Bill Hoff, Neil Lacey, Pat Chumney, and Haldor Nielsen, *House Beautiful* Pace Setter House, State Fair of Texas fairgrounds, 1954. *Photograph by David B. Barrow, Jr.*

Below, Harris, Calvin Antrim house, Fresno, California, 1956. *Photograph by Calvin Antrim*

ight, Harris, garden detail, Ruth
Carter Stevenson house,
1955–56.
Photograph by Paul M. Lamb

above, Ruth Carter Stevenson
planter detail.
Photograph by Paul M. Lamb
right, Ruth Carter Stevenson arc-
shaped balcony.
Photograph by Lisa Germany

Above, Harris, rendering of the
Seymour Eisenberg house, Dallas,
Texas, 1957–58. *Left,* Eisenberg
living room vignette with
exterior view of master bedroom
and study and continuous roof
soffit.
Photograph by Paul M. Lamb

Right, detail of entrance courtyard and porte cochere, Seymour Eisenberg house.
Photograph by Paul M. Lamb
Below, entrance gallery, Seymour Eisenberg house.
Photograph by Paul M. Lamb

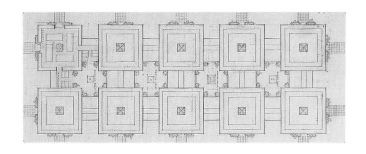

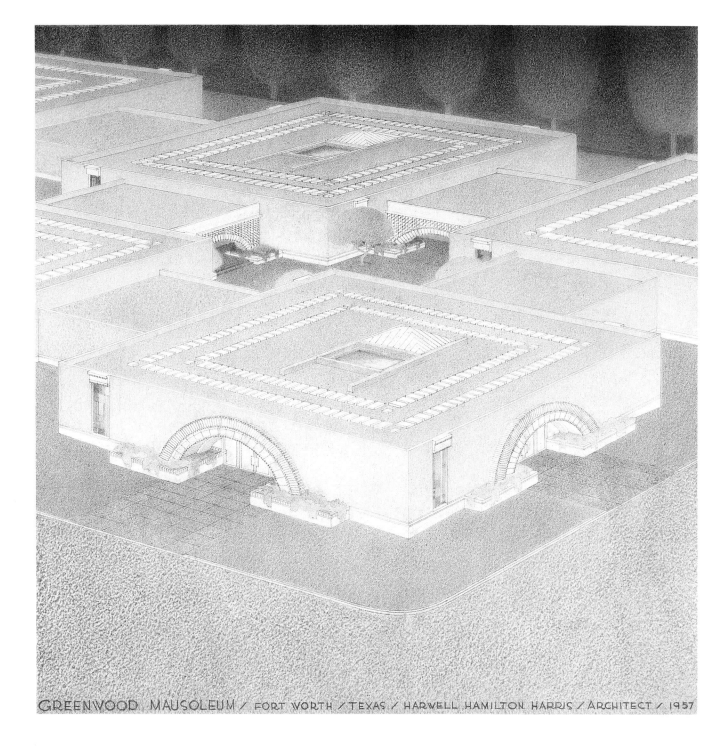

GREENWOOD MAUSOLEUM / FORT WORTH / TEXAS / HARWELL HAMILTON HARRIS / ARCHITECT / 1957

This page, Harris, perspective rendering of the Trade Mart Court, Dallas, Texas, 1958–60, with cable-supported suspension bridges painted in gold and vermilion.

Opposite below, Harris, perspective drawing of the Greenwood Mausoleum, Fort Worth, Texas, 1956–57. *Opposite above,* Harris, Greenwood Mausoleum floorplan indicating layout of future development.

C-21

Opposite above, lake-side, rear elevation of the John Treanor house, 1958–59.
Photograph by Paul Lamb

Opposite below, garden court, John Treanor house.
Photograph by Harwell Hamilton Harris, courtesy of David B. Barrow, Jr.

This page, *right*, entrance corridor of Dr. and Mrs. J. M. Woodall house, Big Spring, Texas, 1958–59.
Photograph by Lisa Germany

below, Woodall living room with its sheltering 30 ft.-square, Philippine mahogany, hipped ceiling, marked off in 3 ft.-square modules.
Photograph by Lisa Germany

Left, living room of Harris's office/home, Raleigh, North Carolina, 1968–70.
Photograph by Louise E. Andrews

Below, two views (side and front) of Harris's office/home.
Photographs by Louise E. Andrews

ight, living and
*a*rden rooms as
*s*en from
*H*arris's
*m*ezzanine
*st*udy.

*Ph*otograph by
*Br*ian Shawcroft

Left, sanctuary, Saint Giles
Presbyterian Church, Raleigh,
North Carolina, 1967–83.
Photograph by Brian Shawcroft
Below, Harris, rendering of Saint
Giles Presbyterian Church
showing his beloved covered
walkways, which the church is
still planning to build.

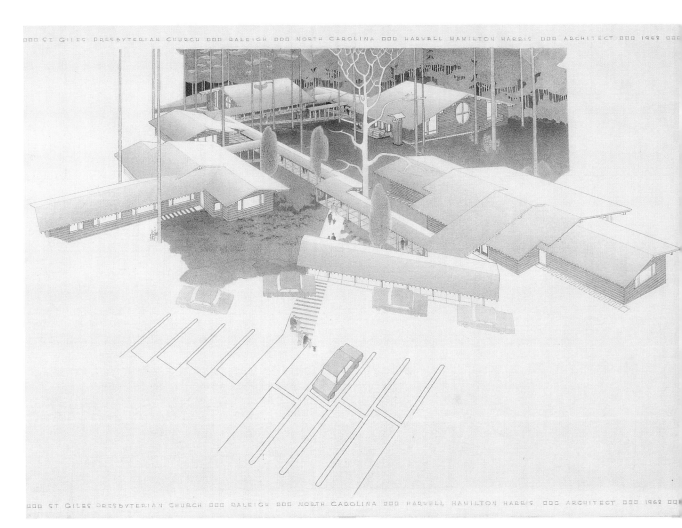

Notes

ABBREVIATIONS

CAA   *California Arts & Architecture*

NCSU   *Harwell Hamilton Harris: A Collection of His Writings and Buildings,* ed. Keller Smith, Jr., and Reyhan Tansal. Student Publication of the School of Design, North Carolina State University, vol. 14, no. 5 (Raleigh: University of North Carolina Printing Plant, 1965).

POAA   "Portrait of an Architect." Jean Harris's title for her collection of Harris's writings, both published and unpublished. Only unpublished writings will be so designated. Published articles will be given full documentation, in accordance with their original publication.

UCLA   Harris interview by Judy Stonefield, August 15, 22, 23, 1985, under the auspices of the Oral History Program, University of California at Los Angeles.

HHH   to author, Tape Series I: Author's interviews with Harris, March 11–18, 1984.

HHH   to author, Tape Series II: Author's interviews with Harris, January 24–28, 1988.

HHH   to author, Tape Series III: Harris's comments while touring Texas buildings, February 5–8, 1988.

HHH   letter to author, followed by the date, will designate individual letters from the active correspondence of Harris, whose address is 122 Cox Avenue, Raleigh, North Carolina 27605, and the author, 201 West 32nd Street, Austin, Texas 78705. Harris answered a series of questions addressed to him during August 1988. Possibly because he thought all the answers were a part of one letter, he did not date them. Instead, in a letter dated July 18, 1988, he wrote to say that he had received my questions and would be sending answers in installments. This he did during the following four or five weeks. The letters have been designated August [n.d.], 1988.

1. Forsaking the Formula, 1903–1921

1. CAA 49 (January 1935). This issue of *California Arts & Architecture* was edited by Pauline Schindler and was devoted completely to Modernism. Besides the homage paid to Frank Lloyd Wright and essays by Richard Neutra and Rudolph Schindler, the issue reproduced photographs of houses by Neutra, Schindler, Lloyd Wright, Morrow and Morrow, and Harwell Hamilton Harris (the Lowe house). For comparisons of Harris's buildings to those of J. R. Davidson, Gregory Ain, and Raphael Soriano, see also Esther McCoy, *The Second Generation* (Salt Lake City: Gibbs M. Smith, Peregrine Smith Books, 1984).

2. HHH letter to author, [n.d.]. According to Harris, Neutra pointed out Gill's Banning house in Los Angeles as they were passing it (ca. 1929) and commented that he had told Frank Lloyd Wright that something should be done to publicize Gill. He further stated that he saw a great similarity between Gill and Adolph Loos, the Viennese architect who had inspired both Schindler and Neutra to come to America. Only through Schindler, however, did Harris begin to admire Gill's work. He wrote: "I must have passed Gill's Dodge house in going to Schindler's, but with my mind on 835 Kings Road I failed to notice [it]. I suppose I would have been more excited by Gill if the parts of his buildings hadn't looked so familiar. I had seen so many stucco walls and windows with semicircular heads. I had always liked the long arcades in the California missions. Instead of seeing these features in a new total form, I simply turned the page. If at that time I had known the walls of some had been cast in concrete in a horizontal position and then up ended just as Schindler's at King's Road, I would have looked differently at Gill. His Dodge house had an intricacy and richness despite the fact its parts remained as simple as before."

3. The reaction of American architects and critics to the meteoric rise in popularity of European design is treated more extensively in Chapter 6 and Chapter 8. However, nowhere is the tone of reaction so strong as it is in Wayne Andrews's popular *Architecture, Ambition, and Americans, a Social History of American Architecture,* 7th ed. (New York: Free Press, 1978), originally published in 1947.

4. HHH conversation with author, March 1984.

5. I am indebted to Judy Stonefield's very fine series of interviews for many of the specific facts regarding Harris's lineage and childhood; UCLA, pp. 1–7. Benjamin Harris's accomplish-

ments were of a particularly interesting and checkered nature. He was admitted to the bar in Virginia, but in 1849 took the difficult overland trail to California with other gold seekers. He seems to have had some success at mining but decided to settle in Sacramento and practice law. There he built up a large clientele, but in 1861 when the Civil War began he immediately headed home to enlist. At the close of the war he successfully launched Nashville University at Nashville, Tennessee, occupying the chair in languages. After his return to California, he served as city attorney for San Bernardino (the first to hold this post) and as city clerk, refusing to accept payment for either job. John Bron, Jr., *History of San Bernardino and Riverside Counties*, vol. 2 (Chicago: Lewis Publishing Company for the Western Historical Association, 1922), pp. 978–979.

6. HHH letter to author, Fall 1988. McCarthy and Mendel, Architects, where Fred Harris served three years as an apprentice, was mentioned in Bron, *History of San Bernardino*, p. 979.

7. UCLA, p. 33.

8. POAA, p. 41.

9. UCLA, p. 19.

10. POAA, p. 40.

11. UCLA, p. 33.

12. The buggy rides to his father's job sites were Harris's earliest exposure to architecture. He believes that evidence survives that indicates that he must have betrayed an obvious interest in it. In the inscription of a book, *The Enchanted Island of Yew* by L. Frank Baum, given as a birthday gift, a building contractor friend of his parents wrote: "To Harwell Hamilton Harris, Architect, on His Sixth Birthday." Harris recalls that he "was hurt, ungrateful and furious because it was actually my seventh birthday." "Why I Became an Architect," Talk to the Student Chapter, AIA, School of Design, North Carolina State University, October 2, 1977; POAA, p. 1.

13. According to Don McCue of the A. K. Smiley Public Library in Redlands, Fred Harris's 1903 house for W. L. Holt survives as one of the city's landmarks. Harris recalls a large watercolor perspective of it hanging in his father's office. In the drawing, a carriage, with a pair of horses and a driver, was parked under the elaborate porte cochere; UCLA, pp. 11–12. The 1911–12 Redlands City Directory records that Fred Harris's office was located in one of his own designs, the Redlands National Bank Building, rooms 14–16.

14. UCLA, pp. 10–11. The Fred Harris residence was located at 103 Nordina; Redlands City Directory, 1911–12. According to early photographs, Harris was about three years old when his parents moved to this large shingle-style house with a wide curving arch over the front door. His birthplace was a rose covered Victorian house at 44 La Verne Street. From May Harris's notes in her son's meticulously kept baby book.

15. Harris recalled that the Redlands freeze occurred in 1912 (UCLA, p. 11), but an article in the centennial edition of the local newspaper indicated that the disaster—the worst in Redlands's history—occurred on January 5, 6, and 7, 1913. Local farmers who believed they were in a frost-free climate were caught unprepared when the temperature dropped to 18 degrees. *Redlands Good News*, October 23, 1988, p. AA3.

16. Among the buildings designed by Fred Harris were the Holt Opera House and the El Centro High School in El Centro, the Lugenia Building in Redlands, and the Mt. Vernon Avenue School, the Metcalf Building, and the Upland School in San Bernardino. Bron, *History of San Bernardino*, p. 979.

17. POAA, p. 41. T. C. Howard, a Harris friend in Raleigh, N.C., has mentioned that the young Harris had two horses at this time. When he did not drive with his father to school, he rode horseback, alternating between the two according to a rather carefully worked out plan.

18. UCLA, p. 13.

19. POAA, p. 41.

20. UCLA, pp. 14–16.

21. Ibid., p. 15.

22. HHH to author, Tape Series I.

23. HHH letter to author, March 30, 1988.

24. UCLA, p. 78.

25. Joan Didion, "Some Dreamers of the Golden Dream," *Slouching towards Bethlehem* (New York: Farrar, Straus and Giroux, 1961; reprint ed., New York: Washington Square Press, 1981), pp. 19–20.

26. Ibid.

27. UCLA, p. 78.

28. Ibid., pp. 78–79.

29. Ibid., p. 80.

30. "Autobiographical Fragments," POAA, p. 42.

31. Ibid. Harris has expressed an admiration for the El Centro Library because, at the time of his childhood, books for young people were shelved alongside those for adults, thus imposing no limitations on his lively curiosity.

32. Ibid., No. 1, p. 41.

33. Ibid., p. 42.

34. Ibid., No. 2, p. 48.

35. HHH to author, Tape Series I.

6. One of Harris's most vivid memories is of an afternoon during spring recess of his senior year, lying on the side of a ravine just below Strawberry Flat in San Bernardino and reading Alfred Russel Wallace's *Social Environment and Moral Progress*. POAA, "Autobiographical Fragments," No. 2, p. 49.

37. Ibid., No. 3, p. 50.

38. Ibid., p. 51.

39. Ibid. Under the influence of Shaw, Harris began to spell words as they sounded. Thus "through" became "thru," "thought" became "thot," "though" became "tho," and so on.

Form in Clay and Color, 1922–1925

1. HHH to author, telephone conversation, September 1988.

2. UCLA, p. 37.

3. Ibid., p. 39.

4. Ibid., p. 38.

5. Ibid., p. 32.

6. Ibid., p. 31.

7. POAA, "Autobiographical Fragments," No. 3, p. 52.

8. Ibid., p. 53.

9. Harwell Hamilton Harris, "Architecture as Art," *Journal of the American Institute of Architects* (November 1952): 216.

10. Harris, "Why I Became an Architect," Talk to the Student Chapter, AIA, School of Design, North Carolina State University, October 2, 1977; POAA, p. 3.

11. UCLA, pp. 47–48.

12. POAA, "Autobiographical Fragments," No. 3, p. 53.

13. Ibid.

14. HHH to author, Tape Series I. See also POAA, "Autobiographical Fragments," p. 55. Swartz asked his students to observe the mouth, the nose, and the eyes of Michelangelo's *David*, forgetting what they were but capturing how they acted. According to Harris, Swartz wanted them to see "how each is made up of many parts, almost indistinguishable at first; how they grow, meet, merge and climax, rhythmic in their sequence and resolution, becoming a single form, a total form, a total harmony." Ibid., p. 54.

15. Gail Levin, *Synchromism and American Color Abstraction 1910–1925* (New York: George Braziller in association with the Whitney Museum of American Art, 1978), pp. 10–12.

16. In addition to these, Harris favored Chinese sculpture and the contemporary works of Maillol, Kolbe, and Lembruch. Harris, "Why I Became an Architect," POAA, p. 3.

17. POAA, "Autobiographical Fragments," No. 3, p. 54.

18. Gail Levin acknowledges that the Parisian artists Sonia and Robert Delaunay also claimed to have invented Synchronism. Morgan Russell and Stanton Macdonald-Wright were, however, more interested in using color to express form. Because they are less intent on the creation of this sculptural quality, the Delaunay paintings seem flatter and more abstract. Levin, *Synchromism*, pp. 17–20.

19. Included in a 1913 Synchromist exhibition at Der Neue Kunstsalon in Munich, both Russell's *Small Synchromy in Green* and Macdonald-Wright's *Dying Slave* depicted the back view of Michelangelo's *Dying Slave* in the Louvre. Russell executed many sketches of this sculpture and at least one synchromy of Michelangelo's *Pieta* in the Cathedral at Florence. Ibid., p. 17, plate 4.

20. Ibid., pp. 20–31.

21. Ibid., p. 46.

22. HHH to author, phone conversation, fall 1984.

23. Levin, *Synchromism*, p. 47.

24. Ibid., p. 24.

25. Ibid., pp. 10–14.

26. HHH to author, Tape Series I.

27. POAA, "Autobiographical Fragments," No. 4, p. 57.

28. Harris's taste for integral interiors may have emerged out of his admiration for Frank Lloyd Wright. Wright made his disdain for the conventional approach explicit in his *The Natural House* (New York: Bramhall House, 1954), pp. 28–29. Like Wright, Harris believed that the architect was to choose and synthesize the plantings, furnishings, and other embellishments to the house. David Gebhard comments that Rudolph Schindler's desire to have total control over all details within his buildings was an inheritance from the turn-of-the-century Arts and Crafts Movement. See *Schindler* (Santa Barbara: Peregrine Smith, 1980), p. 99.

29. Frank Lloyd Wright, *Genius and the Mobocracy* (New York: Horizon Press, 1949), pp. 91–93.

30. Ibid., pp. 91–92.

31. POAA, "Autobiographical Fragments," No. 3, p. 59.

3. Of Organisms, Machines, and the Illusion of Architecture, 1926–1931

1. POAA, "Autobiographical Fragments," No. 4, p. 59. By the time the Sowden house was finished, Harris had become a de-

votee of Frank Lloyd Wright and had very little interest in what his son might have designed. Nevertheless, the house did make an impression on him which shaped his feeling toward the younger Wright's work. Since Lloyd Wright was a popular Los Angeles architect during Harris's time there, Harris's remarks are worth noting. As with all Harris memories, the house is caught in a web of timely events and telling personal detail. "I remember someone accused Lloyd of using corn as the motif for the overall decoration above the entrances. This snide remark was made because the money that built the house came from Ruth who was from the Iowa corn belt. John devoted himself to nonrenumerative activities like music and theatrics. The one time I remember having dinner at their house (this was before the Lloyd Wright house was built) John, to illustrate something got up during the meal, went to the piano and played part of Gershwin's "Rhapsody in Blue." This was the first time I heard it and so I have never forgotten it. In the house design the outdoor theater, stage and studio were John's requirements. Consequently, the theatrical look of the house was Lloyd's response to the client's preferences. Somehow I looked upon this design more as theater than architecture. Lloyd's furniture for the house was a kind of modern-ornate. I didn't care for it." To Harris Lloyd Wright's Sowden house was "decorative form"; his father's Hollyhock House was much, much more. It was "fundamental form." HHH to author, April 26, 1988.

2. Esther McCoy, *Vienna to Los Angeles: Two Journeys*, with a foreword by Harwell Hamilton Harris (Santa Monica: Arts + Architecture Press, 1979), pp. 35–38, 79–83.

3. Art collector Walter Arensberg lived in Cottage A on Olive Hill for a time and, according to Harris, it had opened his eyes to architecture. Harris became quite friendly with the Arensbergs after Neutra returned from Europe in 1932 and wrote them that he had asked Harris to make a model of the Lovell Health House for a special exhibition in New York. The Arensbergs went to see the model, on which Harris had spent his entire fee of $500 in order to ensure that every painstaking detail was absolutely perfect. It wasn't until 1938, however, that he got to know the couple better. This was when Walter Arensberg asked him to design a combination house and gallery to be located on a plot of land only one block from the Beverly Hills Hotel. The idea was that guests could stay at the hotel and that the house could be devoted to art. The house Harris started to design not only had galleries but gardens for sculpture. As it turned out, however, Lucy Arensberg had such an intense horror of the construction aspects of building that Harris had to give up the job eventually. "I have never gotten over my regret for this loss," he wrote to Peter Papademetriou, Houston architect and Eero Saarinen biographer, April 18, 1987.

4. UCLA, pp. 49–51. Harris has described his experience on Olive Hill many times, most notably in his "Architecture as Art," *Journal of the American Institute of Architects* (November 1952) 216–219. This account, which he favors, is most notable for the way in which he relays how immediate was the sense that his life was changed by the event. Speaking of himself in third person, he concluded: "He was alone with his discovery, striding in rhythm to inaudible music. Forms gathering in procession and pouring themselves out in melody; climax following climax. He was in a new world. No halt, no uncertainty, no fumbling, no struggle; only melody, pouring itself out endlessly. With racing pulse he saw life as form, union, plan; and architecture as a kind of crystallized play, regulating life as though it were music." For all this, however, the description caught on Judy Stonefield's tape (as Harris remembered extemporaneously) seems to capture the freshness of the moment of discovery more powerfully.

5. HHH letter to author, August [n.d.], 1988.

6. Ibid.

7. UCLA, p. 91.

8. Ibid.

9. HHH letter to author, August [n.d.], 1988; see also UCLA p. 92.

10. UCLA, p. 92 (emphasis added).

11. Ibid.

12. HHH letter to author, August [n.d.], 1988.

13. See McCoy, *Vienna to Los Angeles*, p. 51, and *The Second Generation*, p. 41. Also, in POAA, p. 60, Harris implies that Neutra asked him to come and work for him at the time of their first meeting.

14. UCLA, p. 52.

15. Harris's comment that "it was unlike any Wright building. Nevertheless it was fresh and it was powerful" may be found in POAA, p. 60.

16. McCoy, *Vienna to Los Angeles*, p. 8.

17. Thomas Hines, *Richard Neutra and the Search for Modern Architecture* (New York: Oxford University Press, 1982), p. 6. Gebhard, *Schindler*, pp. 13–14.

18. Data pertaining to the arrival in America of Neutra and Schindler is drawn from McCoy, *Vienna to Los Angeles*, pp. 22–23, 26–29. Pp. 35–38 treat Schindler's involvement with Wright on the Hollyhock House; pp. 48–49 briefly describe Neutra's

enure with Wright, which she states began in October 1924 and ended at an unknown point in the winter of 1925. Hines, *Richard Neutra*, pp. 53–55, suggests that Neutra started with Wright in November of 1924 and left Taliesin at the end of January 1925. Kathryn Smith in her book *R. M. Schindler House 1921–22* (West Hollywood: Friends of the Schindler House, 1987), p. 34, records that the Neutras moved into the guest studio at Schindler's house, then into the Chaces' former apartments when they were vacated by tenants who had rented them since the Chaces' departure.

19. McCoy, *Vienna to Los Angeles*, p. 13.

20. UCLA, p. 53.

21. Harris's letter of December 16, 1974, to Pauline Schindler on the occasion of the founding of the Friends of the Schindler House quotes him as saying, "After a while Dione Neutra (I didn't know who she was) walked through the room and smiled. She was barelegged, wearing sandals and something resembling a toga (unbleached muslin, I believe) with that ribbon drawn above that completely untroubled brow. She didn't interrupt my thoughts; she merely suggested that this mountain I was on was maybe Mount Olympus." McCoy, *Vienna to Los Angeles*, p. 54.

22. Ibid., p. 56.

23. August Sarnitz in *R. M. Schindler, Architekt* (New York: Rizzoli International Publications, 1988), p. 17, says that Wright's continuing influence was in the "spatial organization, the sense of scale, the fenestration, and the use of materials." "That he had such a close knowledge of contemporary architecture is shown by his personal file of cuttings which contain pages from a good number of the major European architectural journals, including *Die Bau Gilde, Moderne Bauformen, Soziale Bauwirtschaft, L'Amour de l'art, Das Werk* and *International Studio*. Here can be found designs by van Doesburg, Oud, Rietveld, Le Corbusier, Gropius and Mendelsohn. These cuttings were all filed alphabetically by the architect's name and in some instances by building type; and the collection was added to continually right up until the time of his death." Gebhard, *Schindler*, p. 52. See also Sarnitz, *R. M. Schindler*, p. 16; also p. 24, where he mentions the influence of the Japanese magazine *Kokusai-Kentiku-Kyokai*.

24. McCoy, *Vienna to Los Angeles*, p. 12.

25. UCLA, pp. 161–162.

26. Harris, "AIA Gold Medal, First in Five Years, Awarded to Neutra," *North Carolina Architect* (May–June 1977): 8–11, contains reminiscences of Neutra in the 1920s and 1930s.

27. For Sullivan's naturalism, see Narciso G. Menocal, *Architecture as Nature: The Transcendentalist Idea of Louis Sullivan* (Madison: University of Wisconsin Press, 1981), especially pp. 3, 15–16; 79–80 for Whitman's specific influence. For Wright's ideas about a natural architecture, see his *The Natural House* and *Genius and the Mobocracy*. A succinct discussion of Harris's naturalism may be found in his editorial "Why Nature?" *North Carolina Architect* (June–July 1968): 11, a special issue on the conservation of natural resources in North Carolina.

28. Kenneth Frampton, *Modern Architecture, a Critical History*, 2nd ed. rev. and enl. (London: Thames and Hudson, 1985), p. 248.

29. McCoy, *Vienna to Los Angeles*, p. 25.

30. HHH letter to author, August [n.d.], 1988. Harris reports that sometimes, after having met Neutra at the construction site, he would ride with him to the Bethlehem Steel fabrication plant.

31. POAA, Harris comments accompanying Plate no. 1, the drawing for Neutra's class at the Los Angeles Academy of Modern Art.

32. HHH to author, Tape Series I.

33. Ibid.

34. Harris could be calculating and very technical concerning his use of the module, as his article "Rhythmic Integration of Panel Elements," *Practical Builder* (December 1949), suggests. Reprinted in *Perspecta 2, Yale Architectural Journal* 2 (1953): 36–44. He was also romantic on the subject. When he likened the harmony created by the module to that which comes from being in the company of sympathetic people, he hinted at the power of his design technique. "If the modular form is sensitively developed," he said, "you're feeling much more friendly and you don't feel that you are being handicapped, curbed, restricted, upset in any way."

35. Arthur Drexler and Thomas Hines, *The Architecture of Richard Neutra: From International Style to California Modern* (New York: Museum of Modern Art, 1982), p. 7.

36. McCoy, *Vienna to Los Angeles*, p. 9.

37. Harris, "AIA Gold Medal," pp. 8–11.

38. Ibid.

39. Ibid., p. 9.

40. *Programs and Manifestoes on 20th-century Architecture*, ed. Ulrich Conrads, trans. Michael Bullock (Cambridge: MIT Press, 1964, English trans. 1970), pp. 110–113.

41. HHH letter to author, April 26, 1988.

42. UCLA, p. 62.

43. Drexler and Hines, *The Architecture of Richard Neutra*, p. 8.

44. HHH letter to author, August [n.d.], 1988.

45. HHH letter to author, April 26, 1988.

46. HHH to author, Tape Series II.

47. HHH letter to author, August [n.d.], 1988.

48. McCoy's *Vienna to Los Angeles* is the best source for details concerning the growing friction between Schindler and Neutra in the late 1920s and early 1930s.

49. See n. 55 below.

50. In his biography of Frank Lloyd Wright, *Many Masks* (New York: G. P. Putnam's Sons, 1987), pp. 322–323, Brendan Gill quotes a letter from Wright to his son Lloyd expressing his anger at Schindler. He also includes the letter that Wright sent Schindler ending their relationship.

51. Gebhard, *Schindler*, p. 116, and Sarnitz, *R. M. Schindler*, pp. 22–23.

52. HHH letter to author, August [n.d.], 1988.

53. Harris described his feelings about Schindler in UCLA, p. 70. "Well," he said, "Mr. Schindler appeared to be a very easygoing person, a very genial person, one who had fresh ideas and ones that were expressed in a graphic form that was particularly appealing to me."

54. Harris was never an admirer of *De Stijl* art and does not believe he was influenced by it. Conversation with author while standing in front of a Mondrian at the Kimbell Museum in Fort Worth, March 1988.

55. In *Schindler*, pp. 41–42, David Gebhard makes the statement that Schindler prepared the preliminary and working drawings for Cottage A while Wright was in Japan and forwarded them there for his approval. Through stylistic analysis, he further links this house to Schindler, writing, "The Director's house, with its strange fusion of Wright's Prairie and Pre-Columbian modes, and its looser plan, must be credited to Schindler, for all of the initial sketches, finished designs and working drawings are by him. Neither before nor after did Wright in his concrete houses produce a plan such as this, nor did he ever design a house which so successfully brought together his Prairie and Pre-Columbian styles. The bedroom wing of the Director's house is in effect an open sleeping porch with walls of sliding windows on three sides. The dining stair hall spaces overlook the double height living room . . . The centre of the house is treated as a utility core with baths and kitchen and heating placed one above the other. The symmetry of individual surfaces and volumes is maintained on the exterior, but the interior plan weaves in and out in a free and easy fashion."

Sarnitz, *R. M. Schindler*, p. 17, says, "The design for the Director's residence seems to have been largely Schindler's: the initial designs, as well as the final plans and working drawings are all by him. The exterior shows the marked influence of Wright's Prairie Style, with wide eaves to shield the windows from the sun. The interior, with its two-story-high living room and changes of level, recalls Adolf Loos's 'space plan' idea."

In preparation for her forthcoming book on all the buildings that comprised the Barnsdall commission, Kathryn Smith has concluded that "there is no surviving documentation which gives conclusive proof of the attribution of this building." In a note to the author (August 1989), she explained that no conceptual or preliminary sketches have survived. The plans, she believes, were developed between September 1919, when Wright received the commission, and December 1919, when he left for Japan. "It is inconceivable," she concludes, "that Wright would turn over total design responsibility while he was in his office over a period of three months. Although the house could be compared with complex spatial compositions represented in the Imperial Hotel, the abstract interlocking of parts departs to a degree from Wright's vocabulary of the time. Residence A may represent a Wright design that shows influence of Schindler in the Studio."

56. HHH letter to author, August [n.d.], 1988.

57. UCLA, p. 70.

58. HHH letter to author, August [n.d.], 1988.

59. UCLA, p. 72.

60. In his foreword to McCoy, *Vienna to Los Angeles*, pp. 7–14, Harris describes the bohemian crowd who attended the parties at King's Road. His descriptions were undoubtedly added to and rounded out by his wife, Jean Murray Bangs Harris, who began her acquaintance with the Schindlers several years before Harris met them.

61. McCoy, *Vienna to Los Angeles*, p. 13.

62. Harris's letter of December 16, 1974, to Pauline Schindler, POAA, pp. 16–17.

4. Rubbing Aladdin's Lamp, 1932–1934

1. HHH to author, Tape Series I.

2. Bubblestone, consisting of burlap covered in lightweight concrete, was a material that could be used as a substitute for

ood. According to Harris, Bernard Maybeck came up with the idea for it and interested a Berkeley engineer, J. A. Rice, in producing it. McCoy in *The Second Generation*, p. 44, writes that Maybeck adapted Rice's invention. In any case, Harris started thinking about using the material when he saw a brief note about it in the *Architectural Record*. He had just discovered the unit system and had put it to use in the house drawing he made for Neutra's 1929 class. He wrote, "I was ripe for the idea of prefabricated panel construction and used it in all my projects thereafter. Sometimes the panels were load-bearing and other times there were pipe columns to carry the loads. In my design with Bubblestone I made the panels load-bearing by making the panel frames of heavy gauge galvanized sheet iron designed to interlock. Two interlocking frames formed in section something looking like an 'I beam' or an 'H' column. The Bubblestone was to be plastered on both sides of expanded metal-lath stretched inside each metal frame." When he began work on the Lowe house, he contacted Rice, who sent him five or six little cubes of it, about an inch and a quarter in size. He then tested the cubes by soaking them in a pail of water for several days to see how resistant they would be to the elements. Although he was forbidden to use Bubblestone on the Lowe house and never returned to it, he did later use Cemesto, a prefabricated panel consisting of three Celotex panels cemented together and covered on the outside with asbestos cement. HHH letter to author, August 5, 1989.

.. HHH letter to author, August [n.d.], 1988.

.. HHH letter to author, April 26, 1988.

6. William Jordy, *American Buildings and Their Architects*, vol. 4, *The Impact of European Modernism in the Mid-Twentieth Century* (New York: Doubleday and Company, 1972), pp. 175–176.

6. HHH letter to author, August [n.d.], 1988.

7. In addition to Anderson's house, Harris was influenced by a handful of books on Japanese architecture and style. He purchased Edward Morse's *Japanese Homes and Their Surroundings* in Seattle in 1945, but as early as 1936 he had become acquainted with Jiro Harada's *The Lessons of Japanese Architecture* and Okukura's *Book of Tea*.

8. HHH letter to Jan Strand, September 14, 1975, POAA, pp. 99–101.

9. HHH letter to author, August [n.d.], 1988.

10. Ibid.

11. HHH letter to author, August [n.d.], 1988.

12. "Now the building and loan company wouldn't accept a flat roof, so I changed. It's true that it's not a gable roof; it's a hip roof and probably it's because Wright houses had hip roofs that when I came to a pitch roof I used a hip. . . . I like the low-pitched, spreading roof. I was very fond of the sense of shelter that this gave and that the house was something that lived under the roof. The roof wasn't just hardly more than a lid." HHH to author, Tape Series I.

13. In his foreword to McCoy, *Vienna to Los Angeles*, p. 12, Harris described the King's Road plan as "two right angles, reversed one-to-the-other, then put end-to-end forming a simplified 'S.'" He further noted, "Each angle enclosed a patio."

14. Harris's review of three books, "The Brothers Greene," *Architectural Record* 158 (November 1975): 45–47, gave him an opportunity to express his attitude toward outdoor sleeping. Of William R. Current and Karen Current's *Greene & Greene, Architects in the Residential Style*, he wrote: "Photographs and drawings combine to tell more than either does alone. Plan drawings reveal immediately the concept of the sleeping porch as an integral part of each family bedroom. Photographs of exterior details make clear how fully an extension of the interior Greene and Greene meant these porches to be. The sleeping porch is but one of many features of interest to the social historian. Outdoor sleeping, at least during the Summer, was a widespread custom in Southern California at this time, and many called themselves 'fresh air fiends' and some went so far as to eat 'Graham' bread and chew each mouthful of food thirty times—'Fletcherizing' it was called. But then, this was a time when climate was thot to be the best cure for tuberculosis and the foothills above Pasadena were sites of sanitariums. In most families, members shared a single porch, and the children's beds might be under a weeping tree in the backyard. Outdoor sleeping continued past World War I and was architecturally dignified for a later generation by R. M. Schindler in rooftop 'sleeping baskets' in his 1921 house for himself; by Richard J. Neutra in a sleeping porch for each bedroom in his 1927 Lovell house; and by this reviewer in an enclosed private garden for each bedroom in his 1933 Lowe house. With his private room divided into indoor and outdoor halves, one may express his pleasure in the outdoors in privacy, not 'roughing it,' but elegantly. Greene and Greene work expresses a civilized attitude toward nature. It is in this attitude as much as in their use of wood or in the pattern of their construction that one senses the Greenes' affinity with the Far East."

15. Before the 1932 International Style exhibition but after Schindler had learned that he had not been included, he wrote Philip Johnson the following analysis of the new style: "It

seems to me that instead of showing late attempts of creative architecture it [the exhibition] tends toward concentrating on the so-called 'International Style.' If this is the case my work has no place in it. I am not a stylist, not a functionalist, nor any other sloganist. Each of my buildings deals with a different *architectural* problem, the existence of which has been forgotten in this period of Rational Mechanization. The question of whether a house is really a house is more important to me, than the fact that it is made of steel, glass, putty or hot air." Gebhard, *Schindler*, p. 116.

16. HHH to author, Tape Series II.

17. McCoy, *Vienna to Los Angeles*, p. 11.

18. Ibid., emphasis added.

19. See Schindler, "Space Architecture," *CAA* (January 1935): 19. "Modern architecture," he wrote, ". . . will spring of a vision of life as it may be possible in the future. And, regardless of the perfection of its mechanical functioning, the modern house will not have been achieved in its fullest possibilities, until also it achieves that ultimate trait of personal integration—charm."

20. McCoy, *Vienna to Los Angeles*, p. 11.

21. Sarnitz, *R. M. Schindler*, p. 216.

22. "Concerning Competitions," *CAA* 47 (May 1935): 27; "What Constitutes Plagiarism?" *Apéritif* 1, no. 6 (1935): 42; "California Charges," *Architectural Forum* 62 (June 1935): 42.

5. Jean Murray Bangs and a Career Takes Shape, 1934–1937

1. UCLA, p. 82. See also pp. 166–173.

2. HHH letter to author, August [n.d.], 1988.

3. "Houses by Harwell Hamilton Harris," *Architectural Forum* 72 (March 1940): 171–186. It is not exactly clear what "school" Harris refers to here. Most likely, he is thinking of the course he took from Neutra at the Los Angeles Academy of Art, which was about a year and a half before he received the Lowe commission.

4. HHH letter to author, August [n.d.], 1988.

5. Jean Murray Bangs to author, March 11–18, 1984. See also HHH letter to author, April 24, 1985.

6. Jean took the frequently published photograph of Richard and Dione Neutra just after the latter's arrival in California.

7. The reporter was Sophie Treadwell, whom Harris has described as "one of [his] most interesting clients" and for whom he designed a house that was never built. For more on Sophie Treadwell, see HHH letter to author, February 17, 1989. The black dress, which Jean purchased for $1.00, had belonged to Joan Crawford. Jean Harris, comment to author, March 1984.

8. Clarence Muse, a singer and actor, gave the talk at Hollyhock House, and it so impressed Jean that she offered to help him write. Together they wrote a play. This was just before Harris met Jean. Sometime after Jean had introduced Harris to Muse, the architect designed a tribal map of Africa in which the principal territories were shown in differing tones of acoustic cork. Jean suggested to Muse that he emcee a weekly radio program which would be called the Evelyn Preer Memorial after a young black actress who had just died. He did it, and when the show opened in the Lincoln Theater on Central Avenue, the lobby was embellished with a sculpture—a male nude one-third life size, rising and stretching. It was the archetypal symbolic black man, modeled in clay by Harwell Hamilton Harris.

9. UCLA, p. 129.

10. HHH letter to author, August [n.d.], 1988.

11. Ibid.

12. UCLA, pp. 121, 123. Harris met the Laings at a party at Neutra's, but they seemed not to have remembered him until a mutual friend, a seismologist at Cal Tech, suggested that he design their house.

13. Ibid., p. 121.

14. For more on the Bauer house, see "George Bauer Residence," *Architect & Engineer* (March 1939): 38–39 and "The Residence of Mr. and & Mrs. George C. Bauer," *CAA* 56 (August 1939): 19–21.

15. Harris's plan for the De Steiguers also assured that they could see visitors to their shop from their living room. HHH letter to author, August 5, 1989.

16. The colors of the Laing house are noted in "Graham Laing House, Pauline Lowe House," *Architectural Forum* 63 (October 1935): 316–317. HHH to author, Tape Series I.

17. For the planting plan at the Laing house, see, "A Frank Lloyd Wright House with a Hat On," *CAA* 48 (November 1935): 20–21.

18. HHH to author, Tape Series I.

19. HHH letter to author, August 5, 1989.

20. Ibid.

21. Jean's feelings toward Helene Kershner were impressions I formed during a mealtime conversation with her and Harris, March 1984.

22. HHH letter to author, August [n.d.], 1988. This quote was

ulled by Harris from a letter Jean wrote in the 1950s to Elizabeth Gordon, editor of *House Beautiful.*

3. HHH letter to author, August 5, 1989.

4. HHH letter to author, August [n.d.], 1988.

5. HHH letter to author, August 5, 1989.

6. HHH letter to author, August [n.d.], 1988.

7. The California Board of Architectural Examiners forbade the use of the terms "architect" or "designer" to anyone who was not licensed with the state. Because he was not interested in taking the registration examination, Harris was careful to avoid use of either term. When he needed the signature of an architect or engineer, as he did with buildings that cost over $20,000, he asked M. T. Cantell, a member of the Royal Institute of Architects with whom he had studied structure. On at least one occasion, he took plans to Neutra, but was concerned when Neutra suggested that they work together on the job.

During the 1930s Harris was summoned to court on some charges brought up by a private inspector for the state board, known among architects as "the bloodhound." Stella Gramer, the law partner of John Entenza's father, Tony, represented Harris and "made mincemeat of the bloodhound." Later, Harris designed a house for Gramer that was not built because she bought Neutra's "Plywood Modern" house. Harris adapted it to her site. Also, soon after the incident with the bloodhound, Harris had stationery printed that said, "Harwell Hamilton Harris, Not an Architect." Although a member of the State Insurance Commission had recommended this action for legal reasons, Harris seemed to find it drolly amusing. He was to use it for years.

8. The comparison of the Fellowship Park house with the glass houses of Mies and Johnson was suggested by Paul Lamb.

9. Descriptions of colors based on interview, HHH to author, Tape Series I, March 1984, and "A House for Miss Marion Clark at Carmel-by-the-Sea," *CAA* 53 (March 1938): 27–29 and notes made in Harris's handwriting on the back of a kitchen photograph from the Clark house. University of Texas Architectural Drawings Collection.

10. NCSU, pp. 38–40.

11. HHH to author, Tape Series I.

12. "Santa Monica Canyon Residence for John Entenza," *CAA* 52 (July 1937): 33.

13. Ibid.

14. Reyner Banham, *Los Angeles: The Architecture of Four Ecologies*, 1st U.S. ed. (New York: Harper and Row, 1971), p. 226.

15. David Gebhard and Robert Winter, *Architecture in Los An-*

geles (Salt Lake City: Gibbs M. Smith, Peregrine Smith Books, 1985), p. 188.

36. "The Residence of Mr. and Mrs. George C. Bauer," *CAA* 56 (August 1939): 19–21. Colors of the Bauer house are noted in "House for G. C. Bauer, Glendale, California," *Architectural Forum* 17 (July 1939): 17.

37. Drexler and Hines, *The Architecture of Richard Neutra*, p. 11.

6. Houses with Good Manners, 1938–1942

1. "Houses by Harwell Hamilton Harris," *Architectural Forum* 72 (March 1940): 171.

2. "In Designing the Small House," *CAA* 47 (January 1935): 20.

3. Greta Granstedt was an aspiring actress married to a special effects director at Fox Studios, Max De Vega. They came to Harris after De Vega admired the Marion Clark house in a magazine. Their house was published as the Granstedt house in the hope that publicity might help the actress's career. HHH to author, Tape Series I.

4. HHH to author, telephone conversation, January 1985.

5. UCLA, p. 190.

6. NCSU, p. 36.

7. Harris, "A House for a Playwright," in ibid., pp. 7–12. This article, which began as a classroom exercise for architects, describes the essence of Harris's interest in nature and organic form.

8. HHH letter to author, April 26, 1988.

9. Bruno Zevi, *Towards an Organic Architecture* (London: Faber and Faber, 1950), p. 56. Commenting on why organic architecture has a "feeling of movement," he wrote, "The reason is that the spatial arrangement corresponds fundamentally to the actual movement of the man who inhabits it; organic architecture is not abstractly utilitarian but, in the integral sense of the word, functional. We are still too much in the habit of looking at a house as though it were a picture, and even the best critics are often better at analysing plans and sections and elevation than the total structure and the spatial conception of a building. The organic architect concentrates upon the structure, and he regards it not merely from a technical point of view but as the complex of all the human activities and feelings of the people who will use it."

10. UCLA, pp. 188–189.

11. Vincent Scully, Jr., *Modern Architecture: The Architecture*

of *Democracy*, 9th ed. (New York: George Braziller, 1979), p. 15. Carl Anderson recommended Dapprich to Harris and the photographer agreed to shoot the Lowe house on a contingency basis. When Harris won honorable mention in the *House Beautiful* competition, he was able to pay Dapprich $100. Thus began three decades of Harris patronage.

12. HHH letter to David Thurman, October 14, 1986, a response to Thurman's questionnaire of September 24, 1986.

13. Harris, "Wood," *CAA* 55 (May 1939): 16–17, 40.

14. HHH letter to author, August [n.d.], 1988. Louis B. Easton was an Arts and Crafts devotee. Harris said, "He not only designed a house but then put on overalls and built it with his own hands." Mrs. Easton was the sister of Elbert Hubbard, the founder of the Roycrofters. Hubbard had been an associate of Larkin, for whom Frank Lloyd Wright had designed the tall, top-lighted, Larkin Administration Building. Hubbard drowned when the *Lusitania* sank.

15. The current owner uses an electrical lift to bring guests up the steep lot to the front door.

16. Gebhard, *Schindler*, pp. 169–171. In "The Usonian Legacy," *Architectural Review* 182 (December 1987): 26–31, Kenneth Frampton discusses Wright's influence on Modern architecture in Southern California, the work of Schindler and Neutra, particularly before and after the advent of his Usonian house. Harris's opinion coincides with Frampton's in one critical way; namely, that some of Wright's early houses in Los Angeles (the Hollyhock House, for instance) embodied in grand form many of the ideas that were later developed in the much smaller, less varied Usonian houses.

17. Frampton, *Modern Architecture*, p. 62.

18. HHH to author, Tape Series I.

19. Author's interview with Weston Havens, August 1985.

20. HHH letter to author, August 5, 1989.

21. Harris, "The Evolution of an Over-all Form," POAA, pp. 133–148, describes the development of this most impressive of designs. He first delivered this paper as a student lecture at Yale University, February 8, 1979.

22. Man Ray left Paris for New York during the war and seems to have arrived in Los Angeles in 1945. Man Ray, *Self Portrait*, a New York Graphic Society Book (Boston: Little, Brown and Company, 1963; 2nd ed. 1988), pp. 260 ff.

23. Charles Cruze, who drove his car wearing white gloves, was a graphic designer for whom Harris built an office in 1947. Harris recalls that Cruze and his wife, Kay, were a most glamorous couple. The downtown area of Los Angeles has now sur-

rounded the small office (located at 2340 West Third Street) an the elderly couple who now live in it in rather desperate cond tions are terrified of urban crime.

24. HHH to author, Tape Series I, II.

25. HHH to author, Tape Series II.

26. HHH letter to author, August [n.d.], 1988.

27. HHH to author, telephone conversation, December 1 1989.

28. HHH letter to author, August [n.d.], 1988.

29. Ibid.

30. Among Harris's early draftsmen and assistants were Gor don Drake, Emil Becsky, Robert Olwell, Harry Harrison, Aubre Horn, Charles Adams, Gilbert Leong, Carl John Sterner, an Robert Moser. Later, in Texas Eugene George worked for Harri as did David George (no relation), who had formerly been a Ta iesin fellow. David Barrow was an associate during the Dalla years, and engineer Frank Sherwood was briefly a partne when Harris lived in Fort Worth. Howard Garriss and Joe Sar Queen worked for Harris in North Carolina.

31. For more on Harris's New York World's Fair room, se Talbot Hamlin, "Interior Decoration, 1940," *Pencil Points* 2 (July 1940): 438.

7. New York: Glamour and Dissension, 1943–1944

1. HHH to author, Tape Series I.

2. Richard Pratt, "The Browns Build a War Time House wit Peace Aims," *Ladies Home Journal* (July 1942); "Blue Prints c Tom, Tomorrow: Western House of the Future with Bathin, Lounge," *Sunset* (May 1943); "How the Shumways Can Buil Their House," *Women's Home Companion* (December 1943).

3. "For a Quicker Start in 194X," *Architectural Forum* 7 (September 1942): 116. The segmental house had been previ ously published in "The Segmental House, a House with a Fu ture," *Revere Copper & Brass Bulletin* (1941). Also see Harris "From Little House to Big House in Ten Easy Stages," POA/ pp. 161–174.

4. HHH to author, Tape Series II.

5. Ibid.

6. Ibid. See also David Hanks and Jennifer Toher, *Donal Deskey* (New York: E. P. Dutton, 1987), pp. 126–128.

7. Sigfried Giedion, *Mechanization Takes Command* (Ne York: Oxford University Press, 1948), pp. 625–627.

8. HHH to author, Tape Series II.

Hanks and Toher, *Donald Deskey*, p. 128.

0. HHH to author, Tape Series II. Harris expressed some annoyance that the design was streamlined by Deskey. In his experience, graphic designers always wanted to streamline.

1. "Eight Men on a Unit," *Interiors* 105 (May 1946): 87–88. See also "Harwell H. Harris Shows His West Coast Skill in a Midwest Environment," *Architectural Forum* 84 (February 1946): 4–96.

2. HHH to author, Tape Series II.

3. "Eight Men on a Unit," pp. 87–88.

4. Résumé, Jean Murray Bangs.

5. Jean Murray Bangs Harris conversation with author, March 1984.

6. T. H. Robsjohn-Gibbings, "Post War Dream World or . . . Reality?" *House Beautiful* 86 (August 1944): 48, 85, 86, 88, 89. Born in London in 1905, Robsjohn-Gibbings (whom the Harrises called Gibby) had immigrated to the United States in 1929. Only a year after he wrote this pro-American account of Modernism, he became a naturalized American citizen. It's worth noting in this context that Jean Harris was a Canadian.

7. "How to Judge Modern," *House Beautiful* 86 (August 1944): 9–57, 70–71.

8. For an excellent discussion of this issue, see Deborah Frances Pokinski, *The Development of the American Modern Style* (Ann Arbor: UMI Research Press, 1984).

9. HHH letter to author, April 26, 1988.

0. Ibid.

1. UCLA, p. 32.

2. HHH letter to author, August 14, 1988.

3. HHH letter to author, December 18, 1987.

4. Jean Murray Bangs Harris used these words to describe her impression of the European Modernists in a discussion with the author, March 1984.

5. "Meet Harwell Hamilton Harris," *House Beautiful* 87 (July 1945): 55–56.

6. Ibid.

Back West: A Regrouping in Patterns, 1944–1948

. HHH to author, Tape Series I.

. Huston told Harris that he wanted a house he could ride his horse through, and the architect responded by placing two wings of the house on high ground, forming a natural dog trot between them on the lower level.

3. HHH letter to author, August 5, 1989.

4. Pottenger Hospital patients tended to stay for extended visits. To make them as comfortable as possible, Harris called for outdoor sitting places adjacent to their rooms. He endeavored to keep the building from looking like a hospital and he saw to it that the building's organic form encouraged social interaction and companionship. HHH letter to author, August 5, 1989.

5. HHH letter to author, April 26, 1988. When Joe McCarthy, a draftsman in Wurster's office, gave Harris a tour of the architect's work in San Francisco, Harris was impressed. "All the houses," he recalled, "were small and totally unpretentious, looking as tho designed by a very talented carpenter. This is the way Wurster wanted them to look. Everything about his office looked unpretentious. There was no reception room nor receptionist. Dressed in a linen smock, Wurster met every visitor. Each draftsman was put in charge of a job and was present at all conferences with [the] client. The specifications were typed by a stenographer down on the first floor and she was summoned by ringing a cowbell. The specs were not on 8 1/2″ × 11″ sheets but on 24″ × 36″ or 30″ × 42″ sheets of the same size as the drawings sheets and bound in with the drawings. The sheets had to be folded 4 times to fit in the typewriter and care taken that they did not get smeared or wrinkled. Remember this was before the advent of photocopying. One great advantage of Wurster's system was the fact [that] the specs could be blueprinted (later blueline or blackline ozalid) right along with the drawings. Furthermore, the number of sets of specs was not limited to the number of readable carbons possible. Later, instead of folding the paper to make it go into the machine I cut it into pieces 12 or 13 inches wide and the height of the drawings sheets (30″ usually). This way the sheets would fit easily into the machine and, tho narrower than the drawings sheets, they still could be bound in with them and open in the same book-like fashion. That was 1935 and I have been doing it that way ever since. If you want to be facetious, you can say that Wurster's influence on me was in the specs format."

6. Lewis Mumford, "The Skyline," *New Yorker*, October 11, 1947, pp. 94–96, 99.

7. HHH letter to author, August [n.d.], 1988.

8. Ibid.

9. Jean Murray Bangs, "Greene and Greene," *Architectural Forum* 89 (October 1948): 81–88.

10. HHH to author, Tape Series I. Harris was disappointed that the Wyles did not build the guest house, which is shown in his rendering connected to the main house by a porte cochere.

11. Esther McCoy, *The Second Generation* (Salt Lake City: Peregrine Smith Books, 1984), p. 63.

12. Bangs, "Greene and Greene," p. 85.

13. HHH to author, Tape Series I.

14. The Chadwick School, built of concrete blocks and articulated with strong wooden designs, foreshadows Harris's Saint Mary's Episcopal Church in Big Spring, Texas.

15. An outdoor fireplace made the patio, located beneath the dramatic wing of the second floor, a pleasant place to be even on cold nights. It shared the chimney with its counterpart above.

16. Loeb named the place "Sliding Shutters" and used the name on his stationery.

17. HHH to author, Tape Series II.

18. UCLA, p. 157. There is every reason to believe that Jean shared Robsjohn-Gibbings's attitude toward the MoMA. See the final chapter in his *Mona Lisa's Mustache* (New York: Alfred A. Knopf, 1947), pp. 230–265.

19. HHH letter to author, August [n.d.], 1988.

20. Jean's article on Greene and Greene, which was published in *Architectural Forum* (see n. 9), was reprinted in *House Beautiful* as "Prophets without Honor: Greene and Greene," 92 (May 1950): 138–139. See Chapter 9, n. 1, for the reference to her Bernard Maybeck article.

21. Harris, "Bernard Ralph Maybeck, Architect," a talk accompanying an exhibition of photographs of Maybeck's work at the School of Design, North Carolina State University, March 23, 1987.

22. Ibid.

9. The Schism Intensified: Regionalism Becomes an Issue, 1948–1949

1. Jean Murray Bangs, "Bernard Ralph Maybeck, Architect, Comes into His Own," *Architectural Record* 100 (January 1948): 73–79.

2. Harris, "California Soil." A statement written to accompany photographs of HHH work shown in an exhibition, Six California Architects, Melbourne, Australia, 1948, POAA, p. 98.

3. NCSU. See also "Northwest Architects Meet at Eugene," *Architectural Record* (October 1954): 16; and Kenneth Frampton's comments published as "Ten Points on an Architecture of Regionalism: A Provisional Polemic," *Center* 3 (1987): 20–27.

4. Wayne Andrews, *Architecture, Ambition and Americans* (New York: Harper and Brothers, 1947), pp. 252–287.

5. Ibid.

6. Andrea Oppenheimer Dean, *Bruno Zevi on Modern Architecture*, with a foreword by Peter Blake (New York: Rizzoli, 1983), p. 7.

7. Zevi, *Towards an Organic Architecture*, pp. 105–106.

8. Vincent Scully, *Modern Architecture*, p. 15, and "Doldrums in the Suburbs," *Journal of the Society of Architectural Historians* 24, no. 1 (March 1965): 36–37.

9. Lewis Mumford, "Two Chicago Fairs," *New Republic*, January 21, 1931, p. 271.

10. Sigfried Giedion, *Space, Time and Architecture* (Cambridge, Mass.: Harvard University Press, 1941; 5th ed., 1967), p. 500.

11. Deborah Frances Pokinski, *The Development of the Modern American Style*, p. 2. Sarnitz, *R. M. Schindler*, p. 23, pins the crisis of the International Style on the false reasoning that led Hitchcock and Johnson to refer to European Modernism as a style to begin with.

12. James Marston Fitch, "The New American Architecture Started 70 Years Ago," *House Beautiful* 92 (May 1950): 134–137. Fitch was then the architecture editor of *House Beautiful*.

13. Joseph Hudnut, "Post Modern Architecture," from *Architecture and the Spirit of Man*, in *Roots of Contemporary Architecture*, ed. Lewis Mumford (New York: Reinhold Publishing, 1952), pp. 306–315.

14. When Scully discusses the symposium in "Doldrums" (*Journal of the Society of Architectural Historians*), p. 36, he demonstrates Mumford's points about organic architecture using a photograph of a Harris house rather than one of a Bay Area architect. The actual photograph reproduced in the article is the Birtcher house of 1941, not the Johnson house of 1949, as it is labeled. Clearly, Scully intended the Johnson house to be used, as it was this house he described as "Romantic Modern" in his *Modern Architecture*, p. 15. In "Doldrums" he is setting up the same polemic; namely, the one posed by Gropius's "Classical Modern" and Harris's "Romantic Modern."

15. Marcel Breuer at the 1948 symposium, as quoted by Jordy, *The Impact of European Modernism*, pp. 175–176.

16. Ibid., n. 13, p. 436.

17. Ibid., p. 175.

18. Ibid., p. 187.

19. HHH letter to author, August [n.d.], 1988.

20. Sarnitz, *R. M. Schindler*, p. 26; Schindler, "Space Architecture," *CAA* 47 (January 1935): 19.

1. Drexler and Hines, *The Architecture of Richard Neutra*, p. 11–13.

2. Elizabeth Mock, *Built in the U.S.A.* (New York: Museum of Modern Art, 1945), p. 16.

3. *Time*, August 15, 1949—Neutra is "Man of the Year," *tyle*, p. 2.

9. Decline of the West, 1950

Banham, *Los Angeles: The Architecture of Four Ecologies*, p. 54, 226, 229–230.

UCLA, pp. 130–131. Harris and Jean were close to Jere *Johnson*, who published *California Arts and Architecture*. 'hen she was expecting a baby and needed to find someone to *run* the magazine while she was away, they suggested John Entenza, whom she subsequently hired. Soon afterwards, Entenza *acquired* the magazine for very little money and became the *permanent* editor. The Harrises believed that Johnson had *been* cheated, that Entenza's lawyer father and his partner *Della* Gramer had put undue pressure on her to sell it. This *episode* caused the Harrises to break with Entenza, though *they* did remain on speaking terms with him.

See Esther McCoy, *The Case Study Houses 1945–1962* (Los *Angeles*: Hennessey and Ingalls, 1977).

The Harrises knew that *California Arts and Architecture* fed *the* national magazines like *Architectural Record* and *Architectural Forum* and influenced the directors of the Museum of *Modern* Art. They introduced Entenza to the editors and curators they knew in an effort to help him get started. They believed *that CAA* documented the distinctive place that was California. *Making* the magazine national and international obliterated that *distinction.* UCLA, pp. 130–133.

HHH letter to author, August [n.d.], 1988.

Banham, *Los Angeles*, p. 223.

Gebhard, *Schindler*, p. 188.

David Gebhard and Robert Winter, *Architecture in Los Angeles* (Salt Lake City: Gibbs M. Smith, Peregrine Smith Books, *1985*), p. 305.

HHH letter to author, November 23, 1985.

3. Harris, "Client Form," a speech first given as a talk to a student group, School of Design, North Carolina State University, *1981*. It is one of Harris's favorite lectures, perhaps because it *involves* the listener directly in the development of the English *house* organic plan. POAA, pp. 127–132.

11. Ibid., p. 130.

12. HHH to author, Tape Series I.

13. HHH to author, Tape Series II.

14. Ibid.

15. UCLA, pp. 216–219.

16. The discussion of Frank Lloyd Wright's influence on Harris in Fallbrook was enriched by David Barrow's very interesting and thoughtful comments.

11. "We're Not Canning Tomatoes": The University of Texas at Austin, 1951–1955

1. HHH to author and Frank Harmon. Comment made while driving through West Texas on a tour of Harris homes.

2. Harris taught as an instructor at the Chouinard Art Institute from 1938 to 1940 and again in 1944. He was visiting professor at USC in the summers of 1940 and 1942 and spent the summer of 1942 and the spring and winter terms of 1945 at UCLA. Just prior to becoming director of the UT School of Architecture in 1951 he had been a visiting critic at Yale University. He spent a month (November 15 to December 17) again at Yale in 1952. After leaving UT he was a visiting critic at the University of Minnesota (1956) and an adjunct professor at Columbia University (1960 to 1962). He joined the faculty of North Carolina State University in February 1962. In 1967 he was a visiting critic at Ball State University in Muncie, Indiana.

3. David George, former Harris associate in Dallas, to author.

4. Hugo Leipziger-Pearce to author.

5. HHH to author, Tape Series II. Jean Harris mentioned the Goldsmith letter to me, but I have been unable to find it in either *California Arts & Architecture* or *Pencil Points*, the latter of which printed a very critical review by Magonigle, "The Upper Ground" (March 1935): 113.

6. Ibid. See also Harris, letter to David Thurman, October 14, 1986. Opening remarks on Hoesli as well as the answer to Thurman's question no. 8. See also HHH letter to author, August [n.d.], 1988.

7. HHH, letter to David Thurman, October 14, 1986. Answer to Thurman's question no. 3.

8. David Alan Thurman, "Towards a Unified Vision of Modern Architecture: The Texas Experiment, 1951–56," Master's thesis, University of Texas at Austin, 1988, p. 13.

9. HHH to author, Tapes Series II.

10. Ibid.

11. HHH letter to author, March 25, 1987. Harris wrote, "Jean [and Colin] appreciated one another. He was at the house a good deal and I remember Jean's frequent question in proposing an afternoon snack: 'How about smoked oysters?' and his invariable answer: 'Smoked oysters would be fine.' I am afraid you would have to know Colin to enjoy this exchange."

12. Thurman, "Towards a Unified Vision of Modern Architecture," p. 13.

13. Ibid., pp. 20–21.

14. HHH letter to David Thurman, March 25, 1987.

15. Ibid.

16. Ibid.

17. Ibid.

18. Harris's address to the members of the 1955 graduating class at the School of Architecture, University of Texas at Austin, is published in NCSU, p. 14.

19. Barrow acquired Harris's entire collection of drawings and photographs in 1984 and donated them to the Architectural Drawings Collection of the Architecture and Planning Library, a branch of the General Libraries at The University of Texas at Austin.

20. HHH letter to David Thurman, March 25, 1987.

21. The Pace Setter House was sold by Joe Maberry, the Dallas homebuilder who had worked closely with Harris on it in 1954. It was moved in 1957 to 12020 Stone Brook Circle in Dallas. Harris admired Maberry's work, but was somewhat disappointed by the completed house because some of the furnishings— shades and shutters and other such appointments—chosen by the *House Beautiful* staff were not in keeping with the character of the house.

22. HHH letter to David Thurman, March 25, 1987. See also HHH to author, Tape Series II.

23. Jean Murray Bangs Harris, "Escape from Youth," talk before the women's club in San Angelo, Texas, ca. 1956.

24. Ibid.

25. HHH letter to David Thurman, March 25, 1987 and HHH letter to author, August [n.d.], 1988.

26. Joseph Barry, "Report on the American Battle between Good and Bad Modern Houses," *House Beautiful* 95 (May 1953): 172–173.

27. Elizabeth Gordon, "The Threat to the Next America," *House Beautiful* 95 (April 1953): 126–131. For a discussion of this very controversial article, see the open letter to Gordon from *Progressive Architecture* 34 (May 1953): 234; also the June issue, pp. 9–10; and the July issue, pp. 9–10.

28. HHH letter to author, August [n.d.], 1988.

29. Jean Murray Bangs, "Greene and Greene," *Architectural Forum* (October 1948): 88.

30. HHH letter to author, August [n.d.], 1988.

31. Harris was impressed with Mumford's *Sticks and Stones* for the way in which he talked about an architecture that was humanistic. The day after he met Weston Havens (at a beach club belonging to a mutual friend), he recalls that the two of them started talking about the book as they stood in ocean water up to their waists.

32. Jean Murray Bangs, review of *Roots of Contemporary Architecture* by Lewis Mumford, *Progressive Architecture* 34 (March 1953): 166, 168, 170.

33. Colin Rowe, "Roots of American Architecture: An Answer to Mumford's Analysis," *Architectural Review* 116 (August 1954): 75–78.

34. Harris told Judy Stonefield that Giedion was working on *Mechanization Takes Command* when they met; UCLA, p. 180. About the book Harris recalled, "He and Jean had great arguments over that." When pressed to remember what the nature of their argument was, Harris was not sure, but felt it must have had to do with the kitchen, as Jean had a strong interest in these spaces herself. HHH letter to author, August [n.d.], 1988.

12. The Ten-Fingered Grasp of Reality in the Split Culture of Fort Worth and Dallas, 1955–1962

1. HHH to author, Tape Series III.

2. Ibid.

3. Ibid.

4. Gebhard and Winter, *Architecture in Los Angeles*, p. 142.

5. HHH letter to Jan Strand, September 14, 1975, POA, pp. 99–101. Harris also mentions here that he and Jean are considering writing a book on Texas courthouses.

6. The Townsend house appeared under the heading "Simple Plan for Privacy" in an article entitled "Homes that Achieve Most in Livability," *Life Magazine*, September 29, 1958, pp. 60– 61. It was reprinted in *House & Home* 14 (December 1958): 128–129 as "A House to Show the Fun of Family Life."

7. Harris discussed his and Jean's feelings about not having children in HHH letter to author, March 19, 1986.

8. Seymour and Jean Eisenberg to the author, August 1989.

9. Ines Antrim letter to author, September 8, 1989.

10. For more on the Motel-on-the-Mountain, see "Two Mo

s: Atlantic Coast Motel Has Pacific Design," *Architectural* *rum* 105 (August 1956): 124–127; "The Motel on the Moun- n," *Interiors* 116 (September 1956): 102–107; and "Motel ng on a Hilltop," *Life*, August 12, 1957, p. 93.

. "Making a Monument Work," *Architectural Forum* 111 ly 1958): 99–104.

. For more on Sullivan and his banks, see Larry Millett, *The* rve of the Arch: The Story of Louis Sullivan's Owatonna Bank . Paul: Minnesota Historical Society Press, 1985) and Lauren ingarden, *Louis H. Sullivan: The Banks, 1906–1920* (Cam- idge: MIT Press, 1987).

. James F. Fitch, address on the occasion of the rededica- n of Louis Sullivan's Security Bank & Trust Company Build- g, presented at a special meeting of the Minnesota Chapter the American Institute of Architects, Owatonna, Minnesota, ne 12, 1958. (Hereafter designated as Fitch Address.)

. HHH letter to author, February 17, 1989. See also Deborah ances Pokinski, *The Development of the American Modern* le, pp. 77–78.

. Fitch Address.

. Harris, "Divide to Simplify, Multiply to Magnify," a School Design Public Lecture, North Carolina State University, 1965, AA, p. 150.

. Ibid., p. 153.

. The 1946 showroom and repair shop for the Treanor uipment Company in Delano, California, may have been the eans by which Harris realized some of his ideas for the ill- ed Jelton Motor Company project he had designed a year lier with Wurster.

. HHH to author, Tape Series III.

. The Cranfill Apartments with a single run staircase, loft- e room above a kitchen, and double height exposure to the tdoors through a wall of windows also bear a strong connec- n to Harris's own later house in Raleigh (1968).

. Harris wrote an enthusiastic review of Frank Lloyd right's building in 1959 for the book *The Dallas Theater Cen- r*. It was published in NCSU, p. 20.

. Cole Weston sent Harris aerial photographs of his site, owing the soft undulations of the mountains as they curved wnward to meet the violent Pacific. Jean and Harris had own Edward Weston during their time in Los Angeles. They et Cole when they approached the father about photograph- g the elderly Greene Brothers in late 1948. He encouraged em to hire Cole instead.

. HHH to author, Tape Series I.

24. David Barrow to author, telephone conversation, October 1988. Of Aalto's architecture, Harris wrote, "I believe my build- ings share with his a similar lack of tightness and depend for their simplicity on a generic harmony of parts rather than a stylistic strait-jacket." HHH letter to author, February 17, 1989.

25. HHH to author, Tape Series III.

26. Ibid.

27. HHH to author, Tape Series II.

28. David Barrow conversation with author, October 1988.

29. Harris, "The Changing Practice of Architecture," a panel talk before the California Council of Architects, Yosemite Valley, 1960, NCSU, pp. 21–23.

30. Harris believed an ideal commercial client would be someone like Sullivan's Owatonna patron, Carl Bennett, "a small town banker with imagination, forceful character and great respect for his fellow man." Ibid., p. 22. Harris always in- tended to write a book on Bennett, whom he came to know through reading letters the young Bennett had written home to his family from Harvard. Mrs. Bennett was still alive when Har- ris renovated the bank and Harris made a point to interview her on the subject of her husband's collaboration. Harris ex- plained how Carl Bennett "struck sparks in Louis Sullivan" when he gave a talk before the 1965 Northwest Regional Confer- ence of the AIA at Glacier National Park. The talk was published as "Design Dimensions," *North Carolina Architect* (September 1966): 8, 16–17.

31. Harris, p. 22, "Changing Practice," emphasis added.

32. Ibid.

33. Harris told the congregation of Unitarians in Dallas what their building would feel like by describing this analogy. "The interior of the auditorium reminds us of a clearing in the forest. It is as though we had been moving along a narrow path, driven forward by the dark wall of trees pressing against us on each side and closing in behind us. Suddenly the walls are gone. We are in a great open space filled with sunlight from above. We experience an overwhelming sense of release." Har- ris recalled the speech in a talk for a seminar at the Ecumenical Institute in Winston-Salem, North Carolina, entitled "Building as Shelter, Invitation and Presence," October 15–16, 1975, POAA, pp. 7–13.

34. HHH to author, Tape Series II.

35. HHH letter to author, August [n.d.], 1988.

36. Scully, *Modern Architecture*, pp. 51–52.

37. HHH letter to author, August [n.d.], 1988.

38. Harris's complete passage was, "Unfortunately we con-

sider inoffensiveness a virtue in building. Only the positive has virtue, and until one has found a building that is every inch alive and into whose arms he surrenders himself as to a partner in a dance, he has yet to discover architecture." "Houses by Harwell Hamilton Harris," *Architectural Forum* 72 (March 1940): 171.

13. The River Flows On: North Carolina, 1962–1975

1. See Kamphoefner's "Architectural Education," NCSU, vol. 8, no. 1, pp. 3–8.
2. NCSU, p. 3.
3. HHH letter to author, March 1984.
4. NCSU, p. 23.
5. Harris, "Why Nature?" *North Carolina Architect* (June–July 1968): 11.

6. Ibid.
7. Paul Lamb pointed out the connection between the Ma[...] beck roof form and that of Harris's Van Alstyne house.
8. Dr. Kenneth Sugioka to HHH, Tape Series III.
9. Ibid.
10. HHH to author, conversation while touring St. Gil[...] March 1984. When landscape architect Judy Harmon e[...] pressed delight that the focus of the church complex was [...] nature, Harris, in good humor, asked, "Well, have you ev[...] heard of a great revelation that took place *indoors?*"

14. Retirement

1. HHH letter to author, August 17, 1985.
2. HHH letter to author, November 23, 1985.

Chronological Harris Bibliography

Except where noted with an asterisk, all the buildings listed below are represented by drawings in the Architectural Drawings Collection, the Architecture and Planning Library of the General Libraries at the University of Texas at Austin. The collection is also the repository of numerous photographs documenting Harris's work. Because Harris is included in most anthologies of American and Modern architecture, books that refer to him will not be found below. The interested reader will find generous bibliographic information for the most important treatments of Harris in the endnotes, where the writings of Esther McCoy, Bruno Zevi, Wayne Andrews, David Gebhard, Thomas Hines, Vincent Scully, Kenneth Frampton, and others are discussed. This book has overtaken and superseded my own small catalog on Harris, published in 1985 by the Center for the Study of American Architecture, part of the University of Texas at Austin School of Architecture. The little volume *Harwell Hamilton Harris, a Selection of His Work and Writings*, published by the students of the School of Design, North Carolina State University in 1965 (and denoted in the notes as NCSU), is still the best and most direct source of Harris's many thoughtful writings on architecture.

1927
EXHIBITIONS

"Southern California Painters and Sculptors." Los Angeles Museum of History, Art and Science [HHH exhibits sculpture]

1928
EXHIBITIONS

San Diego Museum of Art [HHH exhibits sculpture]

1929
BUILDINGS AND DESIGNS

Proposed residence for Ryland Thomas
Project design for Richard Neutra's class
The Los Angeles Academy of Modern Art

1930
PUBLICATIONS

By Harwell Harris

"Ein amerikanischer Flughafen." *Die Form* 5 (April 1930): 184–185. [Neutra published this article under Harris's byline]

About Neutra and his assistants, including Harris, Gregory Ain, Donald Griffen, and Rognilde Liljedahl

"Projekt für einen Flugverkehrs—Unschlaghof Rush City." *Deutsche Bauzeitung* 64 (February 1930): 21–23

Neutra, Richard. "Terminals?—Transfer!" *Architectural Record* 68 (August 1930): 99–104.

1931
BUILDINGS AND DESIGNS

Multifamily dwelling for Arthur Jensen
Occidental Boulevard
Los Angeles, California
(not built)

Residence and studio for Lewis Gaffney
Silver Lake
Los Angeles, California
(not built)

1932

BUILDINGS AND DESIGNS

Residence remodeling for Fred Hasenauer
717 N. Lafayette Park Place
Los Angeles, California

1933

BUILDINGS AND DESIGNS

Residence for Miss Pauline Lowe
478 Punahou Drive
Altadena, California
(1933–34)

Residence for Barney Rudd
2517 Ivanhoe Drive
Los Angeles, California
(not built)

1934

PUBLICATIONS

About Harwell Harris

"Suggesting the Japanese." *House Beautiful* (October 1934): 72–73. [Pauline Lowe house]

EXHIBITIONS

House Beautiful Traveling Show, exhibited in the leading department stores of the country

AWARDS

Honorable Mention—Class III, 7th Annual *House Beautiful* competition

1935

BUILDINGS AND DESIGNS

Residence for Professor and Mrs. Graham Laing
1642 Pleasant Way
Pasadena, California

Residence for Helene Kershner
3905 Brilliant Way
Los Angeles, California
(addition in 1948 for A. Stewart Ballinger)

*Addition to residence for Marquiset
Altadena, California

Residence for Mr. and Mrs. Harwell Hamilton Harris
The Fellowship Park House
2311 Fellowship Parkway
Los Angeles, California

*Residence remodeling for C. R. Harper

Residence for Stella Gramer
701 Holmby Avenue
Westwood
Los Angeles, California

PUBLICATIONS

By Harwell Harris

"In Designing the Small House." *California Arts & Architecture* 46–47 (January 1935): 20–21. [Pauline Lowe house]

About Harwell Harris

Oyer, George. "Concerning Competitions." *California Arts & Architecture* 46–47 (May 1935): 27. [Charges that the Pauline Lowe house was plagiarized]

"California Charges." *Architectural Forum* 62 (June 1935): 42. [Pauline Lowe house]

"What Constitutes Plagiarism in Architecture?" *Apéritif* 1, no. (1935): 12. [Pauline Lowe house]

Architectural Forum 63 (October 1935): 316–317 and 360–361. [Graham Laing and Pauline Lowe houses, respectively]

"A Frank Lloyd Wright House with a Hat On." *California Arts & Architecture* 48 (November 1935): 20–21. [Graham Laing house]

Architect & Engineer 123 (December 1935): 42–43, 45. [Pauline Lowe and Graham Laing houses]

EXHIBITIONS

House Beautiful Traveling Show

1936

BUILDINGS AND DESIGNS

Residence for W. L. Long
2041 Live Oak Drive
Los Angeles, California
(not built)

Cabin for Dr. and Mrs. Hugo Benioff
Mammoth Lakes, California

Residence and shop for Mr. and Mrs. Edward De Steiguer
0 Glen Sumner Road
Pasadena, California

Residence for Ian Campbell
Pasadena, California
(not built)

Residence for John Carr
Brentwood, California

Residence addition for Mr. and Mrs. Robert Campbell
416 Wilson Avenue
San Marino, California

Residence for Mr. and Mrs. Horace Fraser
Bonnie Avenue
Pasadena, California
(not built)

937

BUILDINGS AND DESIGNS

Residence for Walter Joel
742 Silverwood Terrace
Los Angeles, California

Residence for John Entenza
75 Mesa Road
Santa Monica, California

Cabin for Pierre Dick
Big Tujunga, California

Residence for Marion Clark
Valley View at 17th Street
Carmel-by-the-Sea, California

Buick Sales and Service Building
246–58 Glendon Avenue
West Los Angeles, California

Residence for Lee Blair
Beech Knoll Road
Los Angeles, California
(not built)

Pottenger Elementary School Unit
Monrovia, California
(not built)

* Residence for Roy Rosen
Montrose, California
(not built)

Residence for Greta Granstedt (and Max DeVega)
7922 Woodrow Wilson Drive
Los Angeles, California
(1937–38)

Store and Office Building for Chester Fritz
8500 Sunset Boulevard
Los Angeles, California

PUBLICATIONS

About Harwell Harris

"A House in Fellowship Park, Los Angeles." *California Arts & Architecture* 51 (March 1937): 24–25.

"Oriental Calm for the West." *House Beautiful* 79 (March 1937): 46. [Fellowship Park house]

"House in Fellowship Park, Los Angeles, California." *Architectural Forum* 66 (April 1937): 278–281.

"Residence for John Entenza." *California Arts & Architecture* 52 (July 1937): 33.

"House in Fellowship Park." *Architectural Forum* (August 1937): 75–76, 82–83. [Pittsburgh Glass Institute competition]

"The Los Angeles Home of Miss Helene Kershner." *California Arts & Architecture* 52 (August 1937): 29.

"Novel Nautical House Idea." *LAAC Mercury*, September 25, 1937, p. 8. [Entenza house]

Architectural Forum 67 (October 1937): 264, 353. [Walter Joel house details]

"Southern California Chapter of the American Institute of Architects Honor Awards." *California Arts & Architecture* (November 1937: 12). [Fellowship Park house; Laing singled out also]

EXHIBITIONS

House Beautiful Traveling Show

Pittsburgh Glass Institute, an exhibition that toured the country under the auspices of the American Federation of the Arts

Paris International Exposition, Cercle des Architectes Modernes, Paris, France

Los Angeles City College, Harwell Hamilton Harris—One Man Show, Los Angeles, California

AWARDS

First Prize—Class 1A, 1st Annual Pittsburgh Glass Institute competition [Fellowship Park house]

Honorable Mention—Class III, 9th Annual *House Beautiful* competition [Fellowship Park house]

1938

BUILDINGS AND DESIGNS

Residence for Harold Swann
Hope Ranch
Santa Barbara, California
(not built)

* Residence for W. L. Montgomery
San Dimas, California
(not built)

* Motel Chain for the Winter Company
(not built)

* Second residence for John Carr
Brentwood, California
(not built)

Residence for Anne Bauer
Glen Oaks Boulevard
Glendale, California
(not built)

Residence for Mr. and Mrs. George Bauer
2528 East Glen Oaks Boulevard
Glendale, California

Residence for Edmund Stiff
8420 Yucca Drive
Los Angeles, California

Residence for Mr. and Mrs. J. Musick
3019 Passmore Drive
Los Angeles, California

PUBLICATIONS

About Harwell Harris

Rice, Norman N. "Planning a Physician's Office Suite." *Architectural Record* (February 1938): 59. [Project drawing]

"Industrial Design: Its Parentage and Motives." California Graduate School of Design, Carmelita Garden, Pasadena, January 29–February 27, 1938.

Edgerton, Giles. "The House Unpretentious but Convenient." *Arts & Decoration* 48 (March 1938): 27–29. [Fellowship Park house]

"A House for Miss Marion Clark at Carmel-by-the-Sea." *California Arts & Architecture* 53 (March 1938): 27–29.

"A Dwelling for Mr. John Entenza, Santa Monica, California." *California Arts & Architecture* 53 (May 1938): 26–27.

"A Residence Designed for Miss Greta Granstedt in Hollywood." *California Arts & Architecture* 54 (July 1938): 18

"A House That Grows & Grows." *Sunset* (August 1938): 14–15. [Pauline Lowe house]

"Carmel by the Sea—House for Marion Clark." *Architectural Forum* 69 (September 1938): 213–216.

"House for Miss Helene Kershner, Los Angeles, California." *Architectural Record* 84 (October 1938): 100–102.

"House for John Entenza, Santa Monica, California." *Architectural Forum* 69 (November 1938): 349–351.

Architect & Engineer 135 (December 1938): 42. [Fellowship Park living room]

EXHIBITIONS

Washburn College Art Department, Topeka, Kansas.

"Industrial Design, Its Parentage and Motives," California Graduate School of Design, Pasadena, California

"Modern Domestic Architecture in the U.S." U.S. Housing Authority, exhibition prepared by the Museum of Modern Art

"Harwell Hamilton Harris—One Man Show," Chouinard Art Institute, Los Angeles, California

"Harwell Hamilton Harris—One Man Show," Los Angeles City College, Los Angeles, California

Pittsburgh Glass Institute permanent exhibition, Institute of Decorative Arts and Crafts, Rockefeller Center, New York, New York

"1937 Honor Awards for Residential Architecture and the Allied Arts," Southern California Chapter of the American Institute of Architects, Los Angeles, California

House Beautiful Traveling Show

AWARDS

First Prize Class 1A, 2nd Annual Pittsburgh Glass Institute competition [Bauer house]

onor Award, Southern California Chapter of the American Institute of Architects

939

BUILDINGS AND DESIGNS

Residence for Byron Pumphrey
15 Kingman Avenue
Santa Monica Canyon
Los Angeles, California

Second residence for Mr. and Mrs. Lee Blair
763 Fredonia Avenue
Los Angeles, California

Chemi-Culture Sales Room for Ernest Brundin
26 Poplar
Montebello, California

Residence for Dr. and Mrs. Fred Harris
10 Avenue 64
Pasadena, California
(plans for an addition, 1975)

Residence for Mr. and Mrs. J. E. Power
160 La Canada Boulevard
La Canada, California

Residence for Edwin (Stan) Hawk
421 Silver Ridge
Los Angeles, California

Pottenger Laboratory
Monrovia, California
(not built)

Residence for John Huston
San Fernando Valley, California
(not built)

Residence for Mr. and Mrs. Theodore Blau
33 North Lucile Avenue
Los Angeles, California

Residence for Weston Havens
55 Panoramic Way
Berkeley, California
(1939–40; alterations and additions, 1967–68)

Residence for Dr. and Mrs. Alfred Pellicciotti
Monta Vista Avenue
Tujunga, California
(not built)

PUBLICATIONS

By Harwell Harris

"Wood." *California Arts & Architecture* 55 (May 1939): 16–17, 40. [Illustrated with Easton's Curtis Ranch, Altadena and a Lamella dome structure]

About Harwell Harris

"A House in Fellowship Park, Los Angeles." *Architecture and Building News* (January 27, 1939): 131–132.

"George Bauer Residence." *Architect & Engineer* 136–137 (March 1939): 38–39.

Southwest Builder & Contractor (May 1939): 55. [Buick salesroom's Lamella dome in ad for Summerbell Roof Structures]

"Comfortable." *Studebaker Wheel* (May 1939): 11. [George Bauer living room]

"House for G. C. Bauer." *Architectural Forum* 71 (July 1939): 16–18.

"The Residence of Mr. and Mrs. George C. Bauer." *California Arts & Architecture* 56 (August 1939): 19–21.

"Ein Sommerhaus am Waldersrand." *Das Ideale Heim* (October 1939): 323–324.

Williams, Melvin. "Fireplaces." *California Arts & Architecture* 56 (November 1939): 18. [Robert Campbell house]

EXHIBITIONS

"Harwell Hamilton Harris—One Man Show," Scripps College, Claremont, California

"Modern Architecture and Housing," U.S. Housing Authority, exhibition began in Topeka, Kansas, moved to Denver, Colorado, and made a circuit of the country

"Three Centuries of American Architecture," Museum of Modern Art, New York, New York

"Harwell Hamilton Harris—One Man Show," Chaffee Junior College, Ontario, California

"Harwell Hamilton Harris—One Man Show," University of California at Los Angeles, Los Angeles, California

1940

BUILDINGS AND DESIGNS

Proposed cottage for Fellowship Park
2311 Fellowship Parkway
Los Angeles, California
(not built)

* Remodeling of Francis Pottenger, Jr., Clinic Building
North Canyon Boulevard
Monrovia, California

Highway Hotel
Project for *Architectural Forum*

* Residence for Kenneth Anderson
Flintridge, California
(not built)

* Residence for Sophie Treadwell
Beverly Hills, California
(not built)

Grandview Gardens Restaurant
Castellar Street
New Chinatown
Los Angeles, California

Exhibition room for "America at Home"
South of the Golden Gate
New York World's Fair 1940
Long Island, New York

Cabin for John Adams Comstock
1373 Crest Road
Del Mar, California

Residence for Mr. and Mrs. Elwood E. Schwenk
14329 Millbrook Drive
Van Nuys, California

Alterations to residence for Mrs. Richard B. Fudger
631 North Crescent Drive
Beverly Hills, California

Residence for Mr. and Mrs. Dean McHenry
624 Holmby Avenue
Westwood
Los Angeles, California

Residence for Mr. and Mrs. Linden Naylor
60 Arden Road
Berkeley, California

Residence for Hobart Wong
1001 Castellar Street
Los Angeles, California
(not built)

* Remodeling of residence for Adolph Menjou
727 Bedford Drive
Berkeley, California

Residence for Mr. and Mrs. Milton E. Kahl
Shannon Road
Los Angeles, California

Residence for Mr. and Mrs. Herbert Alexander
2265 Micheltorena Street
Los Angeles, California

Residence for Mr. and Mrs. John Treanor
343 Greenacres Drive
Visalia, California
(Addition, 1949)

PUBLICATIONS

About Harwell Harris:

Sampson, Foster. "Modern Light for Living." *California Arts & Architecture* 57 (January 1940): 28–29. [Living room of Helene Kershner house]

"Houses by Harwell Hamilton Harris." *Architectural Forum* 72 (March 1940): 171–186. [Granstedt, De Steiguer, Hawk, Blair, and Powers houses]

"Weston Havens House on Steep Hill." *California Arts & Architecture* 57 (March 1940): 2+5. [Havens house drawing on cover]

"3 Modern California Houses." *California Arts & Architecture* 57 (April 1940): 18–19. [Greta Granstedt house]

"House in Pasadena." *Architectural Forum* 72 (April 1940): 243. [Fred Harris house]

Hamlin, Talbot. "Interior Decoration, 1940." *Pencil Points* 21 (July 1940): 438. [New York World's Fair room—"South of the Golden Gate"]

"Grandview Gardens Restaurant, China City." *California Arts & Architecture* 57 (August 1940): 22–23.

"The Highway Hotel." *Architectural Forum* 73 (October 1940): 248. [Designed for *Forum*'s "Design Decade"]

"Villa a Los Angeles." *Costruzione Casabella* 13 (December 1940): 42.

"Regional Determinants of Western House Architecture," arranged by California State Association of Architects, Golden Gate International Exhibition at San Francisco World's Fair, San Francisco, California

"Outstanding Examples of American Architecture," New York Architectural League, New York, New York

"What Is Modern Architecture?" Pottenger Galleries, Pasadena, California

"Space for Living," Telesis, San Francisco Museum of Art, San Francisco, California

"America at Home," New York World's Fair, exhibition room entitled "South of the Golden Gate," New York, New York

"Modern Architecture in Southern California," University of California at Los Angeles, Los Angeles, California

"Harwell Hamilton Harris—One Man Show," Los Angeles City College Department of Architecture, Los Angeles, California

"Architecture, Planning and Housing," American Institute of Architects and California Council of Architects, Palace of Fine Arts, San Francisco, California

"The Low Cost House," A & M College Department of Architecture and School of Engineering, College Station, Texas

1941

BUILDINGS AND DESIGNS

Residence for Mr. and Mrs. R. I. Kelsey
Berry Drive
Los Angeles, California

Residence for Dr. and Mrs. Harold Sox
Ridgeview Drive
Atherton, California

Addition to residence of Mr. and Mrs. Bernard A. Forrest
512 Beverly Drive
Beverly Hills, California

Remodeling of residence for W. H. Snyder
10879 Whipple Street
North Hollywood, California

Residence for Mr. and Mrs. Cecil Birtcher
Central Terrace
Los Angeles, California
(1941–42; alterations, 1949 for Mr. and Mrs. Jerome Share)

Residence for Dr. Lodewijk Lek
1600 Mecca Drive
La Jolla, California
(1941–42)

PUBLICATIONS

About Harwell Harris

"Houses." *Architectural Record* 89 (January 1941): 94–95. [Fred Harris house]

Kentiku Sekai (April 1941): 12–14. [This folio of four houses discusses the Granstedt, Entenza, Clark, and Bauer houses]

Hamlin, Talbot. "Architecture in America Today." *New Republic*, August 4, 1941, pp. 156–157.

"Young America Builds." *Mademoiselle* (August 1941): 238. [Personal profile]

"Two-way Cupboards." *Architectural Forum* 75 (October 1941): 281. [Stan Hawk house]

EXHIBITIONS

"Harwell Hamilton Harris—One Man Show," Long Beach Junior College, Long Beach, California

"40 under 40," New York Architectural League, New York, New York

"Harwell Hamilton Harris—One Man Show," Yale University Department of Architecture (arranged by a student group under the direction of Edward Butler Crittenden)

"Design Decade," Baltimore Museum of Art, Baltimore, Maryland

"Fine Arts Exhibition," Pomona County Fair, Pomona, California

"Harwell Hamilton Harris—One Man Show," Redlands University Art Department, Redlands, California

Guatemala Fair (ten photographs, now part of the permanent collection of the goverment school), Guatemala City, Guatemala

George Washington High School, Los Angeles, California

Marlborough School, Los Angeles, California

1942

BUILDINGS AND DESIGNS

Project for the *Ladies Home Journal*

Residence for Mr. and Mrs. Langford Brown
Vista Way
Chula Vista, California
(not built)

Project for the Revere Copper and Brass Company
The Segmental House
(not built)

Project for *Architectural Forum*
Bathing Lounge
(not built)

* Residence for Roy Marquardt
Hawthorne, California
(not built)

Residence for Mr. and Mrs. Fritz Meier
2240 Lakeshore Avenue
Los Angeles, California

* Residence for Mr. Jack Calvin
Sitka, Alaska
(1942–46)

PUBLICATIONS

About Harwell Harris

Hamlin, Talbot. "The Trend of American Architecture."
Harpers (January 1942).

Morley, Dr. Grace L. McCann. "Architects in an Exhibition."
California Arts & Architecture (March 1942): 24–35.
[Exhibition at San Francisco Museum of Art with discussion
and illustrations of the Granstedt house]

"Inn with Cottages." *New York Beaux Arts Institute of Design
Bulletin* 18 (March 1942): 35.

"New California Architecture." *Time*, April 20, 1942, p. 48.
[Granstedt house]

"Chinatown Restaurant." *California Arts & Architecture* 59
(May 1942): 54. [Grandview Gardens]

"The Browns Build a Wartime House with Peace Aims." *Ladies
Home Journal* (July 1942): 66. [Includes plan and model of
the project commissioned by the magazine]

"The New House 194x." *Architectural Forum* 77 (September
1942): 116. [Plan and perspective drawing of the bathing
lounge]

"For a Quicker Start in 194x." *Architectural Forum* 77
(December 1942): 108–109. [Segmental house for Revere
Copper and Brass]

"A House with a Future." Revere Copper and Brass booklet.
[Segmental house]

"Blueprints of Tomorrow." Booklet announcing series. *Sunset*.

EXHIBITIONS

"Western Living: Five Houses under $7,500," San Francisco
Museum of Art, San Francisco, California

"Five Western Architects," Museum of Modern Art (Birtcher
model kept on extended loan, show by appointment), New
York, New York

Los Angeles Museum of History, Art and Science, Los Angeles,
California

"Modern Living," Museum of Modern Art," New York,
New York

1943

BUILDINGS AND DESIGNS

Project for *Sunset*
Postwar house
(not built)

Bathing lounge for *Sunset*

* Alterations to the Airwick Office for W. H. Wheeler
New York, New York

A utility core design for Donald Deskey
New York, New York

PUBLICATIONS

By Harwell Harris

Project and article for *Sunset* (May 1943).

About Harwell Harris

"La Jolla House." *Pencil Points* 24 (May 1943): 50–55. [Louis
Lek house]

"Berkeley Hillside House for Weston Havens." *Architectural
Forum* 79 (September 1943): 76–87.

"Multiple Dwelling in 194X." *Architectural Forum* 79 (September 1943): 26.

"Multiple Dwelling in 194x." *Pencil Points* 24 (September
1943): 27.

"A House with a View." *Interiors* 103 (September 1943): 18–23.

1944

BUILDINGS AND DESIGNS

Residence for the Headmaster at North Country School
Lake Placid, New York

Project for *Woman's Home Companion*
"House for the Shumways"
Greenfield, Connecticut
(not built)

Project for *Architectural Record* and *Petroleum News*
Motor Lodge and Service Station
Pennsylvania Turnpike
(not built)

Chemical Plant for Gallowhur Chemical Company
Claremont, New Hampshire
(not built)

Salt Water Laboratory for Gallowhur Chemical Company
Fire Island, New York
(not built)

Honeymoon cottage/hunting lodge for George Gallowhur
Windsor, Vermont

PUBLICATIONS

About Harwell Harris

"Scene from Above." *House & Garden* (January 1944): 54–55.
[Weston Havens house]

"Student's Room." *New York Beaux Arts Institute of Design
Bulletin* 20 (February 1944): 19.

"Station for a Highway Hostelry." *Architectural Record* 95
(February 1944): 78–80.

"How to Judge Modern." *House Beautiful* 86 (August 1944):
47–49, 70–71. [Weston Havens house]

"Harwell Hamilton Harris, arquitecto. Obra casa para el Sr.
Weston Havens." *Revista de Arquitectura* 29 (August 1944):
364–372.

"Our Homes and Our Children." *Household Magazine*
(October 1944): 1. [De Steiguer house]

"Berkeley House for Weston Havens." *Studio Yearbook* 128
(October 1944): 101–103.

"Dining Kitchens." *Better Homes & Gardens* (November 1944):
20–21. [HHH designed "dining kitchen" for the magazine]

"How the Shumways Can Build Their House." *Women's Home
Companion* 71 (December 1944): 78–80.

"Residencia en Pasadena." *El Arquitecto Peruano* 8 (December
1944): 11–12.

EXHIBITIONS

Industrial Design Exhibition, Museum of Modern Art, New
York, New York

"New Architecture in the U.S." (traveling exhibition prepared
by the Museum of Modern Art), shown by the Société de
L'Art, Cairo, Egypt

1945

BUILDINGS AND DESIGNS

Residence for Mr. and Mrs. Lewis Allen
Ridgeview Drive
San Mateo, California
(not built)

Caretaker's apartment for Mr. and Mrs. Austin Longcroft
1653 Rancho Avenue
Glendale, California

* Residence 2 for Richmond Kelsey
North Hollywood, California

Residence and music studio for Mr. and Mrs. John
Pennington
Pasadena, California
(not built)

* Residence for W. L. Montgomery
(not built)

* Display rooms for Cannel & Chaffin
Los Angeles, California

Lodge, portable cabin, and studio for John Nesbit
Circle M Ranch
Big Sur, California
(1945–46)

Sport Center
Ice Rink and Amusement Center
West Los Angeles, California
(not built)

Hospital for Francis Pottenger
Monrovia, California
(1945–46, not built)

Studio for Harwell Hamilton Harris
2311 Fellowship Parkway
Los Angeles, California

A highway hotel for Pauline Lindbloom
El Monte, California
(not built)

Garage and sales building for Jelton Motor Company with
   Wurster, Barnard and Emmons, Associates
Oakland, California
(not built)

* Residence for George Taylor
Hollywood, California
(not built)

Salen Emergency Hospital
Wilcox Street
Hollywood, California
(not built)

* Residence for O. K. Meyers
Visalia, California

Project for *Mademoiselle*
(not built)

Tool and tea house for John Pennington
Pasadena, California

A house for the Ingersoll Steel and Disc Division of the Borg
   Warner Corporation
U-8 Crown Street, Hillsdale Park
Kalamazoo County, Michigan

* Office for the Kimbal Advertising Agency
Los Angeles, California
(not built)

PUBLICATIONS

By Harwell Harris

"Modern or Traditional?" *Better Homes and Gardens* 23
   (February 1945): 28+.

About Harwell Harris

Architectural Forum 82 (April 1945): 58. [Portrait of HHH]

"House of Timber in California." *Architects' Journal* 101 (May
   1945): 387–392.

"People Who Influence Your Life—Meet Harwell Hamilton
   Harris." *House Beautiful* 87 (July 1945): 54–55. [Profile of
   Harris with photo by Karsh]

"Motel." *New York Beaux Arts Institute of Design Bulletin* 21
   (October 1945): 18–19.

EXHIBITIONS

"Harwell Hamilton Harris—One Man Show," Bennington
   College, Bennington, Vermont

"Outstanding Examples of Modern Architecture in the Last
   Decade," Museum of Modern Art, 15th Anniversary
   Exhibition, New York, New York

"Harwell Hamilton Harris—One Man Show," Yale University,
   New Haven, Connecticut

"New Architecture in the U.S.," U.S. Office of War Information

1946

BUILDINGS AND DESIGNS

Residence for *Good Housekeeping*
(not built)

House and garage for *Mademoiselle*
(not built)

A solar house for Libbey-Owens-Ford Glass Company
San Marino, California
(not built)

* Cottage for Irvine Chapman
Balboa Beach, California
(not built)

Fashion Lounge for W. J. Schminke
2845 West Seventh Street
Los Angeles, California

Residence addition for Mrs. Allan Lee Hancock
2000 North La Brea Terrace
Los Angeles, California

Residence for Mr. and Mrs. John G. Sobieski
1420 Sierra Madre Boulevard
San Marino, California

Showroom and repair shop for the Treanor Equipment
   Company
U.S. Highway 99
Delano, California

Residence and stables for Mr. and Mrs. Austin Longcroft
1653 Rancho Avenue
Glendale, California

Residence for Mr. and Mrs. F. M. Hatz
Palos Verdes Drive
Palos Verdes, California
(additions in 1950)

antvoort Residence
a Canada, California
(1946–47; not built)

Residence for Mr. and Mrs. Clarence Wyle
964 Rancho Drive
Ojai, California
(1946–48)

PUBLICATIONS

About Harwell Harris

La vivienda de mañana." *Proyectos y Materiales* 1 (February
1946): 7.

Sales Building for Souvenirs in a National Park." *New York
Beaux Arts Institute of Design Bulletin* 22 (February 1946): 29.

Harwell H. Harris Shows His West Coast Skill in a Midwest
Environment." *Architectural Forum* 84 (February 1946):
94–96. [Ingersoll house with utility core]

Pageant (March 1946). [Havens house]

Home of Mr. Weston Havens, Berkeley, California." *Homes &
Interiors* 2nd quarter (1946): 72–74.

Eight Men on a Unit." *Interiors* 105 (May 1946): 87–88.
[Ingersoll house]

Inventive Design." *House & Garden* (May 1946): 78. [Havens
house photograph]

How to Successfully Mix New and Old." *House Beautiful*
(September 1946): cover, 110–113.

Hillside Sites Make the Most Interesting Houses." *House
Beautiful* (October 1946): 165–168. [Blair house]

San Mateo Country House for L. Allen." *Architectural Record*
100 (November 1946): 84–85.

Three Houses in Western U.S.A." *Architectural Review* 100
(December 1946): 157–160.

Good Housekeeping (December 1946): 59. [Home designed for
the magazine]

Mademoiselle (December 1946). [Project for a house and
garage]

1947

BUILDINGS AND DESIGNS

Residence for Henry Sarber
Oakland, California
(not built)

Palos Verdes College
Remodeling of an abandoned army camp for temporary
college quarters
Palos Verdes Peninsula, California

Residence for Mr. and Mrs. Werner Huthsing
2446 Ronda Vista Drive
Los Angeles, California

Office for Charles Cruze
2340 West Third Street
Los Angeles, California

Residence for Mr. and Mrs. Ralph Johnson
10280 Chrysanthemum Lane
Los Angeles, California
(1947–48)

Pavilion for Mr. and Mrs. Gerald M. Loeb
Redding, Connecticut
(1947–50)

Library at Palos Verdes College
Rolling Hills Campus
Crest Road
Palos Verdes, California
(1947–49; not built)

PUBLICATIONS

About Harwell Harris

Scott, Walter Hylton. *Nuestra Arquitectura* (January 1947):
3–31. [HHH folio]

"Dress for the Sun." *Holiday* (February 1947): 82. [Fellowship
Park house]

"Adroit Handling of Wood Marks This Hilltop House."
Architectural Forum 87 (December 1947): 102–103. [Cecil
Birtcher house]

1948

BUILDINGS AND DESIGNS

The Chadwick School
Rolling Hills, California
(1948–50; administrative office addition, 1948; senior
classroom, 1948; recreation room, 1949; faculty cottages,
1950; activities building, 1950; swimming pool and dressing
rooms, 1950; senior boys dormitory, 1951)

Exhibition buildings for the National Orange Show
San Bernardino, California
(1948–55)

Exhibition rooms for Baker Furniture
Grand Rapids, Michigan

Residence for Mr. and Mrs. Robert Ryan
15946 Woodvale Road
Los Angeles, California
(not built)

Display and office building for Cecil Head
Sixth and D Street
San Bernardino, California
(not built)

Residence for Mr. and Mrs. Frederick Hoffman Wood
Mill Hill
Fairfield, Connecticut
(1948–49)

Telex Office—Professional Building
San Bernardino, California
(1948–49)

Residence for Mr. and Mrs. J. J. Mulvihill
580 Hermosa Avenue
Sierra Madre, California
(1948–49; alterations in 1977)

Addition to the Wayside Chapel in association with Walter
    Steilberg and George C. Hodges of Berkeley
Santa Rosa, California
(1948–49)

Residence for Mr. and Mrs. Harold M. English
1261 Lago Vista Drive
Beverly Hills, California
(1948–50)

PUBLICATIONS

About Harwell Harris

"North Country House for Many Children." *Architectural
    Record* 103 (February 1948): 106–111. [Russell S. Johnson,
    associate architect on the house; Lake Placid house for W. E.
    Clark]

"Lookout Station." *New York Beaux Arts Institute Design
    Bulletin* 24 (May 1948): 30.

"Sales Suite, Los Angeles, California." *Progressive Architecture*
    29 (July 1948): 62.

"Architects Will Exhibit in Australia." *Architect & Engineer*
    (August 1948): 34–35.

"Architects 'Down Under.'" *Fortnight*, September 10, 1948,
    pp. 8–11.

EXHIBITIONS

"Six West Coast Architects," Australian-American Association
    and the Royal Victoria Institute of Architects, shown in
    Melbourne and Sidney, Australia [Havens and Birtcher]

1949

BUILDINGS AND DESIGNS

Cottage for Constance
Malibu Beach
Los Angeles, California

Residence for Mr. and Mrs. A. H. Hopmans
1753 North Dillon Street
Los Angeles, California

Residence for Dr. and Mrs. Floyd Ross
Aubrey Horn, architect of record
Paseo Del Mar
Palos Verdes, California
(not built; Horn, who worked for Harris, signed the drawings
    as Harris was not yet registered)

Apartment Units for Weston Havens
Milvia and Blake Streets
Berkeley, California

Phillips X-Ray and Clinical Laboratory
Professional Building
San Bernardino, California

* Residence for *Household Magazine*
(not built)

* Residence for Mrs. Arthur Shepard
Palos Verdes, California

PUBLICATIONS

By Harwell Harris

"Rhythmic Integration of Panel Elements." *Practical Builder*
    (December 1949): 76–79.

About Harwell Harris

"San Francisco Houses." *Life*, September 5, 1949, pp. 44–63.
    [Houses by Corbett, Hilmer and Callister, Anshen and Allen,
    Harris, and Esherick]

950

ILDINGS AND DESIGNS

sidence for Mr. and Mrs. H. W. Aldrich, Jr.
alnut Lane
igene, Oregon
ot built)

sidence for Mr. and Mrs. Alvin Ray
irma Road
llbrook, California

sidence for Mr. and Mrs. S. E. Weaver
540 Thurston Circle
is Angeles, California
ot built)

sidence for Dr. and Mrs. W. H. Snyder (second remodeling)
879 Whipple Street
orth Hollywood, California
950–51)

ach Cottage for Rex Hardy, Jr.
rtuguese Bend Club
is Angeles County, California
950–51)

sidence for Mr. and Mrs. James Elliott
443 Woodbridge
orth Hollywood, California
950–51)

sidence for Mr. and Mrs. H. E. Hanson
05 West Silverlake Drive
is Angeles, California
950–51)

JBLICATIONS

out Harwell Harris

tch, James Marsten. "The New American Architecture
Started 70 Years Ago." *House Beautiful* (May 1950): 134–137.
[Fellowship Park house]

House with Disappearing Walls—Or How to Live
Attractively in One Room." *House & Garden* (June 1950): 118.
[Gerald Loeb house]

Iotion Pictures Document Growth of Architecture's Western
Movement." *Redwood News* (Summer 1950): 14.
[Announcement of the Havens house]

Igerg, Gosta. "Bostadsbygge i Californien." *Byggmastaren*
(November 1950): 102–104. [Wyle and Havens houses]

"Private Retreat: Redding, Connecticut." *Progressive
Architecture* 31 (December 1950): 45–48. [Gerald Loeb
house]

EXHIBITIONS

VII Pan American Congress of Architecture (exhibit requested
by Committee on International Relations of AIA), Havana,
Cuba

New York Architectural League, New York, New York

1951

BUILDINGS AND DESIGNS

Residence for Mr. Edward Adams
2331 Cove Avenue
Los Angeles, California
(not built)

Residence for Mr. and Mrs. Arthur W. Colley
Lancaster, Pennsylvania

* Residence for Alvan Palmer
Benedict Canyon
Beverly Hills, California

* Residence for Lee Blair
Long Island, New York
(not built)

Residence for Mr. and Mrs. Harwell Hamilton Harris
Mission Road
Fallbrook, California
(1951–52)

PUBLICATIONS

About Harwell Harris

"A House to Grow with Your Future." *Home Magazine, Los
Angeles Times,* June 3, 1951, pp. 6–7. [The Segmental House
for Revere Copper & Brass]

Burden, Jean. "Timeless California." *Home Magazine, Los
Angeles Times,* July 29, 1951, cover, pp. 3–5. [Mulvihill
house]

"Named by University of Texas." *Architectural Forum* 95
(August 1951): 68.

"Harwell Hamilton Harris Heads Texas School of
Architecture." *Architectural Record* 110 (September
1951): 232.

"Fields of Light." *Sunset* (October 1951): 47. [Stair hall of the Harold English house]

"Three California Houses and a Tradition Revitalized." *Architectural Forum* 95 (October 1951): 162–170. [Ralph Johnson, Alvin Ray, and Harold English houses]

EXHIBITIONS

Philadelphia Architectural Club, Philadelphia, Pennsylvania

"Contemporary Architecture in the U.S.," U.S. State Department (this exhibition won the Grand Prize of Honor at the Pan American Congress; in the form of a traveling exhibition it met with tremendous success in South America and Europe)

"New Directions in American Archihtecture," Contemporary Arts Association, Houston, Texas (organized by Howard Barnstone)

"Distinguished Buildings outside the Philadelphia Area," Philadelphia Chapter of the AIA, Philadelphia, Pennsylvania

1952

BUILDINGS AND DESIGNS

Residence for Mr. and Mrs. David Barrow
Northwest Hills
Austin, Texas
(not built)

Residence for Professor Thomas M. Cranfill
1901 Cliff Street
Austin, Texas
(proposed additions, 1955 and 1958)

Residence for Mr. and Mrs. Sylvan Lang
700 Alta Street
San Antonio, Texas

PUBLICATIONS

By Harwell Harris

"Architecture as an Art." *AIA Journal* 18 (November 1952): 216–219. [Harris's discovery of Frank Lloyd Wright; originally requested for a proposed catalog of the Frank Lloyd Wright exhibition at the Museum of Modern Art, New York, 1940, that was never published]

About Harwell Harris

"Television Sales Room." *New York Beaux Arts Institute of Design Bulletin* 17 (February 1952): 28. [Comments on awards]

"Casa en Fellowship, Los Angeles." *Nuestra Arquitectura* (March 1952): 82–85.

"Oasis for Good Living." *House & Home* (March 1952): 90–93. [Havens apartments, Berkeley]

"Japanese Details Gave Drake's Houses Lightness and Grace." *House & Home* (March 1952): 102.

"Modern with a Warm Look." *Home Magazine, Los Angeles Times*, May 11, 1952, pp. 4–5. [James Elliott house]

"The Small House on the Cover." *Sunset* (September 1952): cover, 44, 45, 77, 78. [Rex Hardy house]

EXHIBITIONS

"New Directions in Domestic Architecture," New York Architectural League, New York, New York

1953

BUILDINGS AND DESIGNS

* Residence for Mrs. Frederick J. Duhring
Greenwood Commons
Berkeley, California

PUBLICATIONS

By Harwell Harris

"Observations on Mexico's University City." *AIA Journal* 19 (January 1953): 13–14.

"How a House Can Enrich the Life Within." *House Beautiful* 9. (May 1953): 157.

"Rhythmic Integration of Panel Elements." *Perspecta* 2, Yale Architectural Journal (1953): 37–44. [Reprint of December 1949 article for *Practical Builder*]

About Harwell Harris

"Simple Ideas from a Complex House." *House & Home* (January 1953): 126–131. [Clarence Wyle house]

"Above the Valley." *Home Magazine, Los Angeles Times*, June 7, 1953. [Wyle house]

"Like Your Veblen Hotter?" *Saturday Review*, July 25, 1953. [Review by Wayne Andrews of *Built in the U.S.A.: Postwar Architecture*]

EXHIBITIONS

"Harwell Hamilton Harris—One Man Show," Student Home Show, University of Florida, Gainesville, Florida

Harwell Hamilton Harris—One Man Show," University of
Oklahoma, Norman, Oklahoma

Harwell Hamilton Harris—One Man Show," University of
Arkansas, Fayetteville, Arkansas

954

UILDINGS AND DESIGNS

les office for David B. Barrow
rry Lane
ustin, Texas
954)

esidence for David B. Barrow
orthwest Hills
ustin, Texas
ot built)

ouse Beautiful Pace Setter House (Texas State Fair House)
air Park
allas, Texas
954–55; student architects from the University of Texas who
    worked with Harris were Neal Lacey, David Barrow, Jr.,
    Patrick Chumney, William Hoff, Haldor Nielson, and Donald
    Legge; the house was moved in 1957 to 12020 Stone Brook
    Circle in Dallas and altered by Harris to suit its owner,
    Robert Phillips, Jr.)

UBLICATIONS

y Harwell Harris

Architectural Trends." *Review*. Society of Residential
    Appraisers (February 1954): 7–11. [HHH talk and pictures]

The Art of Building." *Alcalde*, University of Texas Alumni
    Magazine (June 1954): 282.

ook review of Gershon Canaan's *Rebuilding the Land of Israel*.
    Dallas Morning News, August 15, 1954.

bout Harwell Harris

Work Has Begun at Fair Grounds on Harwell Harris's 'Model
    House.'" *Dallas Morning News*, July 4, 1954.

Northwest Architects Meet at Eugene." *Architectural Record*
    (October 1954): 16. [Photo and quote from "Regionalism and
    Nationalism" speech]

The Pace Setter House." *Alcalde*, University of Texas Alumni
    Magazine (October 1954): 26.

Pace Setter House. *Dallas Morning News*, October 10, 1954.

Pace Setter House. *Dallas Times Herald*, October 10, 1954.

Sunset (November 1954): 54. [Ralph Johnson fireplace]

1955

BUILDINGS AND DESIGNS

Balcones House No. 1, Austin Corporation
4002 Edgemont Drive
Austin, Texas

Balcones House No. 2, Austin Corporation
Austin, Texas

Residence for Mr. and Mrs. David B. Barrow
4101 Edgemont Drive
Austin, Texas

Kitchen for Frigidaire Division of General Motors
(advertised in *House & Home* [August 1955]; not built)

* Residence remodeling for Robert Hardwick
Eagle Rock Ranch
Wimberley, Texas
(not built)

Residence remodeling for Mr. and Mrs. Theo Davis
2210 Windsor Road
Austin, Texas
(1955–56)

Entrance to Eternity Park Cemetery
Aldine at Spring Road
Harris County, Texas
David B. Barrow, Jr., Associate Architect

House for the Southwest Homestyle Center Foundations
Exhibition, Lot 22
Homestyle Center
Grand Rapids, Michigan
(1955–56; not built)

Motel-on-the-Mountain, in association with Perkins and Will
Mount Hillburn, New York

Residence for Mrs. Ruth Carter Stevenson, in association with
    Frank Sherwood, engineer, and Thomas Church, landscape
    architect
1200 Broad Avenue
Fort Worth, Texas
(1955–56; alterations, 1957–60, 1963)

Residence for Dr. and Mrs. Courtney M. Townsend
2301 Simpson Street
Paris, Texas
(1955–56; proposed addition, 1974)

PUBLICATIONS

By Harwell Harris

"A Regional Architectural Expression." *Architectural Record* 117 (January 1955).

"Air Conditioning." *New York Times*, May 15, 1955.

About Harwell Harris

"Pace Setter Home Took Best of the Old and Best of the New." *House & Home* 7, no. 1 (January 1955): 146–147.

Sunset (January 1955): 50. [Ralph Johnson dressing table]

"The Pace Setter House." Entire issue of *House Beautiful* (February 1955).

"The Pace Setter House." *House Beautiful* (March 1955).

House & Home (March 1955): 65. [Ad for the Pace Setter House]

Kennedy, Robert Woods. "Architecture and the New Package Style." *New Republic*, April 4, 1955, p. 15.

"The Pace Setter House." *House Beautiful* (April 1955).

House & Home 7, no. 5 (May 1955): 290. [Pace Setter House in California Redwood Association ad]

Redwood News (Spring 1955): 15. [Pace Setter House]

House & Home 8, no. 1 (July 1955). [Frigidaire "Kitchen Plan" program]

"Harris Resigns as Head of Texas University School of Architecture." *Architectural Forum* 103 (August 1955): 29.

"News from the Educational Field." *AIA Journal* (November 1955): 234. [HHH resignation and succession at the University of Texas]

1956

BUILDINGS AND DESIGNS

Pool Shelter for Mr. Ernest Allen, Jr.
Fort Worth, Texas

* Residence for Mr. and Mrs. C. R. Antrim
6160 North Van Ness
Fresno, California
(1956–57)

Dr. Tom B. Bond Radiological Group
Remodeling of clinic
1217 West Cannon Street
Fort Worth, Texas

* Office remodeling for Harris and Sherwood
2613 West Seventh Street
Fort Worth, Texas

Tile Council of America Exhibition Room
Fuller, Smith and Ross Advertising Agency
New York, New York

* Convair Division of General Motors Dynamic Corporation
Cafeteria remodeling
Convair Plant
Fort Worth, Texas

Residence for Mr. and Mrs. Louis B. Frederick
Barrington, Illinois
(not built)

Mt. Olivet Cemetery Association
Mausoleum and lake
Sylvania Street at 28th Street
Fort Worth, Texas
(only lake was built; 1956–57)

Saint Mary's Episcopal Church
Big Spring, Texas
(1956–58; additions in 1960)

Restoration and alterations to the Security Bank and Trust
Original 1908 National Farmers Bank designed by Louis Sullivan
Owatonna, Minnesota
(1956–57; alterations in 1967–70, 1972)

Greenwood Mausoleum
White Settlement Road at University
Fort Worth, Texas
(1956–58)

Residence for Mr. and Mrs. Andrew Kirkpatrick
Fairfield, Connecticut
(1956–57)

PUBLICATIONS

About Harwell Harris

"American Beauty." *New Yorker*, March 3, 1956, p. 24. [Motel-on-the-Mountain]

allion, Arthur. "Architecture of the Los Angeles Region."
  Architectural Record 119 (May 1956): 159–166. [Wyle house]

he Contemporary House in the American Southwest."
  Roswell Museum Bulletin 4, no. 3 (Summer 1956).

wo Motels: Atlantic Coast Motel Has Pacific Design."
  Architectural Forum 105 (August 1956): 124–127. [Motel-on-
  the-Mountain]

he Motel on the Mountain." *Interiors* 116 (September 1956):
  102–107.

XHIBITIONS

Built in the U.S.A.," Museum of Modern Art (under the
  auspices of the International Program of the Museum of
  Modern Art, this show traveled to São Paulo, Rio de Janeiro,
  Mexico City, Guadalajara, Monterrey, London, Dublin, Paris,
  Zurich, Barcelona, Frankfurt, The Hague, Vienna, and
  Belgrade)

WARDS

ward of Merit, *House & Home* (in recognition of outstanding
  contribution to Housing Progress in 1956)

957

BUILDINGS AND DESIGNS

acation house for Hollis Baker
Northport Point, Michigan

Remodeling of residence for Mr. and Mrs. August C. Esenwein
505 Rivercrest Drive
Fort Worth, Texas

Helsinki Embassy and staff housing
U.S. State Department Office of Foreign Buildings
Helsinki, Finland
1957–58; not built)

Residence for Mr. and Mrs. Horace Garrett
Big Spring, Texas
not built)

Residence for Dr. and Mrs. Seymour Eisenberg
9624 Rockbrook Drive
Dallas, Texas
1957–58)

Container Corporation Factory and Warehouse
Dallas, Texas

PUBLICATIONS

By Harwell Harris

"What's Your Line?" University of Oklahoma 17th Annual
  Career Conference, April 1957. [HHH talk and
  announcement]

"Regionalism and Nationalism." *U.T. Record* (Winter 1957–58).
  [Announcement of *Texas Quarterly*]

About Harwell Harris

"By-Passed Land." *House & Home* (February 1957): 108–113.
  [Greenwood Common]

"One Hundred Years of Significant Building." *Architectural
  Record* 121 (February 1957): 199–206. [Havens house
  mentioned in brief description by Talbot Hamlin, "Houses
  since 1907," p. 205]

"Architect Designs 'House for Southwest.'" *Royal Report* (April
  1957): 4. [Finnish Embassy news]

"Contemporary: The Hotels, the Holidays." *Vogue* (July 1957):
  74–75. [Motel-on-the-Mountain]

"Motel Hung on a Hilltop." *Life*, August 12, 1957, p. 93.

"One Hundred Years of the American House." *House & Home*
  11 (May 1957): 119. [Fellowship Park house under heading
  "Glamourous Vernacular of the 1930s"]

EXHIBITIONS

Home Show in the Coliseum, New York Chapter AIA, New
  York, New York (Gerald M. Loeb house, one of sixteen
  houses selected to illustrate the progress of architecture in
  one hundred years)

"One Hundred Years of American Architecture," AIA,
  Washington, D.C. (celebrating the centennial of the AIA. It
  was the first exhibition held in the National Gallery of Art.
  Three copies of the exhibition circulated simultaneously in
  Europe, Asia, and America.)

Undicesima Triennale de Milano

1958

BUILDINGS AND DESIGNS

Residence for Dr. and Mrs. Milton Talbot
1508 Dayton Road
Big Spring, Texas
(1958–59)

Residence for Dr. and Mrs. J. M. Woodall, Jr.
808 West 14th Street
Big Spring, Texas
(1958–59)

Addition to the residence of Mr. and Mrs. Obie Bristow
Big Spring, Texas
(not built)

Residence for Dr. and Mrs. Leon B. Cohen
Dallas, Texas
(not built)

Cliff Street Apartments for Professor Thomas M. Cranfill
1911 Cliff Street
Austin, Texas

Residence for Mr. and Mrs. John S. Treanor
2617 Oldham Road
Abilene, Texas
(1958–59)

* Apartment interior for Mr. and Mrs. Harwell Hamilton Harris
3525 Turtle Creek, 8-C
Dallas, Texas

Apartment interior for Mr. and Mrs. Edmund J. Kahn
3525 Turtle Creek, 21-A
Dallas, Texas

Trade Mart Court
Stemmons Expressway
Dallas, Texas
(1958–60)

Revisions to residence of Mr. and Mrs. John Muth
8211 Inwood Road
Dallas, Texas
(not built)

PUBLICATIONS

About Harwell Harris

Sunset (February 1958): 73. [Pace Setter House in California Redwood Association ad]

Fitch, James M. Speech on the occasion of the rededication of Sullivan's National Farmers Bank in Owatonna, Minnesota, June 12, 1958. [When HHH renovated the bank, the name had been changed to Security Bank and Trust Company]

"Making a Monument Work." *Architectural Forum* 109 (July 1958): 99–103. [HHH renovation of Sullivan's National Farmers Bank in Owatonna, Minnesota]

"HHH Apartment in Howard Meyers' Building." *Architectural Forum* (September 1958): 109.

"Simple Plan for Privacy." *Life*, September 29, 1958. [Townsend house]

House Beautiful (November 1958). Reprint. [Dining Room 7, Garden for the Ceramic Tile Council]

"A House to Show the Fun of Family Life." *House & Home* 14 (December 1958): 128–129. [Article on the Townsend house reprinted from "Simple Plan for Privacy," *Life*, September 29, 1958]

"Eight Houses to Help Home Buyers Raise Their Sights." *House and Home* 14 (December 1958): 120–140.

1959

BUILDINGS AND DESIGNS

Addition to building for J. D. Arthur
Abilene, Texas

* Dallas Home Center for Leslie Hill
Dallas, Texas

Remodeling for Headmaster's House
North Country School
Lake Placid, New York
(1959–60)

Stemmons Building for Trammell Crow
Stemmons Expressway
Dallas, Texas
(not built)

Residence for Mrs. Louise Brown
Monte Vista Drive
San Bernardino, California
(not built)

Residence remodeling for Mr. and Mrs. Wesley Francis Wright, Jr.
5409 Farquhar Lane
Dallas, Texas
(not built)

Residence for Mr. and Mrs. Cole Weston
Big Sur
Carmel, California
(not built)

Valley View Shopping Center for Trammell Crow
Valley View at Preston Road
Dallas, Texas
(not built)
Building Materials Mart for Trammell Crow
Stemmons Expressway
Dallas, Texas
(1959–60; not built)
Office Building for David B. Barrow, Sr.
Northwest Hills
Austin, Texas
Alpha Radio
Dallas, Texas
(sketches only)

PUBLICATIONS

By Harwell Harris

"The Architecture." Dallas Theatre Center Brochure (1959).
    [Harris's commentary and praise of Wright's building]

About Harwell Harris

"On View in Moscow." *Dallas Morning News*, July 6, 1959.
    [Feature Exhibits Building from the National Orange Show]
"Motel près de New York." *Architecture d'Aujourd'hui* 30
    (October 1959): 48. [Motel-on-the-Mountain]

EXHIBITIONS

New York Architectural League [Motel-on-the-Mountain]
U.S.S.R. Exhibition in Moscow [National Orange Show]

1960

BUILDINGS AND DESIGNS

Residence for Mr. and Mrs. Wesley Francis Wright, Jr.
3504 Lexington Avenue
Dallas, Texas
(1960–61)
Veteran's Memorial for Eternity Park Cemetery
Aldine at Spring Road
Harris County, Texas
David B. Barrow, Jr., Associate Architect
Apartment Group for Trammell Crow
Stemmons Expressway
Dallas, Texas
(not built)

John Weston Havens Fountain Plaza
A gift to the city from Weston Havens in memory of his father
Berkeley, California
(1960–61; demolished to make way for subway)
Phi Chi Fraternity House for Trammell Crow
Dallas, Texas
(not built)
Drive-in stores for Mr. and Mrs. John Cimaglia
10427 Harry Hines Boulevard
Dallas, Texas
Master Market Center Office Building for Trammell Crow
Dallas, Texas
Project for an insurance company
Ross Street
Dallas, Texas
(not built)
Maple Tower apartment building for Joe Maberry
Robert White, Architect
Harwell Hamilton Harris, Consultant
Dallas, Texas
(1960–61; not built)

PUBLICATIONS

By Harwell Harris

"Measuring the Architect's Professional Philosophy," *St. Louis
    Construction Record*, April 12, 1960. [Harris's speech before
    the Missouri Association of Registered Architects]

About Harwell Harris

Architectural Design (January 1960). Frank Lloyd Wright
    memorial issue, written and designed by Lloyd Wright.
    [Includes Havens and Ruth Carter Stevenson houses]
"1960 National Gold Medal Exhibition of the Building Arts."
    Architectural League of New York. [Motel-on-the-Mountain]

EXHIBITIONS

"1960 National Gold Medal Exhibition of the Building Arts."
    New York Architectural League (Motel-on-the-Mountain)
American Federation of the Arts, traveling show

AWARDS

Honor Award, Texas Society of Architects (Greenwood
    Mausoleum)
Award of Merit, Texas Society of Architects (Treanor
    residence)

1961

BUILDINGS AND DESIGNS

Apartment Group for Hal Anderson
Dallas, Texas
(not built)

Market Towers for Trammell Crow
Stemmons Expressway
Dallas, Texas
(not built)

Cookson Company Office Building for Trammell Crow
4000 Stemmons Freeway
Dallas, Texas
(not built)

* Fina Building for Trammell Crow
Dallas, Texas
(not built)

Preston Road Apartments for Trammell Crow
Dallas, Texas
(not built)

* Tracy-Locke Building
Dallas, Texas
(not built)

Summer Cottage for Henry Miller, Jr.
Marsh Lane and Keller Springs Road
Dallas, Texas
(not built)

New church building for the First Unitarian Church in
association with Beran and Shelmire
Preston Road at Normandy Avenue, University Park
Dallas, Texas
(1961–63)

Remodeling of Fort Sill National Bank
Fort Sill, Oklahoma
(not built; 1961–62)

PUBLICATIONS

By Harwell Harris

"The Mind of an Architect." *Berkeley Review*, November 30,
1961. [HHH talk at the dedication of Havens Fountain Plaza]

About Harwell Harris

"Oasis amid Showrooms—Dallas Trade Mart Court."
Architectural Forum 114 (April 1961): 119.

Lynes, Russell. "Everything's Up-to-date in Texas . . . but Me."
Harpers (May 1961): 38–42.

"An Island of Beauty on a Main Street." *Architectural Record*
(May 1961): 32–33. [Havens Memorial Fountain Plaza]

1962

BUILDINGS AND DESIGNS

Residence for Mr. and Mrs. Francis Paschal
1527 Pinecrest
Durham, North Carolina
(1962–63)

PUBLICATIONS

About Harwell Harris

"Architects in the News. HHH to join faculty of School of
Design." *AIA Memo* (Raleigh, North Carolina), January 15,
1962.

"What's New with Harwell Hamilton Harris?" *House & Home*
(January 1962): 100–107. [Folio of seven buildings, four
old—Ralph Johnson, Alvin Ray, Clarence Wyle, Weston
Havens—and three new—J. Lee Johnson (Ruth Carter
Stevenson), Treanor, and Pace Setter]

"Internationally Renowned Architect to Join N.C.S. School of
Design Faculty." *Statelog*, North Carolina State College
(January 1962).

"First Person Bliss." *House Beautiful* (January 1962): 96. [Rex
Hardy house]

"The Why of an Architect's Design." *Architectural Record*
(February 1962): 32–38. [Havens Memorial Plaza]

1963

BUILDINGS AND DESIGNS

A classroom building for music, art, and social sciences
Fayetteville State College
Fayetteville, North Carolina
MacMillan and MacMillan, Associates
(1963–64)

Security Bank and Trust Motor Bank
Broadway and Cedar
Owatonna, Minnesota
(1963–64)

964

BUILDINGS AND DESIGNS

Residence remodeling for Dr. and Mrs. Frank W. Klingberg
Hawthorne Lane
Chapel Hill, North Carolina

Residence no. 1 for Dr. and Mrs. V. Watson Pugh
Buggs Island
Kerr Lake, Virginia
(not built)

Residence for Dr. and Mrs. Roy Lindahl
05 Clayton Road
Chapel Hill, North Carolina
(1964–65)

Residence for Henry Zaytown
Raleigh, North Carolina
(not built)

Drafting Room for Harwell Hamilton Harris
0 Maiden Lane
Raleigh, North Carolina

EXHIBITIONS

Faculty Show, North Carolina State University, Raleigh, North
    Carolina

The Twentieth Century Home," Museum of Modern Art
    Traveling Exhibition

965

BUILDINGS AND DESIGNS

North Carolina state government center plan
Raleigh, North Carolina
(with Brian Shawcroft and Lewis Clarke; not built)

Residence no. 2 for Dr. and Mrs. V. Watson Pugh
Buggs Island
Kerr Lake, Virginia

Residence for Mr. and Mrs. William Van Alstyne
Woodburn Road
Durham, North Carolina
(1965–67)

Alterations and additions to the residence of John Headley
Laurel Hill Road
Chapel Hill, North Carolina

PUBLICATIONS

About Harwell Harris

Andrews, Wayne. "The Important Evolution of the American
    House." *House Beautiful* (February 1965): 91.

Harwell Hamilton Harris, a Selection of His Work and Writings.
    Student Publication of the School of Design, North Carolina
    State University, vol. 14, no. 5 (1965).

"Home of Mr. Weston Havens, Berkeley, California." *Homes &
    Interiors* (second quarter, 1965): 72–74.

"Honor Fellowships for 37 Members." *Journal of the American
    Institute of Architects* (June 1965): 22.

"A.I.A. Selects 37 Fellows." *Architectural Record* (May 1965).

EXHIBITIONS

"Modern Architecture in U.S.A.," Museum of Modern Art, New
    York, New York (selective survey of building achievements in
    this country from 1900 to 1965, arranged by Arthur Drexler
    and sponsored by the Graham Foundation for Advanced
    Studies in the Fine Arts)

AWARDS

FAIA; elevated to the College of Fellows of the AIA

Citation in recognition of outstanding contribution in the field
    of architecture by editors of *Who's Who in the South and
    Southwest*

1966

BUILDINGS AND DESIGNS

Residence for Dr. and Mrs. Wayne Andrews
Grosse Pointe, Michigan
(not built)

Four Cottages for the North Country School
Lake Placid, New York
(1966–67)

Residence for Mr. and Mrs. G. T. Sweetser
Laurel Park
Hendersonville, North Carolina

PUBLICATIONS

By Harwell Harris

"Design Dimensions." *North Carolina Architect* (September
    1966): 16–17. [Talk before the Northwest Regional
    Conference of the AIA in Glacier National Park, 1965]

1967

BUILDINGS AND DESIGNS

Residence, Tara Farm, for Mr. and Mrs. V. Watson Pugh
Raleigh, North Carolina
(1967–68; not built)

Residence for Dr. and Mrs. Kenneth Sugioka
#1 Bayberry Drive
Chapel Hill, North Carolina
(1967–68)

St. Giles Presbyterian Church
5105 Oak Park Road
Raleigh, North Carolina
(1967–69; additions: elementary grades building, 1973;
  working drawing for sanctuary building, adult classroom
  building, preschool classroom building, 1976–77;
  construction postponed, 1983)

Garden House for Drs. Joseph and Cynthia Hardison
2801 Lakeview Drive
Raleigh, North Carolina

Cumberland County Public Library
MacMillan and MacMillan, Architects
Fayetteville, North Carolina
(not built)

PUBLICATIONS

By Harwell Harris

"A Museum Building Is Special." *North Carolina Architect*
  (May/June 1967): 38–39, 42, 45.

1968

BUILDINGS AND DESIGNS

Office and residence for Mr. and Mrs. Harwell Hamilton Harris
122 Cox Avenue
Raleigh, North Carolina
(1968–70; alterations, 1971, 1977)

Residence for Mr. and Mrs. Duncan Stuart
6710 Leesville Road
Raleigh, North Carolina
(1968–71; alterations, 1983)

* New Rialto Theater
Durham, North Carolina
(not built)

PUBLICATIONS

By Harwell Harris

"Why Nature?" *North Carolina Architect* (June/July 1968): 11.

1969

BUILDINGS AND DESIGNS

Residence for Mr. and Mrs. Ralph C. Bryant
Lake Dam Road
Raleigh, North Carolina

John Weston Havens Memorial Fountain
First proposal for replacement of 1960 Havens Fountain Plaza
  destroyed to make way for subway
Shattuck Avenue
Berkeley, California
(not built)

1970

BUILDINGS AND DESIGNS

John Weston Havens Memorial Fountain
Second proposal for replacement of 1960 Havens Fountain
  Plaza destroyed to make way for subway
Shattuck Avenue
Berkeley, California
(not built)

1971

BUILDINGS AND DESIGNS

Residence for Dr. and Mrs. Stanley Bennett
Jones Ferry Road
Chapel Hill, North Carolina

Deck for residence of Mr. and Mrs. William A. Creech
1202 College Place
Raleigh, North Carolina

1972

BUILDINGS AND DESIGNS

Residence for Mr. and Mrs. Jonathan Brezin
Shady Lawn Court
Chapel Hill, North Carolina
(1972–73; not built)

Hotel Kinabalu for Sharikat Pembangunan Azam

HHH was consulting architect for the International Executive
   Service Corps.

Hotel and resort for small island, Kota Kinabalu
Meruntum Bay
East Malaysia (formerly North Borneo)
(not built)
Village Hall
Whispering Pines, North Carolina
(1972–73)

1974

BUILDINGS AND DESIGNS

Alterations to the residence of Mr. and Mrs. Harold R. Love
109 Sampson Place
Raleigh, North Carolina
(not built)
Church of Reconciliation
110 Elliott Road
Chapel Hill, North Carolina
(1974–75; not built)

PUBLICATIONS

About Harwell Harris

McCoy, Esther. "Architecture West." *Progressive Architecture*
   55 (May 1974): 38+.

1975

BUILDINGS AND DESIGNS

Residence for Dr. and Mrs. John T. Caldwell
1101 Marlow Road
Raleigh, North Carolina
(not built)
Alterations to residence for Dr. and Mrs. John T. Caldwell
10 Granville Drive
Raleigh, North Carolina
(1975–76)

PUBLICATIONS

By Harwell Harris

"The Brothers Greene." *Architectural Record* (November 1975):
   45, 47. [HHH review of three books: *A Greene & Greene Guide*
   by Janann Strand, *Greene & Greene, Architects in the*

Residential Style by William R. and Karen Current, and *A Guide
   to the Work of Greene & Greene* by Randall L. Makinson]

1976

BUILDINGS AND DESIGNS

Cullowhee Presbyterian Church
State Road 1101
Cullowhee, North Carolina
Apartment building for Mr. T. D. Eure
Bogue Sound, North Carolina
(not built)
North Raleigh United Methodist Church
Raleigh, North Carolina
(1976–77; not built)

PUBLICATIONS

About Harwell Harris

"Highlights of American Architecture, 1776–1976." *AIA Journal*
   (July 1976): 125–126. [Havens and Fellowship Park houses]

1977

BUILDINGS AND DESIGNS

Vacation residence for Mrs. Ruth Carter Stevenson
Valley View Drive
Roaring Gap, North Carolina
(not built)
Residence for Mr. and Mrs. W. J. Watson
Barton's Creek Road
Raleigh, North Carolina
* Project for the International Executive Service Corps
Hotel
San Salvador, El Salvador
(not built)

PUBLICATIONS

By Harwell Harris

"A. I. A. Gold Medal, First in Five Years, Awarded to Neutra."
   North Carolina Architect (May/June 1977): 8–10.

1978

BUILDINGS AND DESIGNS

* Project for the International Executive Service Corp.

Design review and suggestions for a four-story block of shops and a twenty-seven story tower of offices
Goldhill Plaza
Newton Road
Singapore, Republic of Singapore
(not built)

PUBLICATIONS

By Harwell Harris

"The Search for a Postmodern Architecture." *Crit 4,*
Architectural Student Journal of North Carolina State
University (Fall 1978): 18.

"Regionalism." *North Carolina Architect* (January/February 1978): 11–12.

About Harwell Harris

Kamphoefner, Henry. *North Carolina Architect*
(January/February 1978): 14. [Comments about Harris's regionalism]

1979

BUILDINGS AND DESIGNS

Renovation of the Hinsdale House for Mrs. Barbara Campbell
330 Hillsboro Street
Raleigh, North Carolina
(1979–80)

1980

BUILDINGS AND DESIGNS

Residence for Pamela Gann and William Van Alstyne
1714 Tisdale Street
Durham, North Carolina
(not built)

* Dental building for Dr. Stephen Renner
5901 Falls of the Neuse Road
Raleigh, North Carolina
(not built)

PUBLICATIONS

About Harwell Harris

Lamb, Paul, and Lawrence Speck. "Rediscovering Harwell
Hamilton Harris." *Texas Architect* (March/April 1980):
36–42.

"The Horizontal City." *New Yorker,* September 15, 1980,
pp. 17–21.

McKinley, C. C. "Renewal: Blending Architecture and Decor."
Architectural Digest (November 1980:) 76–83. [The English
house with new interior by Gil Garfield]

EXHIBITIONS

"Harwell Hamilton Harris—One Man Show," North Carolina
Museum of Art, Raleigh, North Carolina

1982

PUBLICATIONS

About Harwell Harris

Weinell, Eleanor. "Harwell Hamilton Harris: The Architect as
Artist." *North Carolina Architect* (May/June 1982): 17–21.

EXHIBITIONS

"Harwell Hamilton Harris—One Man Show," Fayetteville
Museum of Art, Fayetteville, North Carolina

AWARDS

Richard Neutra Medal for Professional Exellence

1983

BUILDINGS AND DESIGNS

Fred G. Bond Metropolitan Park
Cary, North Carolina
(1983–present)

PUBLICATIONS

About Harwell Harris

Devins, Kim. "Reverence for Nature." *Spectator,* sec. 2, June 16
1983.

1985

BUILDINGS AND DESIGNS

Proposal for an entrance to Greenwood Memorial Park using
replicas of the horses in the church of San Marco, Venice
(August 1985; not built)

PUBLICATIONS

About Harwell Harris

Germany, Lisa. "Home Maker: The Architecture of Harwell Hamilton Harris." *Texas Monthly* (March 1985): 160–165.

Matustik, Vicki. "Exhibit Looks at Work by Former Head of Architecture." *On Campus*, Publication for Faculty and Staff at the University of Texas at Austin. March 25–31, 1985, pp. 4–5.

Dillon, David. "Regional Design with Universal Appeal." *Dallas Morning News*, March 27, 1985, pp. 1F, 3F.

McCombie, Mel. "Architect Exhibit Mirrors 'Comfort' Goal." *Austin American-Stateman*, April 12, 1985, p. G5.

Harmon, Frank. "Harwell Hamilton Harris: A Tribute." *North Carolina Architect* (May/June 1985): 10–15.

Fuller, Larry Paul. "Harwell Hamilton Harris: Rediscovering a Tastemaker of the '50s." *Texas Homes* (July 1985): 35–37.

Holmes, Ann. "Honoring Harwell Hamilton Harris." *Houston Chronicle*, July 14, 1985.

Germany, Lisa. "H. H. Harris in Texas." *Texas Architect* (July/August 1985): 66–69.

EXHIBITIONS

"Harwell Hamilton Harris—One Man Show," Center for the Study of American Architecture, School of Architecture, University of Texas at Austin, Austin, Texas (This show was sponsored by a grant from the Amon Carter Foundation of Fort Worth, Texas. It traveled to the San Antonio Museum of Art, San Antonio, Texas; University of Texas at Arlington, Arlington, Texas; Graham Foundation, Chicago, Illinois; and Columbia University, New York, New York)

1986

AWARDS

Honorary doctorate, North Carolina State University

PUBLICATIONS

Litt, Steven. "Master Plan for State Government." *News and Observer* (Raleigh, North Carolina), May 25, 1986, pp. 1b, 5b.

Litt, Steven. "Unbuilt Raleigh." *News and Observer* (Raleigh, North Carolina), September 21, 1986, pp. 1c–2c.

1988

PUBLICATIONS

About Harwell Harris

Litt, Steven. "The Naturalistic Modernism of Harwell Hamilton Harris." *Arts Journal* (August 1988): 9–11.

Herget, J. Barlow. "Harwell Hamilton Harris: A Raleigh Architect of International Repute." *Architecture in the Triangle* (third quarter 1988): 20A–21A.

Robinson, Mark. "Success is a Joint Venture for the Landscape Architect and Architect." *Architecture in the Triangle* (third quarter 1988): 26A–27A. [Landscape and architecture at St. Giles Presbyterian Church]

1989

PUBLICATIONS

About Harwell Harris

Bouknight, Joanne Kellar. "Two Houses by Harwell Hamilton Harris." *Fine Homebuilding* (August/September 1989): 70–74. [The Fellowship Park house and Harris's studio/home in Raleigh, called here the "Pullen Park home"]

Selby, Holly. "The Man of the House." *News and Observer* (Raleigh, North Carolina), October 8, 1989, pp. 1C–2C.

Long, Christopher. "Harwell Hamilton Harris." *Texas Architect* (November/December 1989): 57. [Harris was one of fifty architects celebrated in this special issue of the magazine, commemorating the fiftieth anniversary of the AIA in Texas]

Miscellaneous undated drawings

Cross House
San Bernardino, California

San Bernardino Housing Project
San Bernardino, California
(ca. 1930s)

Remodeling for James Fuller

Residence for Mr. and Mrs. P. E. Griffin
Buena Vista Way
Berkeley, California

Proposed "Theatre 3"
Dallas, Texas
(no date, but may have been late 1950s; not built)

Index

Page numbers for illustrations are given in **boldface** type.

arris at work in the drafting
oom of his office/home;
anslucent glass windows, in the
oirit of rice paper, allow light in
ut keep out an undesirable
iew.
notograph by Brian Shawcroft